# wet moon™

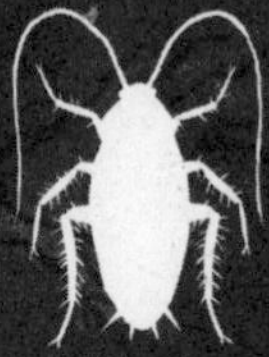

## book 4:
## drowned in evil

# wet moon™

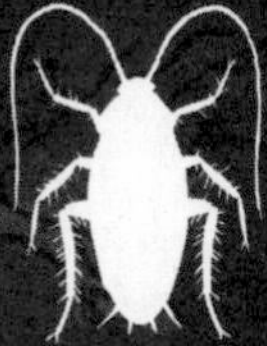

## book 4:
## drowned in evil

*written & illustrated by*

**Ross Campbell**

*Cleo's diary pages by* Jessica Calderwood

*design by* Ross Campbell & Keith Wood

*edited by* Douglas E. Sherwood & James Lucas Jones

*Published by*

**Oni Press, Inc.**

**Joe Nozemack,** *publisher*

**James Lucas Jones,** *editor in chief*   **Randal C. Jarrell,** *managing editor*

**Cory Casoni,** *director of marketing*   **Keith Wood,** *art director*

**Jill Beaton,** *assistant editor*   **Douglas E. Sherwood,** *production assistant*

*Darkstalkers/Vampire Savior* characters property of Capcom.

**Oni Press, Inc.**
1305 SE Martin Luther King Jr. Blvd.
Suite A
Portland, OR 97214

Become our fan on Facebook: facebook.com/onipress
Follow us on Twitter: @onipress
www.onipress.com • mooncalfe.blogspot.com

First Edition: November 2008

ISBN 978-1-934964-09-5

3 5 7 9 10 8 6 4 2

1. Bowden House
2. Vance House
3. Smith House
4. Westmiller House
5. Weitz Hall
6. Polsky Hall
7. Yardley Hall
8. Joseph Hall
9. Simmons Hall
10. Page Hall
11. Meyer Hall
12. Steve Hall
13. Burial Grounds
14. Head-Butt Video
15. House of Usher
16. Denny's
17. Marco's Diner
18. Trilby's Apartment
19. Swamp Things
20. Flower Power
21. Sundae Best
22. Audrey's apartment
23. Penny's apartment
24. Glen's apartment
25. Lorelei Cemetery
26. Polly Poster
27. Zurah Cemetery
28. softball field

wet moon

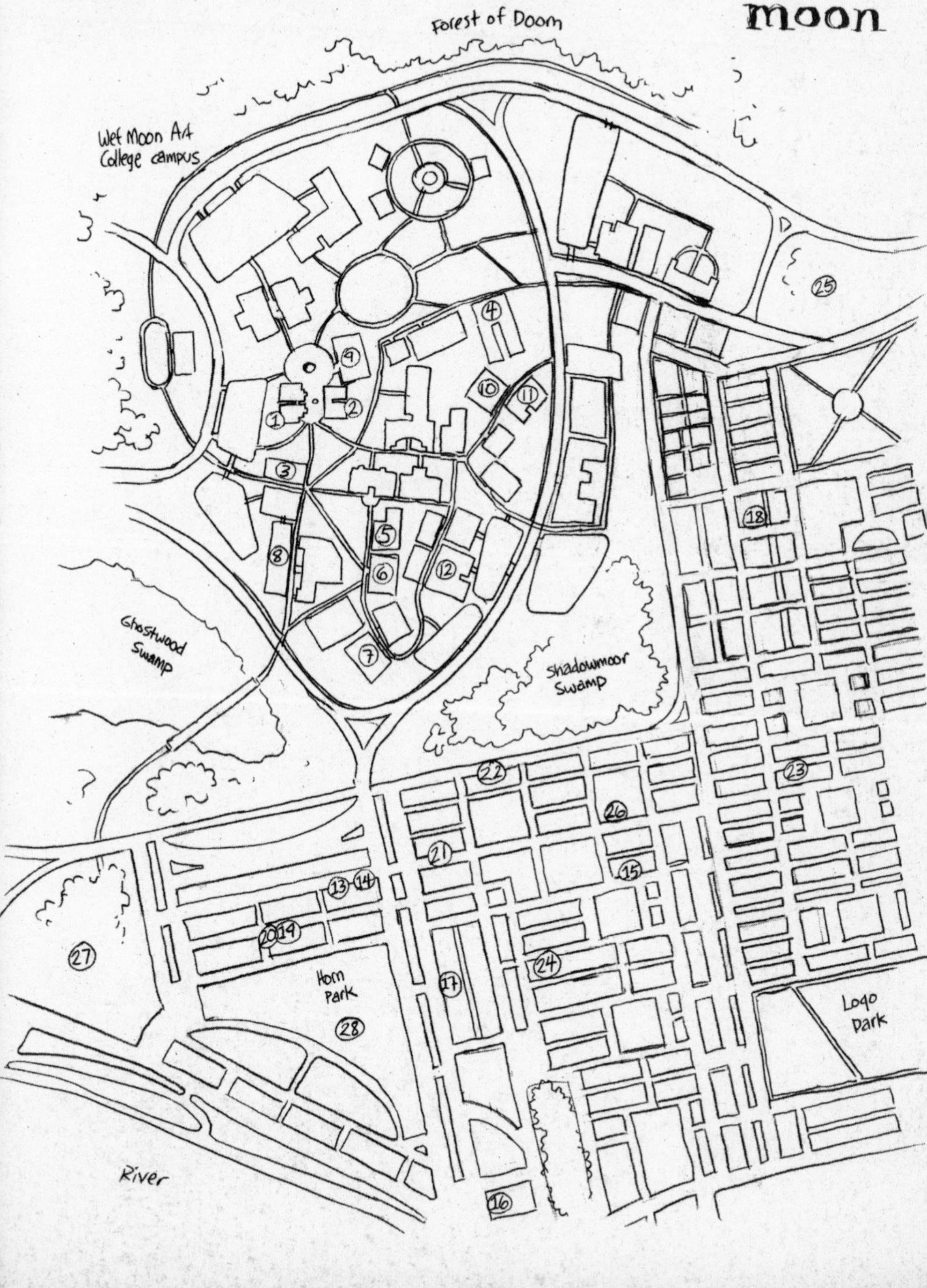
Forest of Doom
Wet Moon Art College campus
Ghostwood Swamp
Shadowmoor Swamp
Horn Park
Logo Park
River

28. The Lovedrop Residence
29. The Swanhilde Residence
30. Wet Moon High School
31. The Shoe Tree
32. The Bernarde Residence
33. The Zuzanny Residence

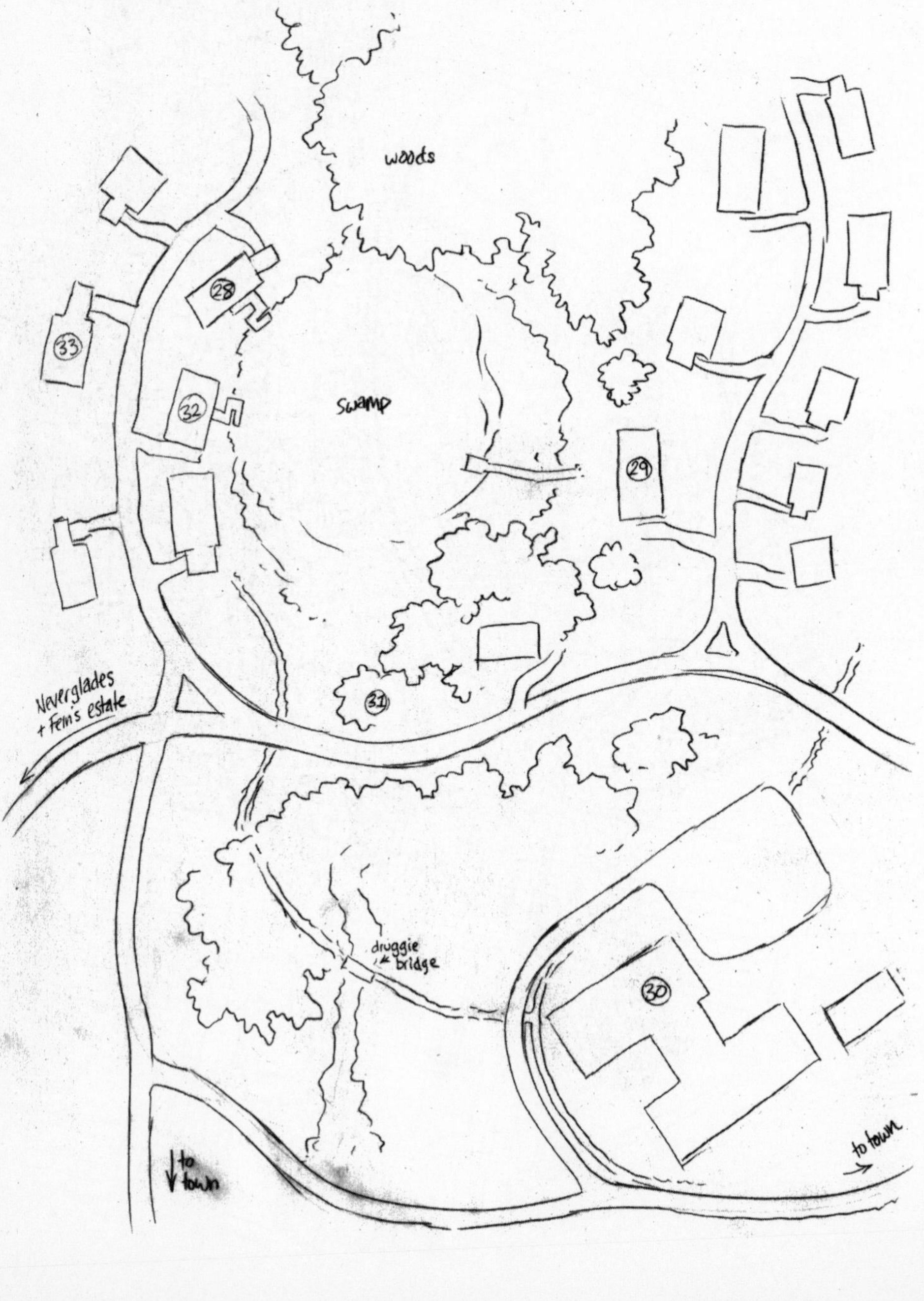

woods
swamp
28
29
30
31
32
33
Neverglades
+ Fern's estate
druggie
bridge
to town
to town

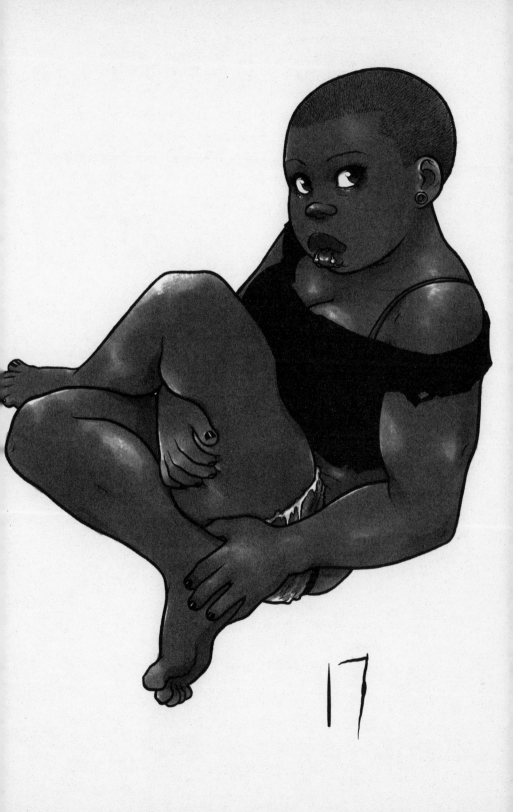

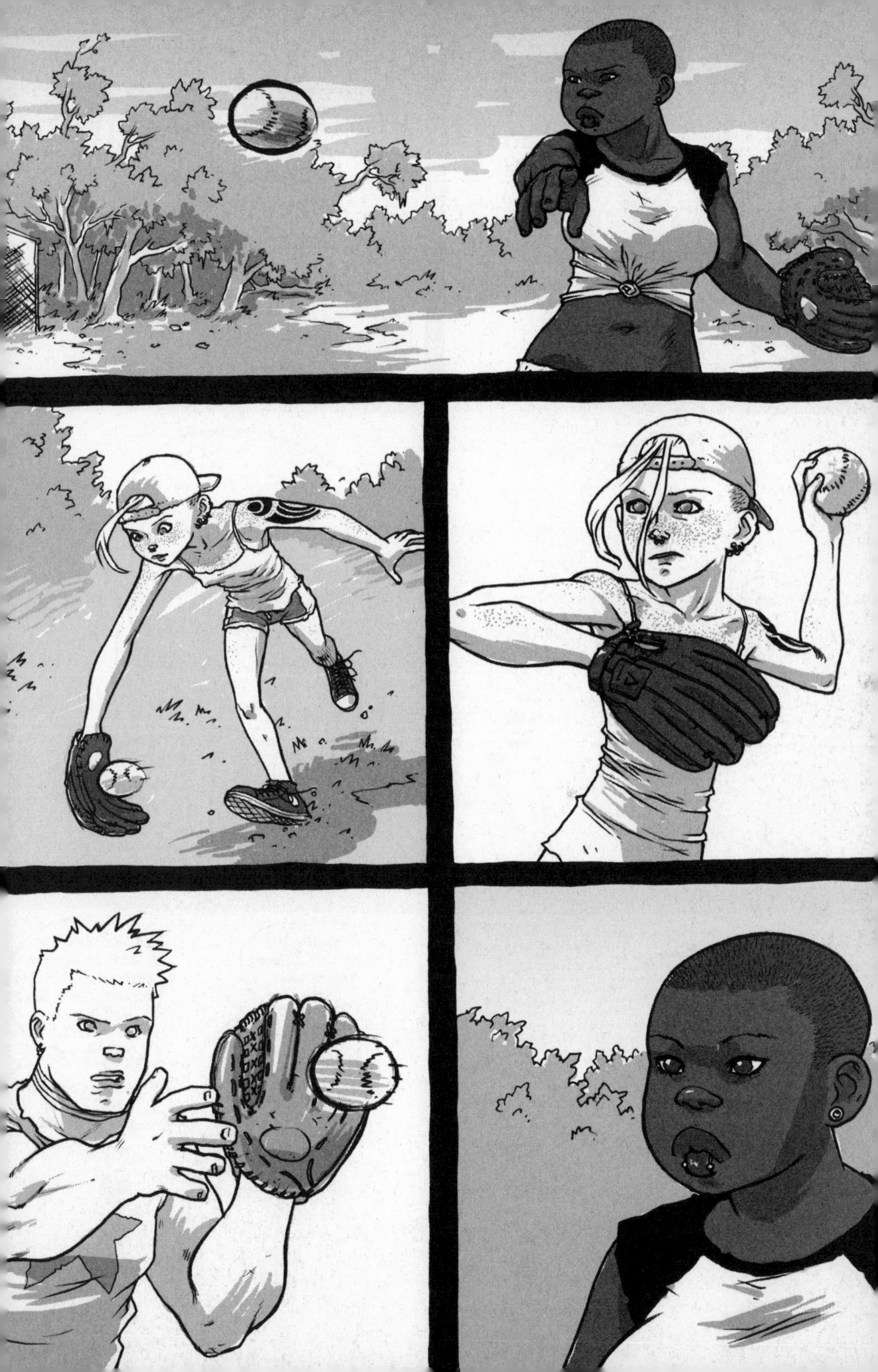

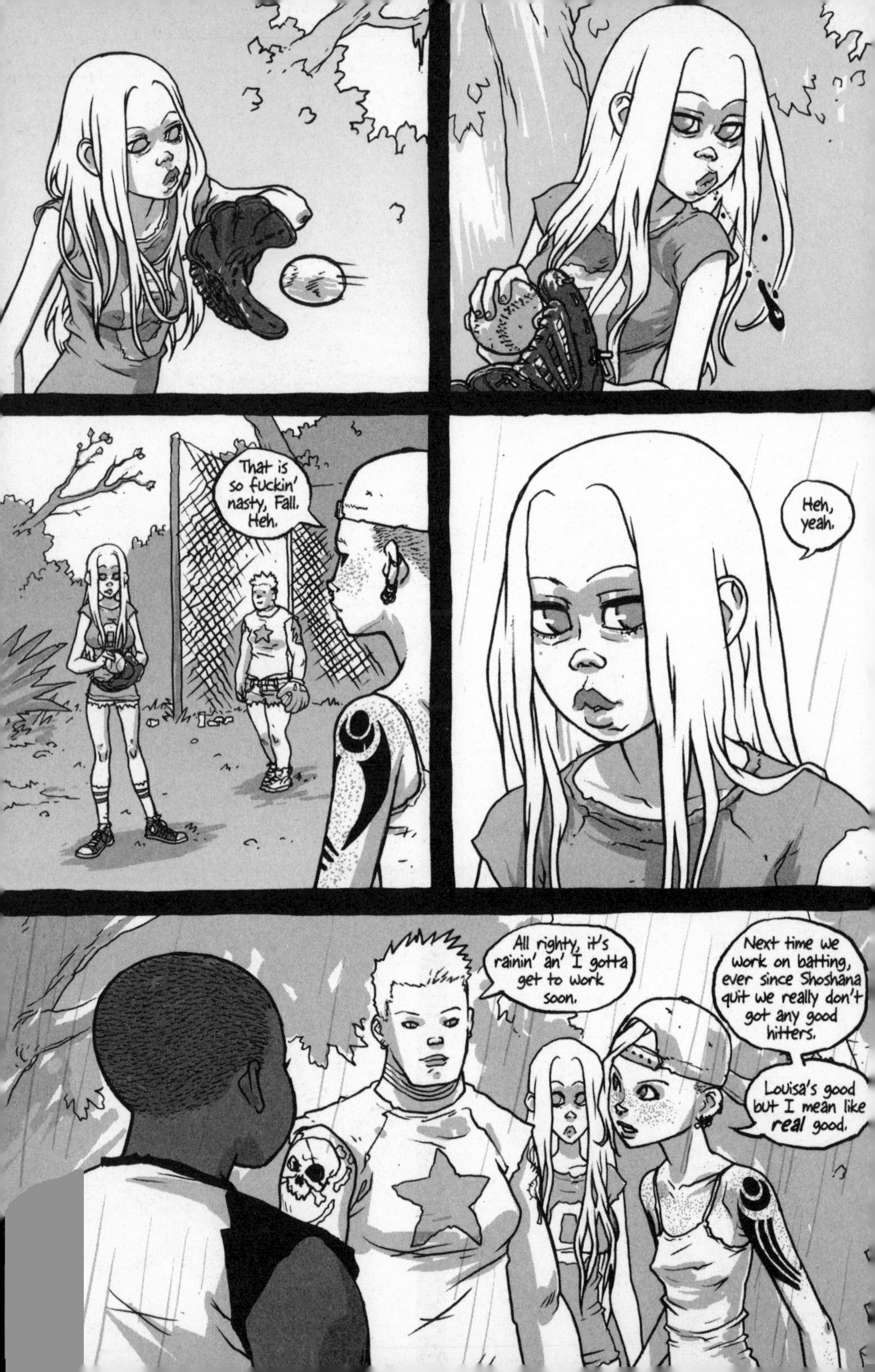
That is so fuckin' nasty, Fall. Heh.
Heh, yeah.
All righty, it's rainin' an' I gotta get to work soon.
Next time we work on batting, ever since Shoshana quit we really don't got any good hitters.
Louisa's good but I mean like real good.

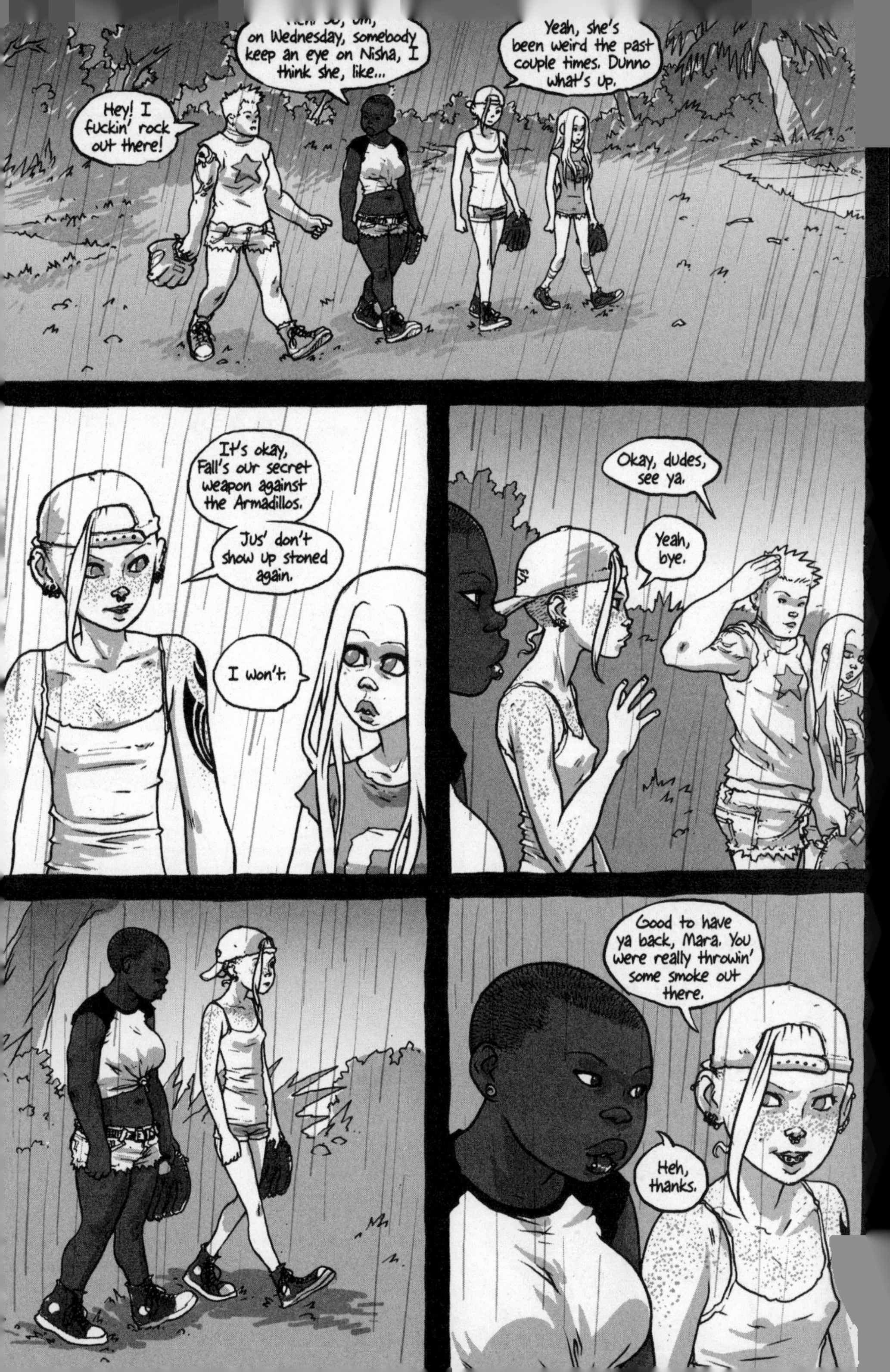
Hey! I fuckin' rock out there!
on Wednesday, somebody keep an eye on Nisha, I think she, like...
Yeah, she's been weird the past couple times. Dunno what's up.
It's okay, Fall's our secret weapon against the Armadillos.
Jus' don't show up stoned again.
I won't.
Okay, dudes, see ya.
Yeah, bye.
Good to have ya back, Mara. You were really throwin' some smoke out there.
Heh, thanks.

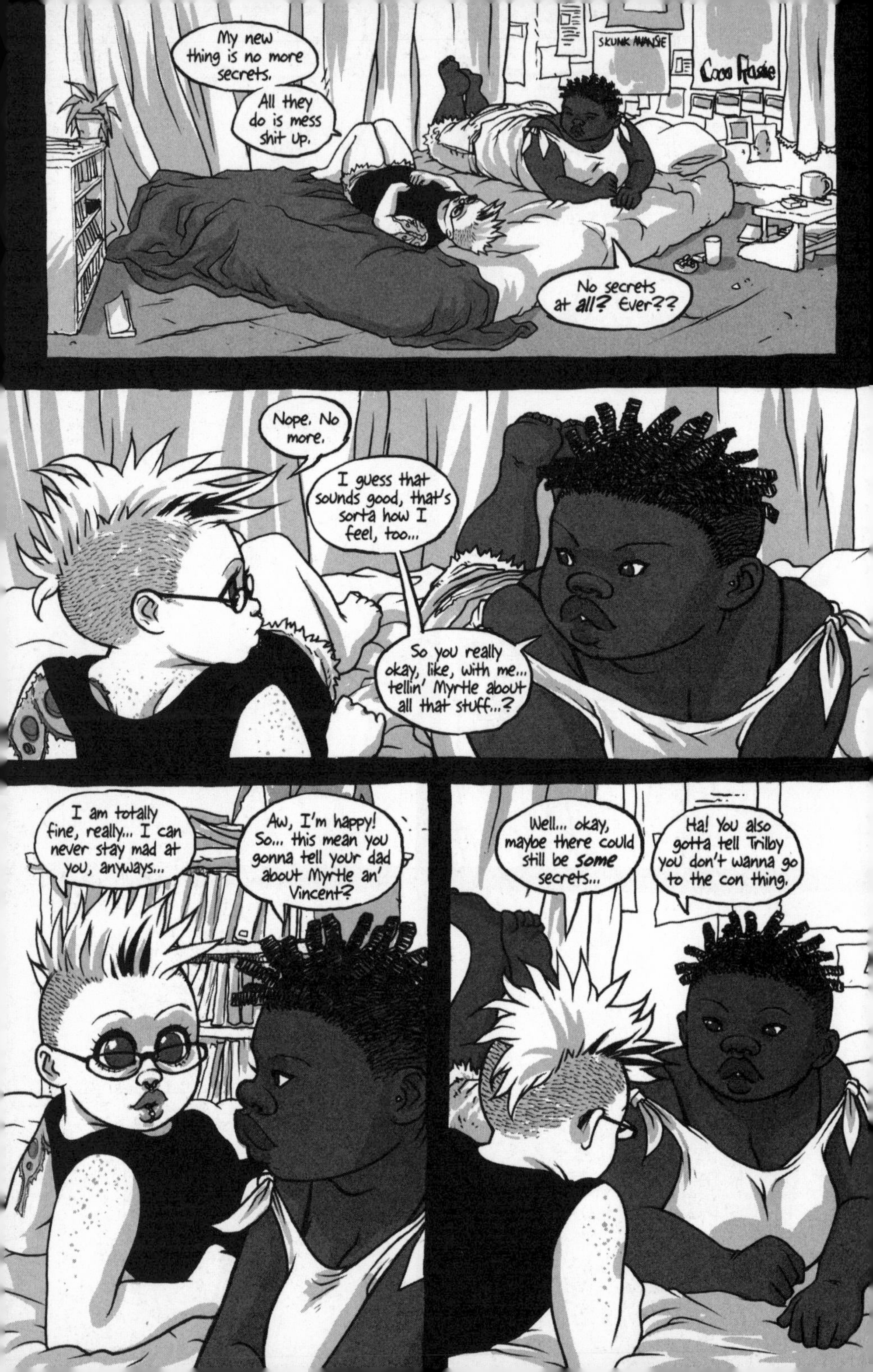

My new thing is no more secrets.
All they do is mess shit up.
SKUNK ANANSIE
Coco Rosie
No secrets at all? Ever??
Nope. No more.
I guess that sounds good, that's sorta how I feel, too...
So you really okay, like, with me... tellin' Myrtle about all that stuff...?
I am totally fine, really... I can never stay mad at you, anyways...
Aw, I'm happy! So... this mean you gonna tell your dad about Myrtle an' Vincent?
Well... okay, maybe there could still be some secrets...
Ha! You also gotta tell Trilby you don't wanna go to the con thing.

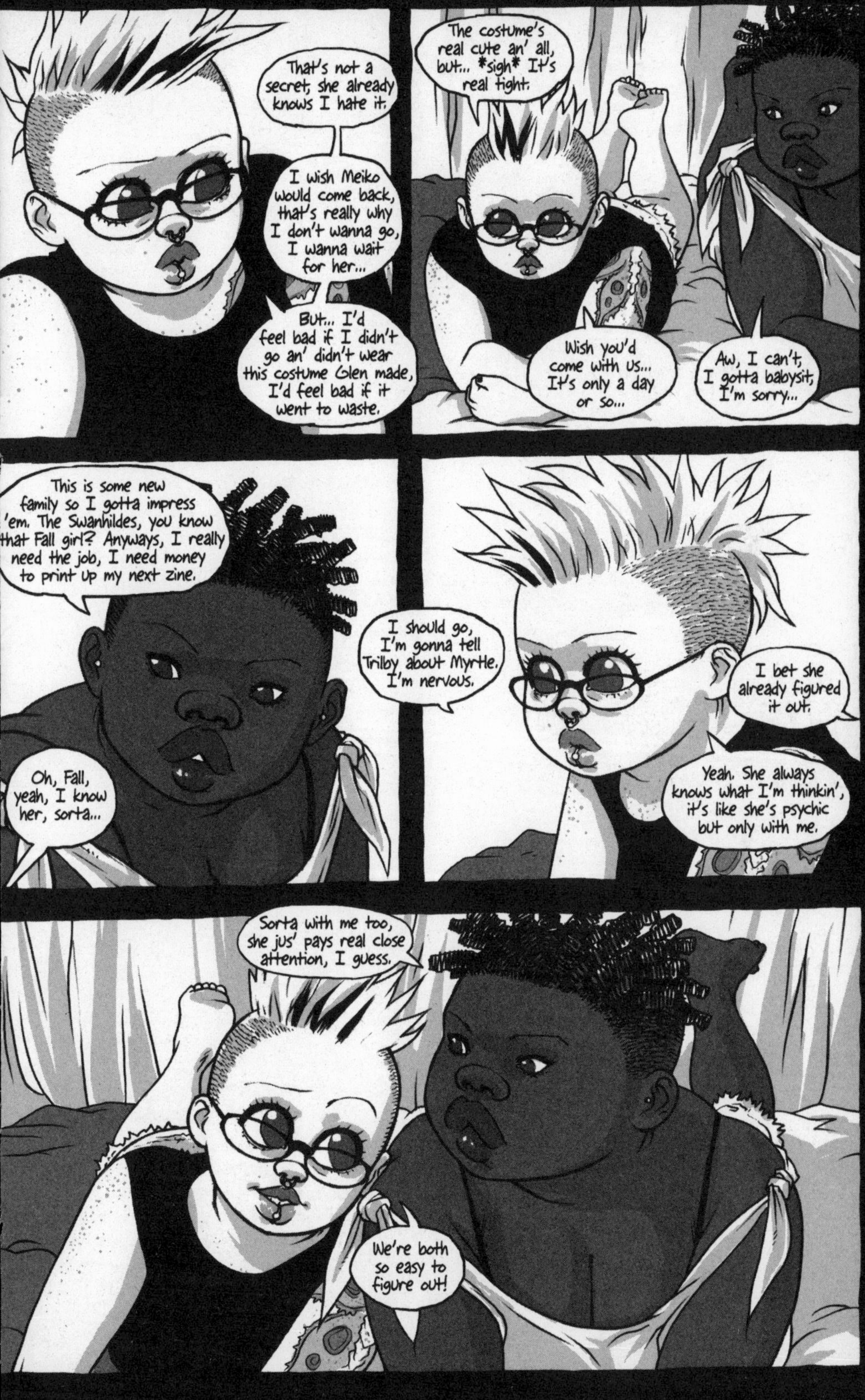
That's not a secret, she already knows I hate it.
I wish Meiko would come back, that's really why I don't wanna go, I wanna wait for her...
But... I'd feel bad if I didn't go an' didn't wear this costume Glen made, I'd feel bad if it went to waste.
The costume's real cute an' all, but... *sigh* It's real tight.
Wish you'd come with us... It's only a day or so...
Aw, I can't, I gotta babysit, I'm sorry...
This is some new family so I gotta impress 'em. The Swanhildes, you know that Fall girl? Anyways, I really need the job, I need money to print up my next zine.
Oh, Fall, yeah, I know her, sorta...
I should go, I'm gonna tell Trilby about Myrtle. I'm nervous.
I bet she already figured it out.
Yeah. She always knows what I'm thinkin', it's like she's psychic but only with me.
Sorta with me too, she jus' pays real close attention, I guess.
We're both so easy to figure out!

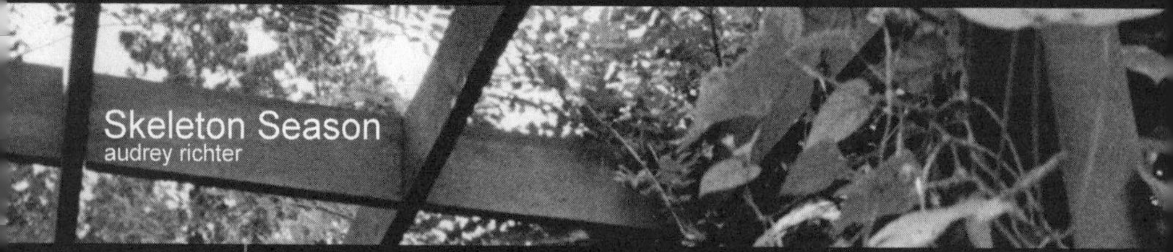
Skeleton Season
audrey richter

Profile

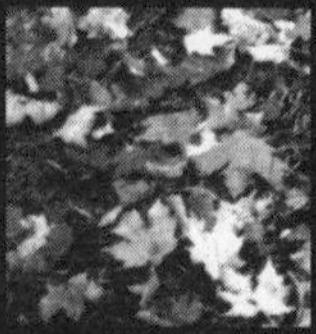

kittyhawk1

Latest Month

October

| S | M | T | W | T | F | S |
|---|---|---|---|---|---|---|
| | | | | 1 | 2 | 3 |
| 4 | 5 | 6 | 7 | 8 | 9 | 10 |
| 11 | 12 | 13 | 14 | 15 | 16 | 17 |
| 18 | 19 | 20 | 21 | 22 | 23 | 24 |
| 25 | 26 | 27 | 28 | 29 | 30 | 31 |

View All Archives

Links

trilbyhatescomics

friendtoroaches

drop-dead

Backyard Birds

Vegans of Color

iamtheshadows.com

kenosha's tomb

230,000 Years Hence

Sisters of Battle

secretcrystal

Evil Galaxy

wetflame

hollow oasis

Twinfold Halfnot

Previous 20

# 97%!

**October 24th, 5:25pm**

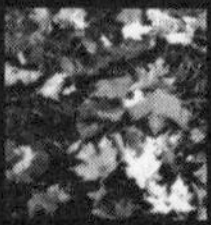

Big babysitting gig this weekend! Actually it's not any different than any others, but I always feel more apprehensive when I get started with a new family who doesn't know me and I don't know how the kids will end up being. But the woman I'm working for, the kids' aunt, said they can be a handful, but I guess every parent/guardian says that.

Anyway, it'll net me a good chunk of cash I can use to put together the next Social Abattoir issue, from which I'll post some pages soon as a teaser! It's like twice the size of the last issue, and I have some interviews with local bands like the Slutty Angels, Nephele, and Gorgon. a friend of mine is dating the vocalist of the Slutty Angels, so I'm getting special treatment! :) I thought about having an advice column either by me or somebody else, in the zine, but I haven't had time to figure it out yet.

Slicer and I are going to visit his parents at some point, probably for Thanksgiving. How terrible. This will be the first time I've gone anywhere for Thanksgiving in about six years, and it's always so awkward explaining to people that you don't eat meat or dairy anymore, and do I say something beforehand so I don't arrive and they only have turkey and I starve? Maybe I could convince them to come HERE, but I guess our apartment isn't big enough... maybe they could stay in my room or whatever and I could stay... ugh, in Slicer's room...? Still, something to think about, so then I could make the Thanksgiving meal! Thanksgiving is kind of a dumb holiday anyway, it doesn't even mean anything anymore, it's been so distorted into just a day where you get together and eat. That's fine, though, but they should have a different day for it, like... Feast Day or some new thing they could make up that doesn't have any historical or sensitive background. I'd be into Feast Day. Dinner Day? Maybe I'll start my own withmy friends. My friend Cleo is big into baking, she'd be into it.

I got a new pair of binoculars the other day, they can see so far and clear! There are some weird swamp birds here in Wet Moon that I want to go take a look at. I hear al these strange bird calls at night and I always think that maybe since the marshes here are so expansive and mysterious, that I'll someday discover a new species of bird nobody knew about. Maybe a bird that lives underwater and comes up to breathe lik a whale? Oh wait I guess that's a penguin. But this one would live in swamps. Or jus a bird with gills? haha. I think a lot about new species, how so many species become extinct every day but we also find new ones to replace them (maybe not at the same rate, but maybe it will be when we can fully explore the ocean!), and there is still so much of Earth left unexplored. I went to a lecture last week and the speaker said tha we've only explored 3% of our oceans!! What is in that other 97%?? Who knows what's out there! Waterbreathing swampbirds? maybe...

**Mood:** inquisitive
**Current Music:** Fugees- temple
**Tags:** social abattoir, babysitting, slicer, birds

3 comments | Leave a comment

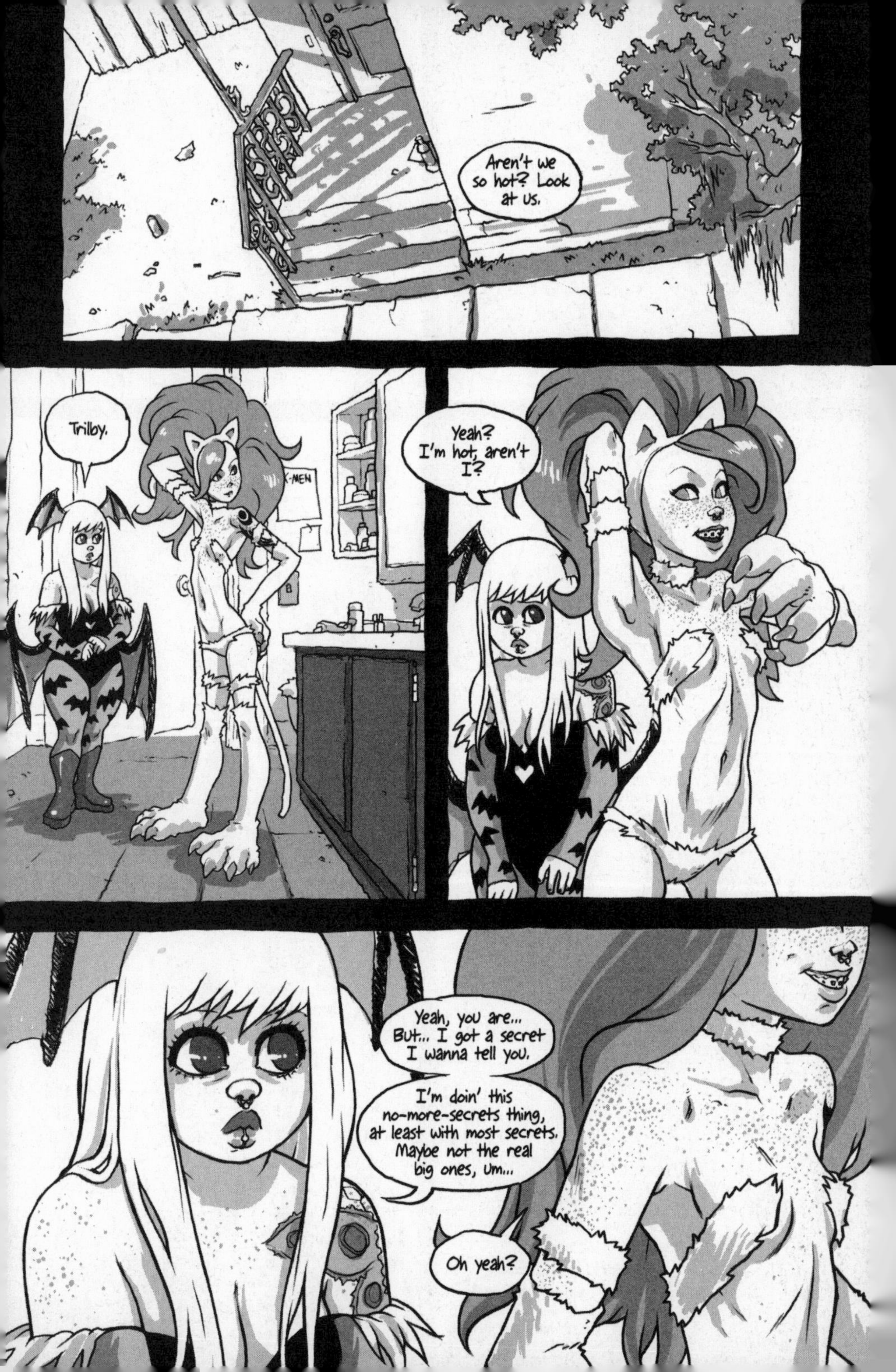
Aren't we so hot? Look at us.
Trilby.
K-MEN
Yeah? I'm hot, aren't I?
Yeah, you are... But... I got a secret I wanna tell you.
I'm doin' this no-more-secrets thing, at least with most secrets. Maybe not the real big ones, um...
Oh yeah?

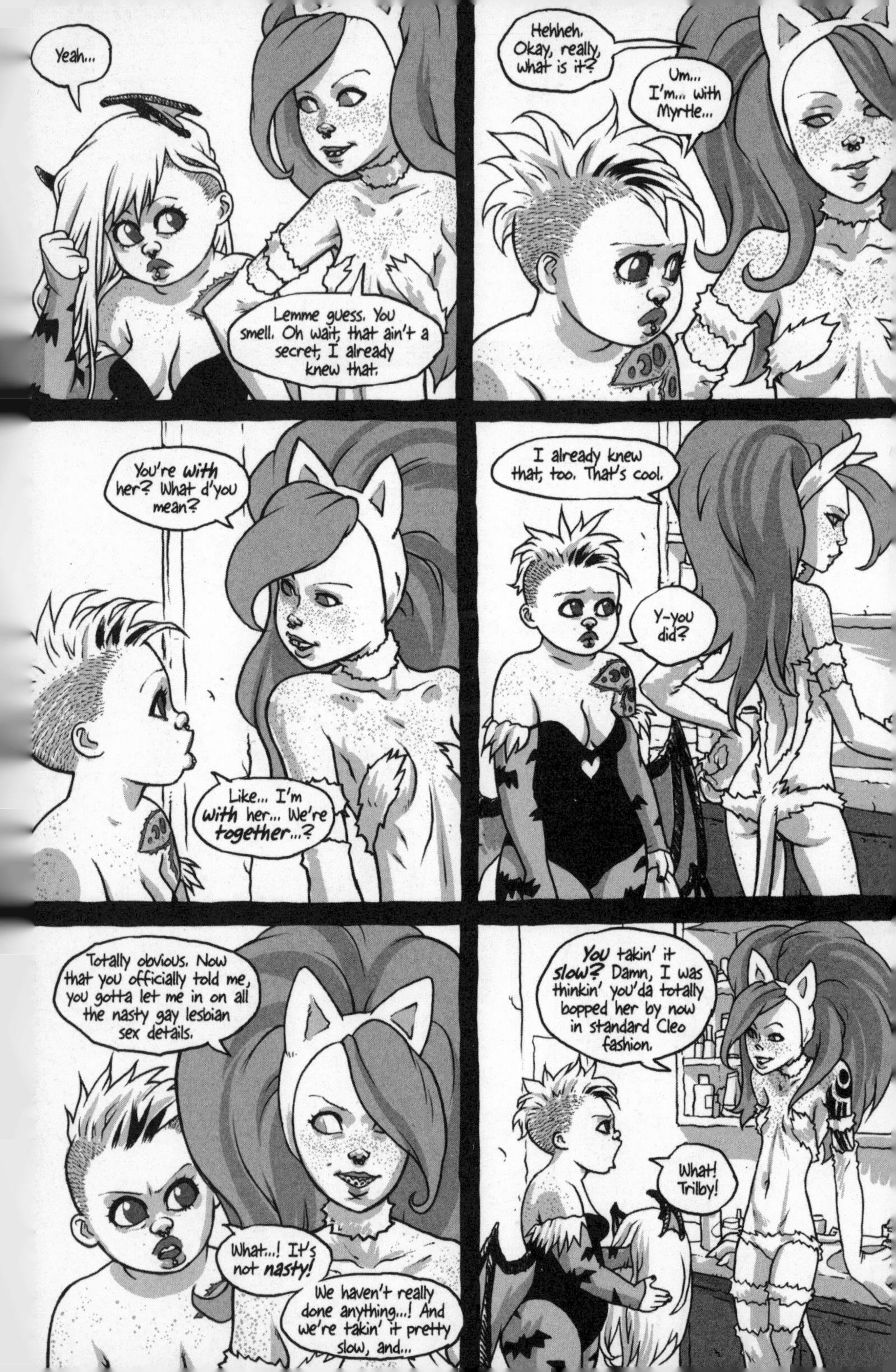

Yeah...
Lemme guess. You smell. Oh wait, that ain't a secret, I already knew that.
Hehheh. Okay, really, what is it?
Um... I'm... with Myrtle...
You're *with* her? What d'you mean?
Like... I'm *with* her... We're *together*...?
I already knew that, too. That's cool.
Y-you did?
Totally obvious. Now that you officially told me, you gotta let me in on all the nasty gay lesbian sex details.
What...! It's not *nasty!*
We haven't really done anything...! And we're takin' it pretty slow, and...
*YOU* takin' it *slow?* Damn, I was thinkin' you'da totally bopped her by now in standard Cleo fashion.
What! Trilby!

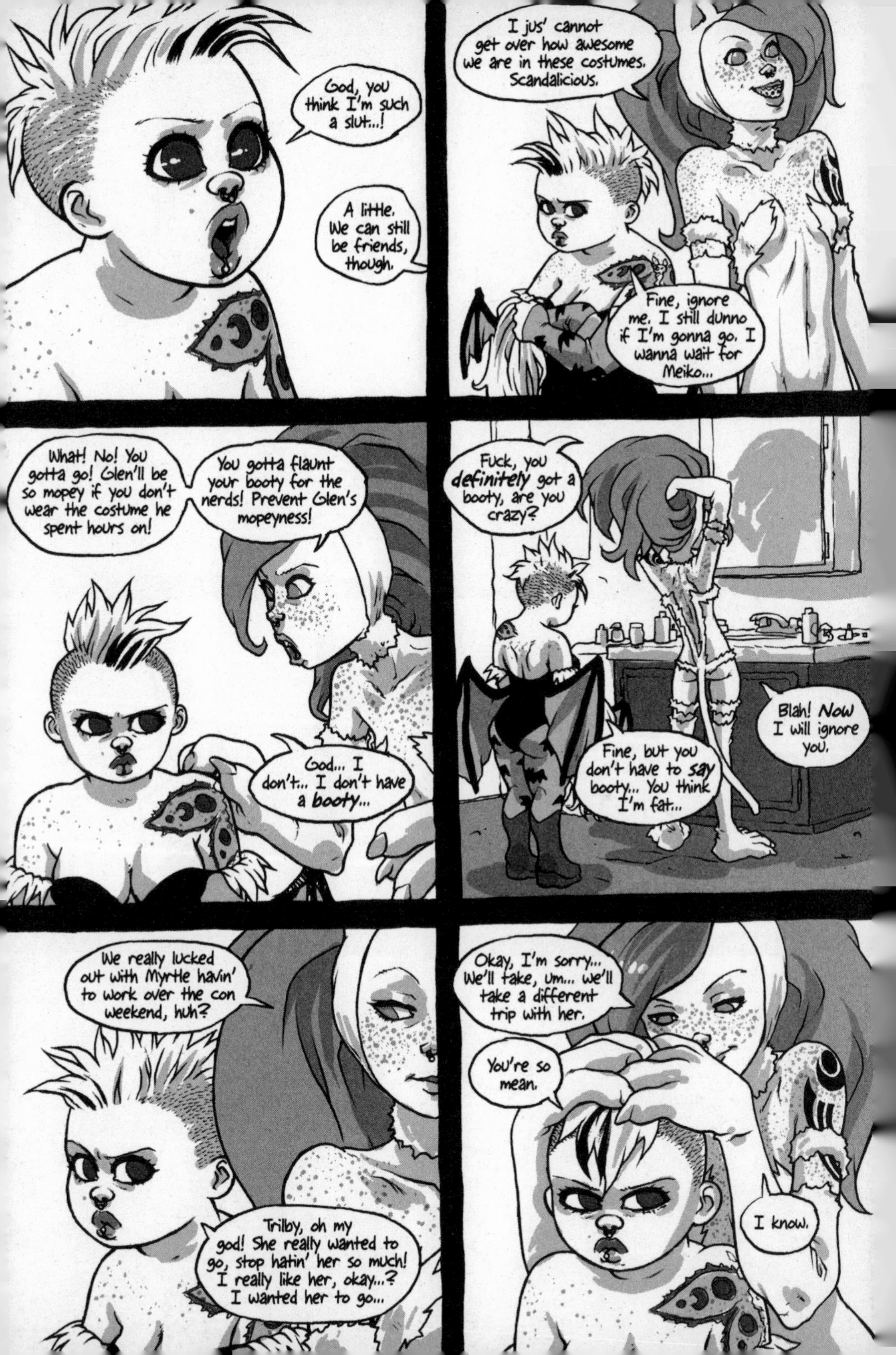
God, you think I'm such a slut...!
A little. We can still be friends, though.
I jus' cannot get over how awesome we are in these costumes. Scandalicious.
Fine, ignore me. I still dunno if I'm gonna go. I wanna wait for Meiko...
What! No! You gotta go! Glen'll be so mopey if you don't wear the costume he spent hours on!
You gotta flaunt your booty for the nerds! Prevent Glen's mopeyness!
God... I don't... I don't have a booty...
Fuck, you definitely got a booty, are you crazy?
Fine, but you don't have to say booty... You think I'm fat...
Blah! Now I will ignore you.
We really lucked out with Myrtle havin' to work over the con weekend, huh?
Trilby, oh my god! She really wanted to go, stop hatin' her so much! I really like her, okay...? I wanted her to go...
Okay, I'm sorry... We'll take, um... we'll take a different trip with her.
You're so mean.
I know.

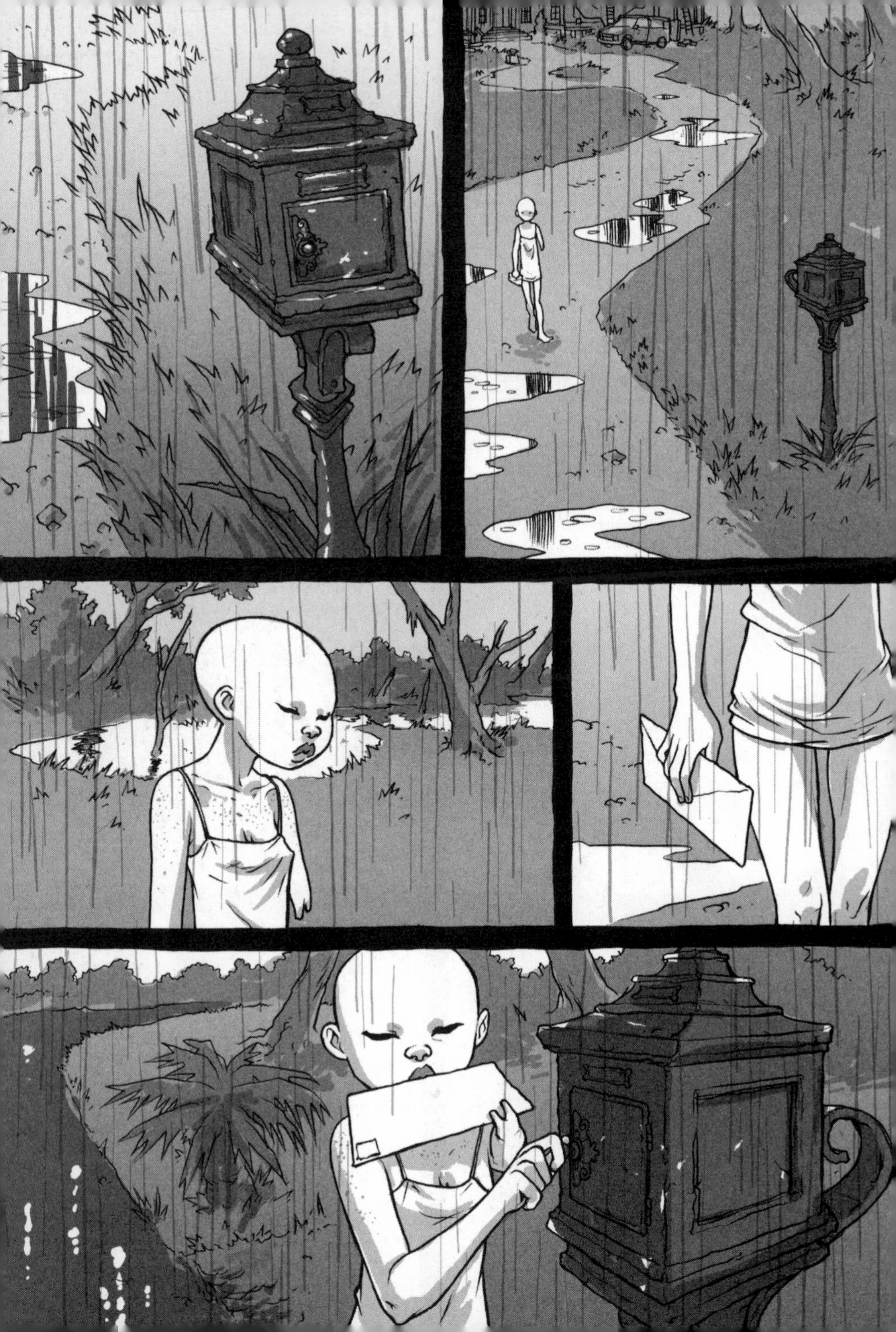

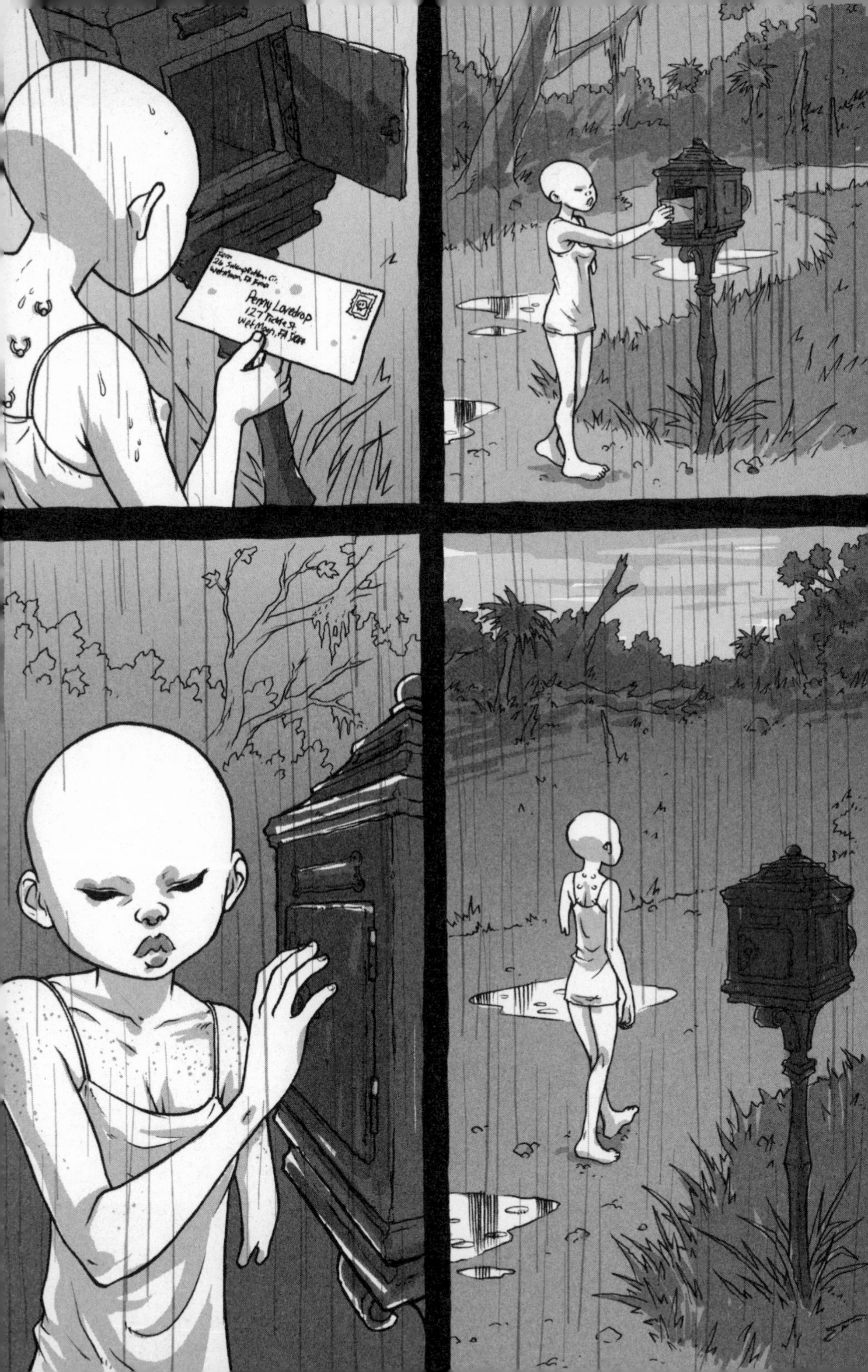
Penny Lovedrop
127 Tickle St.
Wet Moon, FL

October 25

I've been keeping an eye on Malady like Trilby said to. I'm supposed to look for suspicious behavior but I haven't been able to tell if there's been any... Malady's just all ~~around~~ around weird all the time, so if she WAS acting suspicious I'd never be able to ~~tell~~ tell. It could be that she knows I'm onto her, and that's ~~why~~ why she isn't putting up any new fliers. I don't even care anymore.

I told Trilby about me and Myrtle. I should have known it wouldn't be a big deal, Trilby said she didn't even care. Or at least she acted like she didn't care. Or tried to. I know she does, like she's weirded out by me liking other girls. Even though she always championed me getting together with Myrtle before. I think maybe I should just go ahead and tell other people, maybe even my dad and Penny, because everyone else seems to be taking it so casually, but I still can't work up the courage. I don't know what'll happen. I don't know where this came from, this me liking girls thing, I don't know if it means I'm a real lesbian or what... Is it okay for me to be with a girl? I still like guys, though... Even though I haven't been with a guy since Vincent... But I've had sex with a bunch of other ~~guys~~ guys since I was 13, what does that mean? I could be bi, but Trilby always makes fun of bisexual people and stuff, so she'd probably tell me to knock it off, pick a gender and stick with it. I don't know. I think that's kind of sad.

i'm jealous of everyone's looks. Penny especially, i think, I wish i had her body so much. Trilby, Mara... and Audrey has these extraordinary curves and boobs... I could never get like that. i'd love to have Trilby's body too. she works at a lot but even if I did too I could never get like that, she's always been naturally svelte. she says it's genetics. she can scarf down so much food and not gain a pound, she burns it off so fast! i'm jealous of the whole world!

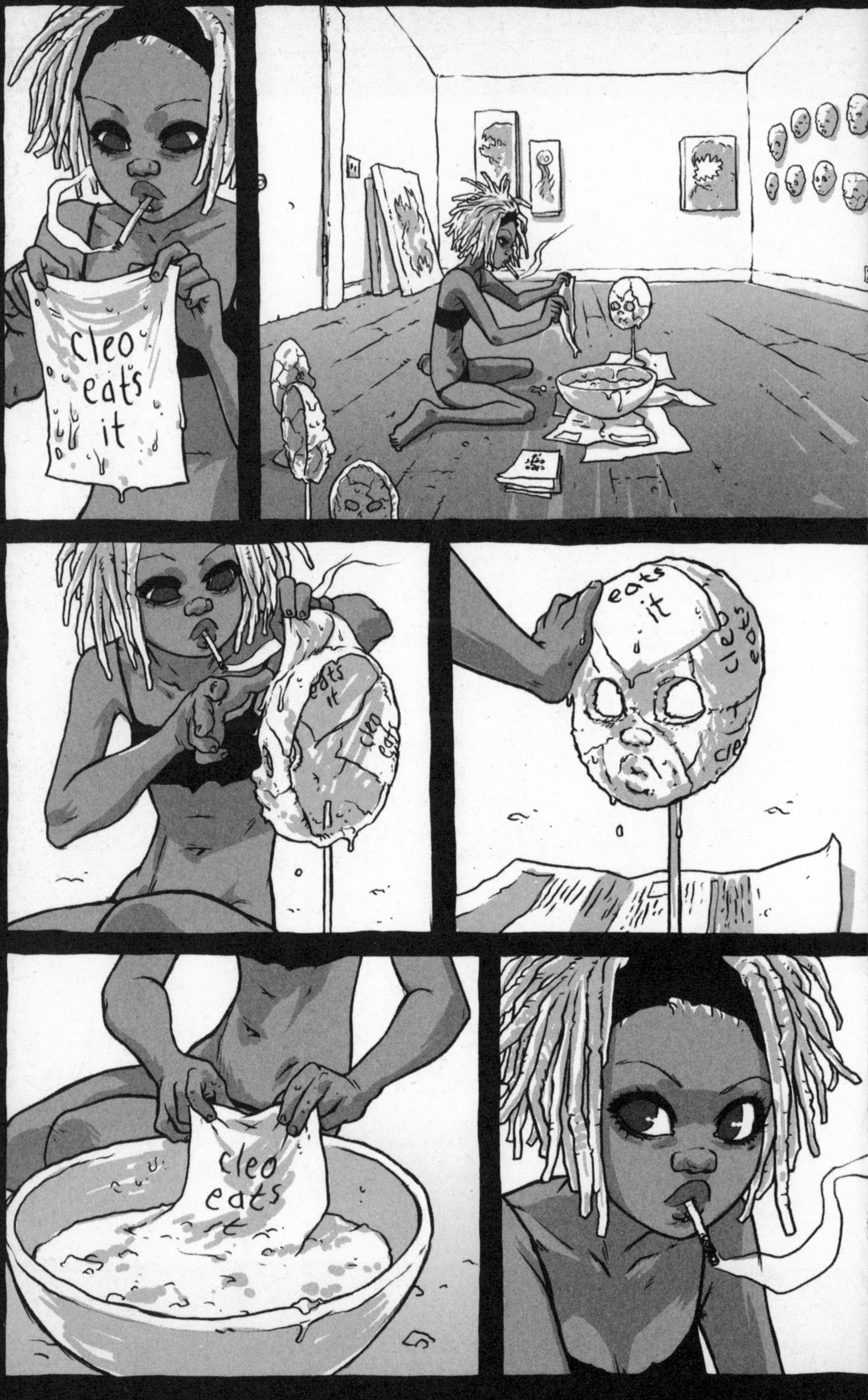
cleo eats it
eats it
cleo eats
eats it
cleo eats

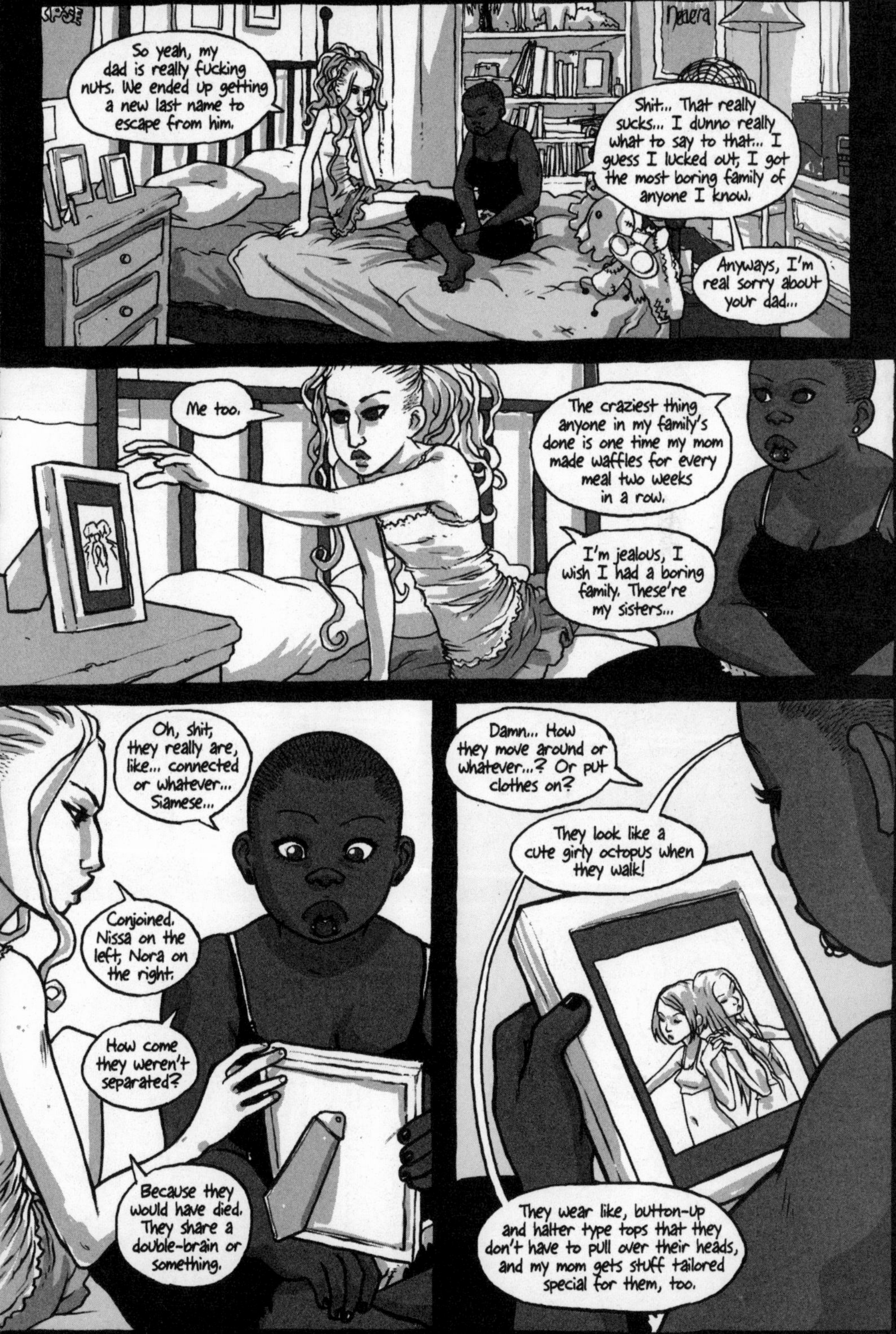
So yeah, my dad is really fucking nuts. We ended up getting a new last name to escape from him.
Shit... That really sucks... I dunno really what to say to that... I guess I lucked out, I got the most boring family of anyone I know.
Anyways, I'm real sorry about your dad...
Me too.
The craziest thing anyone in my family's done is one time my mom made waffles for every meal two weeks in a row.
I'm jealous, I wish I had a boring family. These're my sisters...
Oh, shit, they really are, like... connected or whatever... Siamese...
Conjoined. Nissa on the left, Nora on the right.
How come they weren't separated?
Because they would have died. They share a double-brain or something.
Damn... How they move around or whatever...? Or put clothes on?
They look like a cute girly octopus when they walk!
They wear like, button-up and halter type tops that they don't have to pull over their heads, and my mom gets stuff tailored special for them, too.

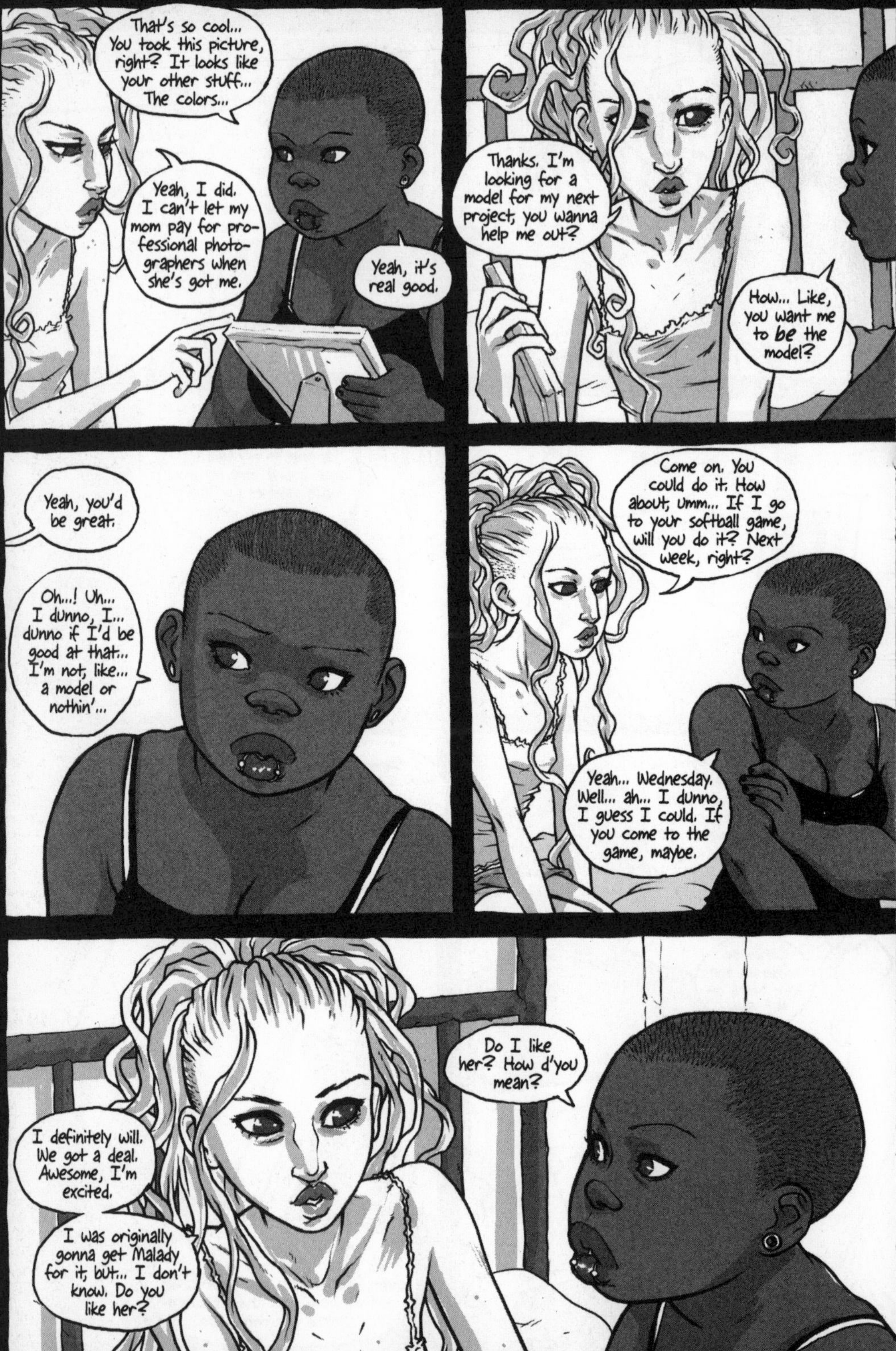
That's so cool... You took this picture, right? It looks like your other stuff... The colors...
Yeah, I did. I can't let my mom pay for professional photographers when she's got me.
Yeah, it's real good.
Thanks. I'm looking for a model for my next project, you wanna help me out?
How... Like, you want me to *be* the model?
Yeah, you'd be great.
Oh...! Uh... I dunno, I... dunno if I'd be good at that... I'm not, like... a model or nothin'...
Come on. You could do it. How about, umm... If I go to your softball game, will you do it? Next week, right?
Yeah... Wednesday. Well... ah... I dunno, I guess I could. If you come to the game, maybe.
I definitely will. We got a deal. Awesome, I'm excited.
I was originally gonna get Malady for it, but... I don't know. Do you like her?
Do I like her? How d'you mean?

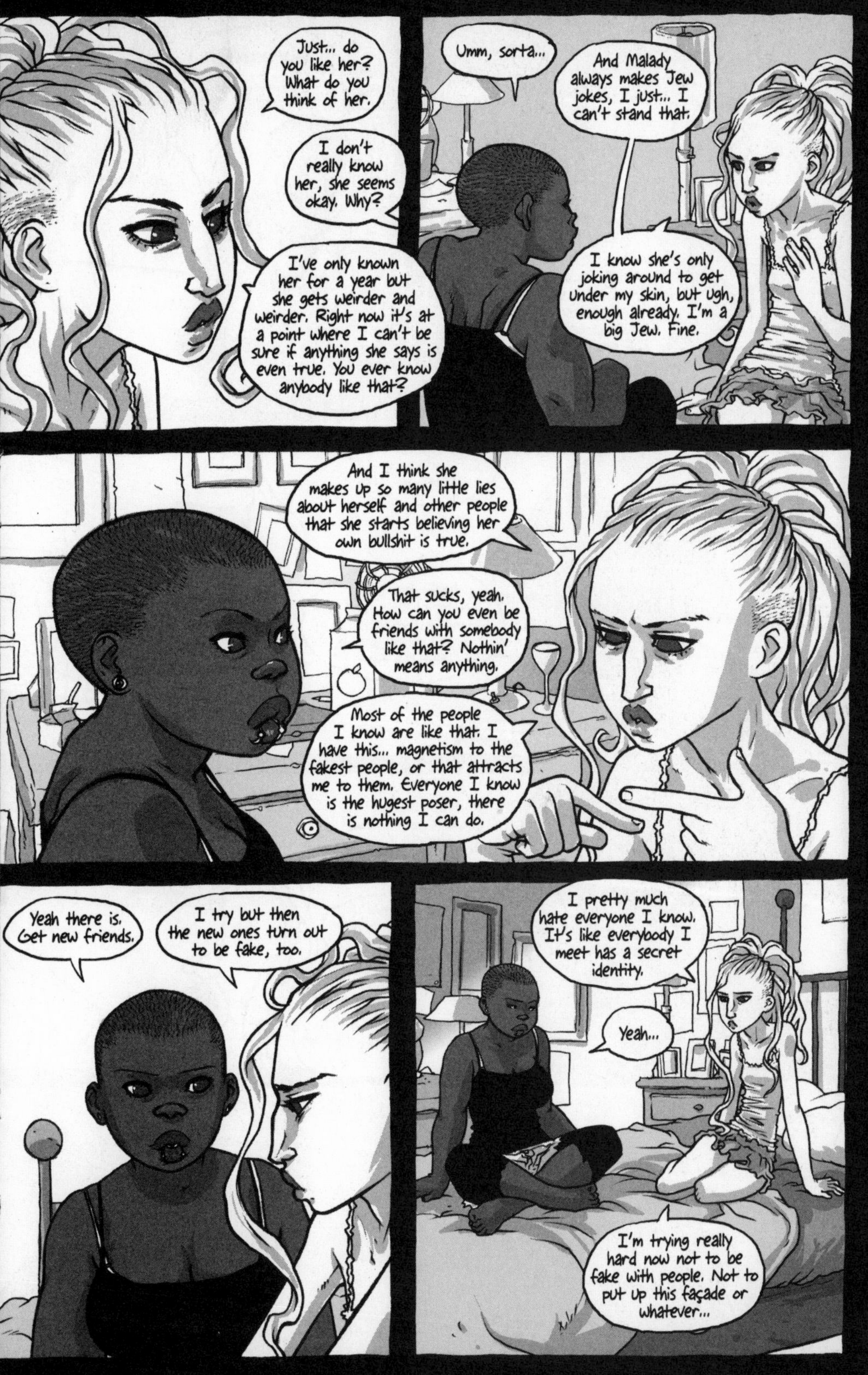
Just... do you like her? What do you think of her.
I don't really know her, she seems okay. Why?
I've only known her for a year but she gets weirder and weirder. Right now it's at a point where I can't be sure if anything she says is even true. You ever know anybody like that?
Umm, sorta...
And Malady always makes Jew jokes, I just... I can't stand that.
I know she's only joking around to get under my skin, but ugh, enough already. I'm a big Jew. Fine.
And I think she makes up so many little lies about herself and other people that she starts believing her own bullshit is true.
That sucks, yeah. How can you even be friends with somebody like that? Nothin' means anything.
Most of the people I know are like that. I have this... magnetism to the fakest people, or that attracts me to them. Everyone I know is the hugest poser, there is nothing I can do.
Yeah there is. Get new friends.
I try but then the new ones turn out to be fake, too.
I pretty much hate everyone I know. It's like everybody I meet has a secret identity.
Yeah...
I'm trying really hard now not to be fake with people. Not to put up this façade or whatever...

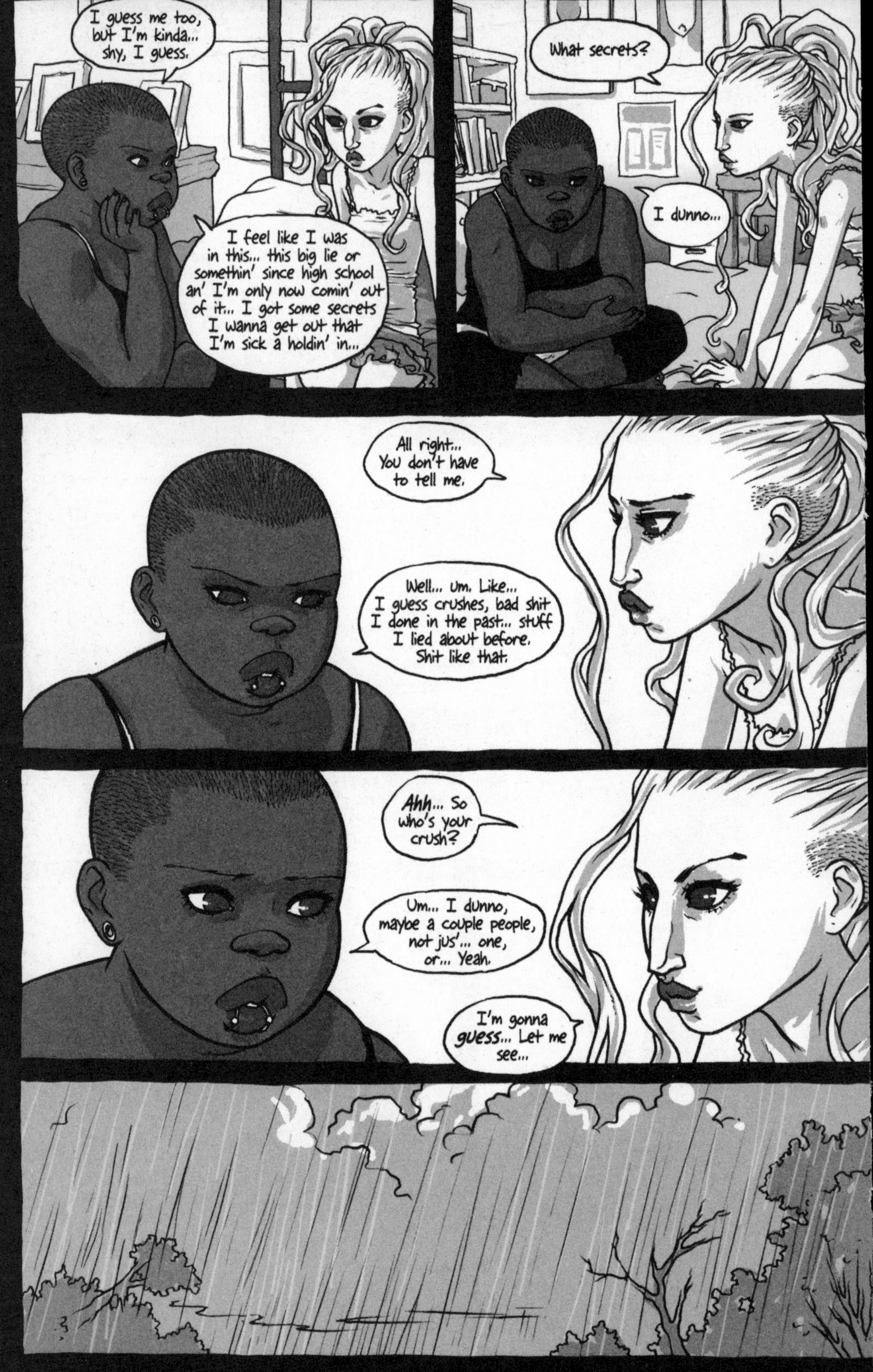
I guess me too, but I'm kinda... shy, I guess.
I feel like I was in this... this big lie or somethin' since high school an' I'm only now comin' out of it... I got some secrets I wanna get out that I'm sick a holdin' in...
What secrets?
I dunno...
All right... You don't have to tell me.
Well... um. Like... I guess crushes, bad shit I done in the past... stuff I lied about before. Shit like that.
Ahh... So who's your crush?
Um... I dunno, maybe a couple people, not jus'... one, or... Yeah.
I'm gonna guess... Let me see...

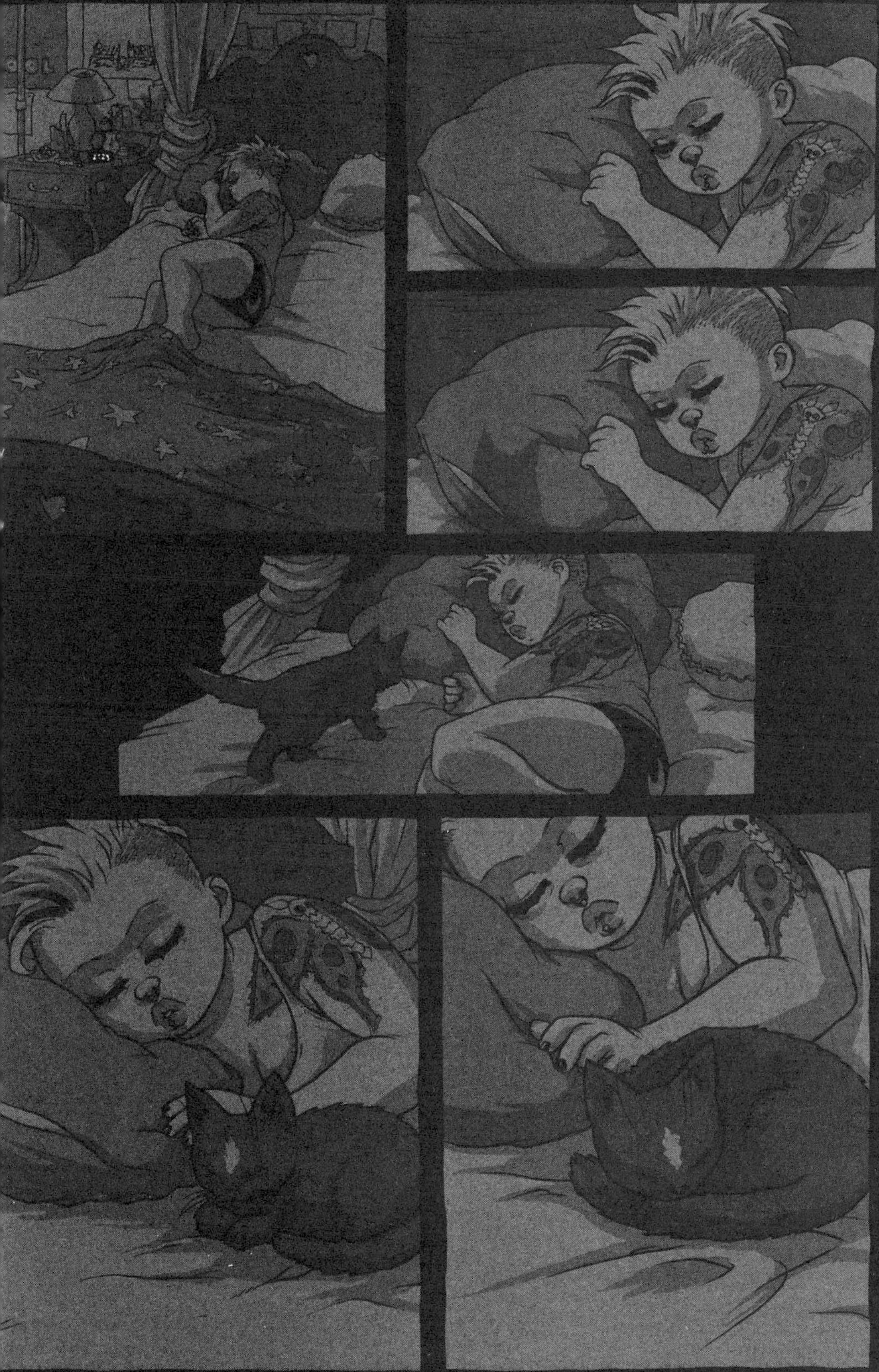

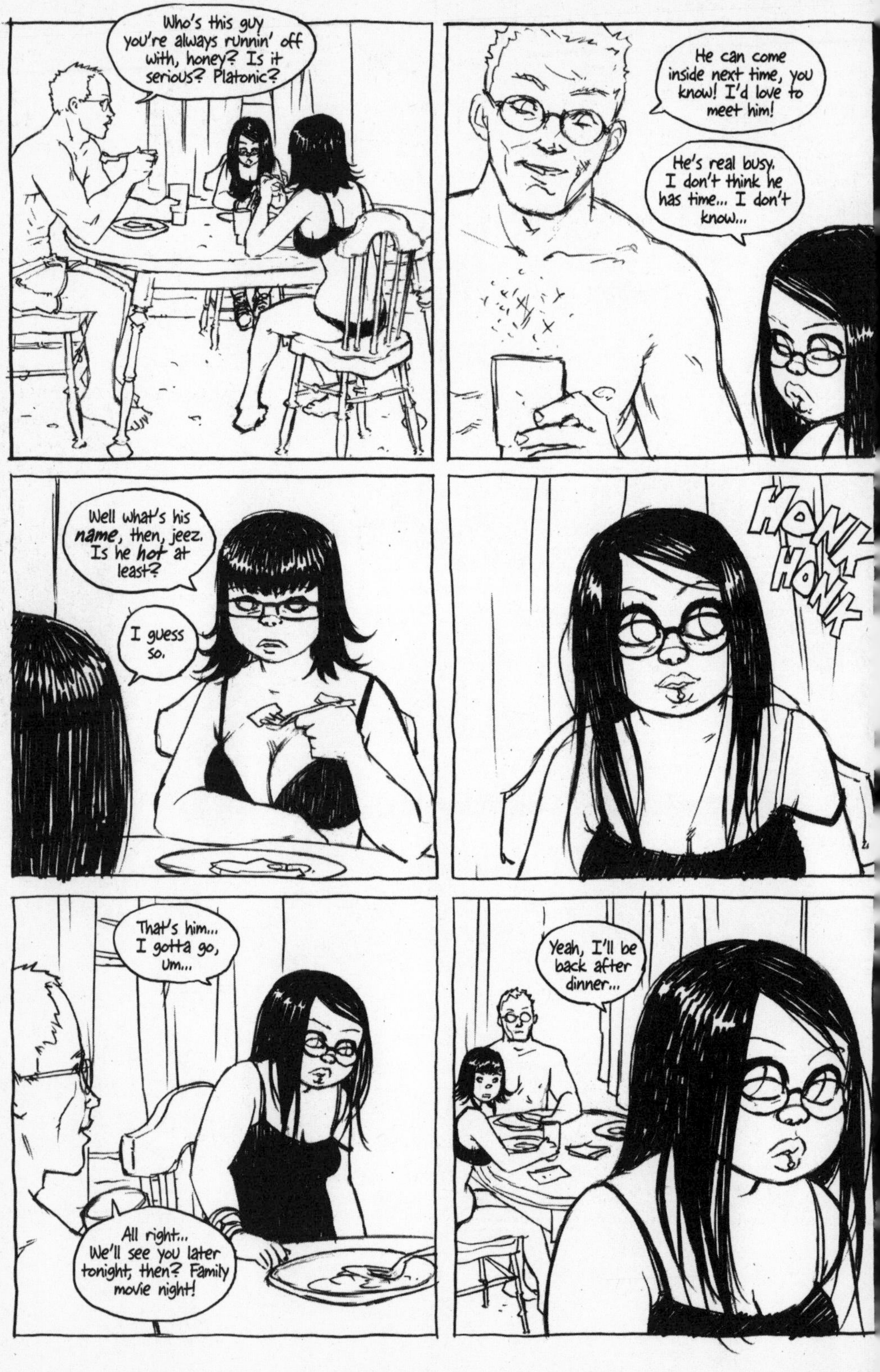
Who's this guy you're always runnin' off with, honey? Is it serious? Platonic?
He can come inside next time, you know! I'd love to meet him!
He's real busy. I don't think he has time... I don't know...
Well what's his *name*, then, jeez. Is he *hot* at least?
I guess so.
HONK HONK
That's him... I gotta go, um...
All right... We'll see you later tonight, then? Family movie night!
Yeah, I'll be back after dinner...

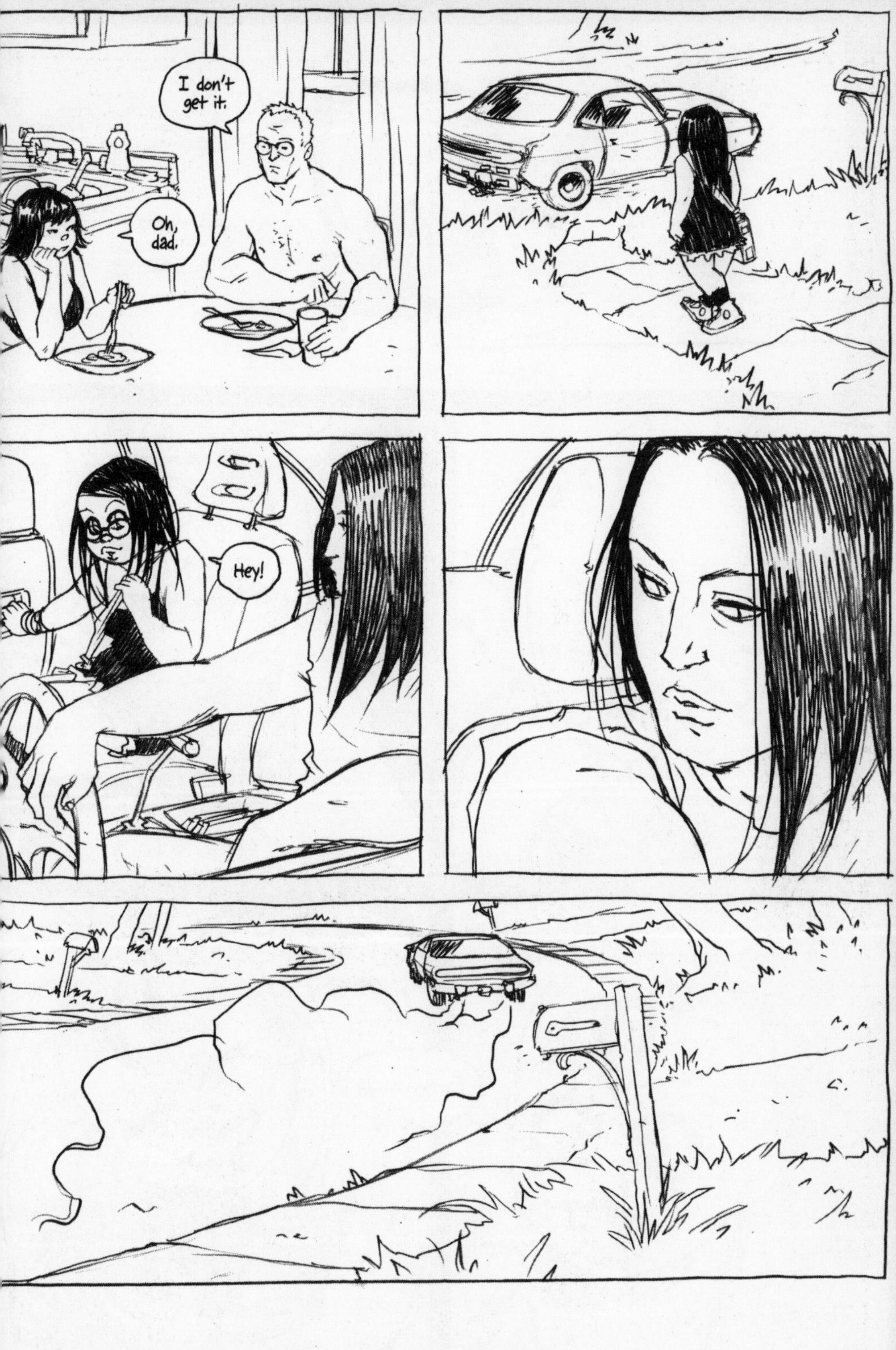
I don't get it.
Oh, dad.
Hey!

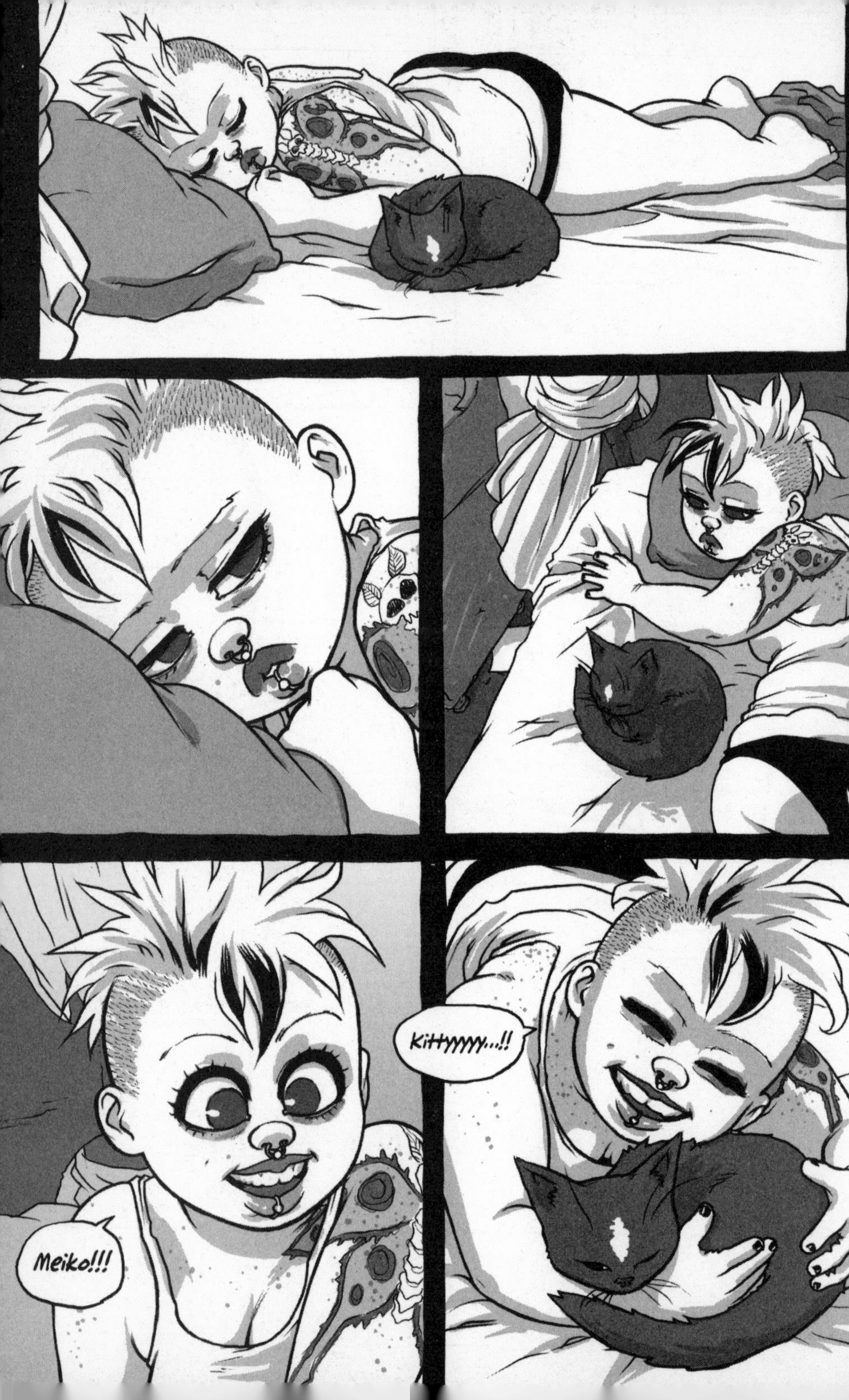
Meiko!!!
Kittyyyyy...!!

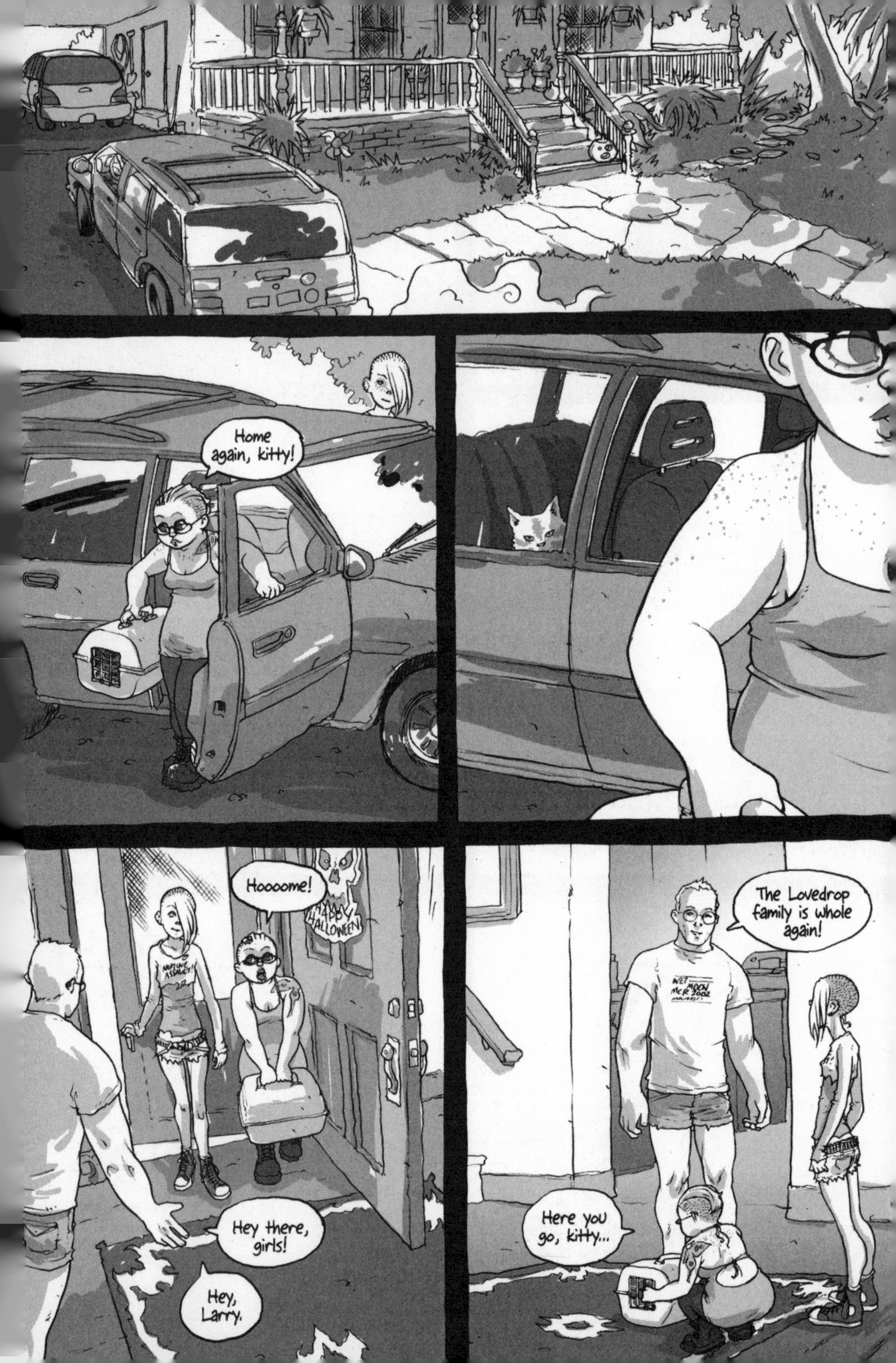
Home again, kitty!
Hoooome!
HAPPY HALLOWEEN
Hey there, girls!
Hey, Larry.
The Lovedrop family is whole again!
Here you go, kitty...

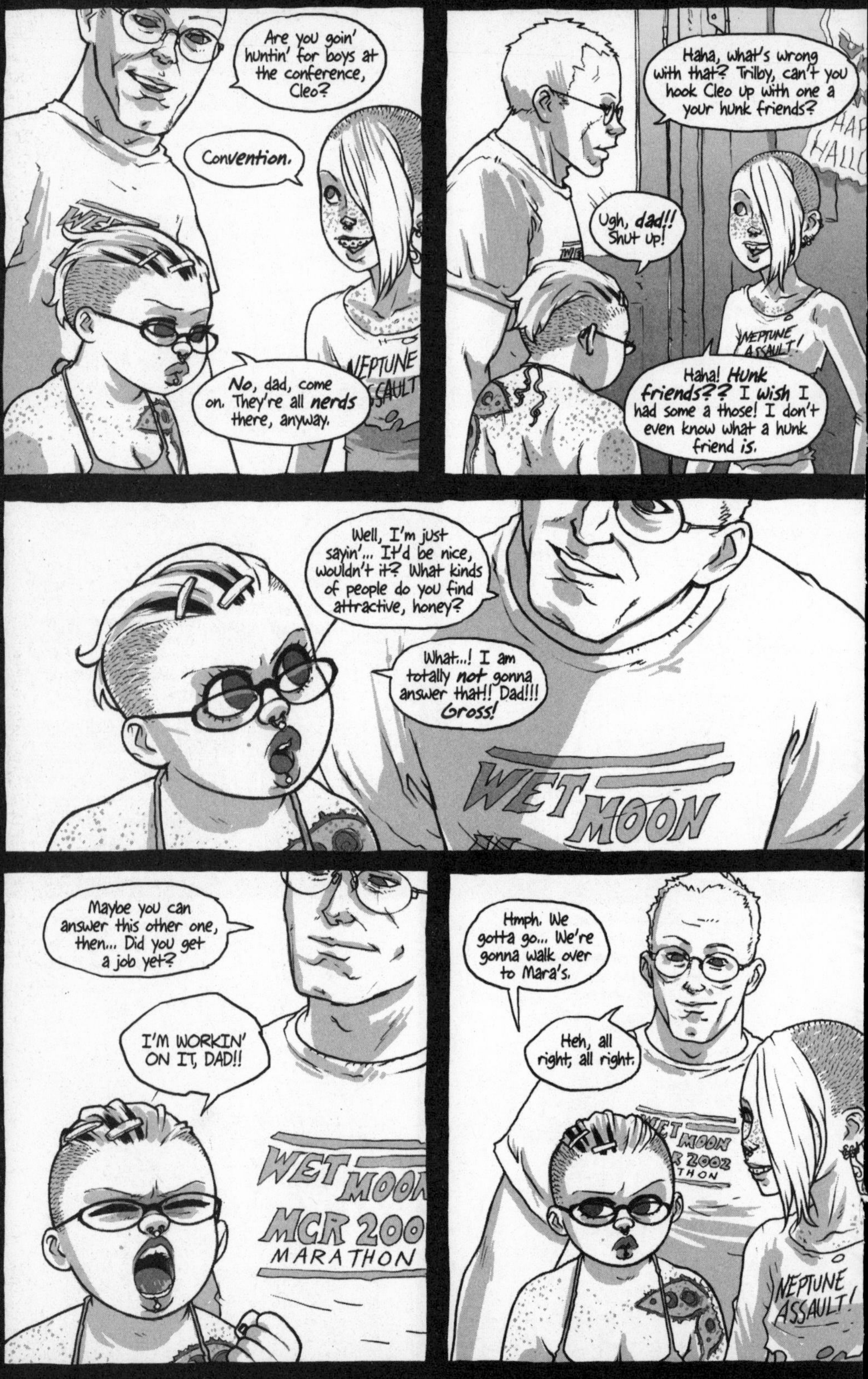
Are you goin' huntin' for boys at the conference, Cleo?
Convention.
No, dad, come on. They're all **nerds** there, anyway.
Haha, what's wrong with that? Trilby, can't you hook Cleo up with one a your hunk friends?
Ugh, **dad!!** Shut up!
Haha! ***Hunk friends??*** I ***wish*** I had some a those! I don't even know what a hunk friend ***is.***
NEPTUNE ASSAULT!
Well, I'm just sayin'... It'd be nice, wouldn't it? What kinds of people do you find attractive, honey?
What...! I am totally ***not*** gonna answer that!! Dad!!! ***Gross!***
WET MOON
Maybe you can answer this other one, then... Did you get a job yet?
I'M WORKIN' ON IT, DAD!!
MARATHON
Hmph. We gotta go... We're gonna walk over to Mara's.
Heh, all right, all right.
NEPTUNE ASSAULT!

October 26

# Meiko is HOME!!!

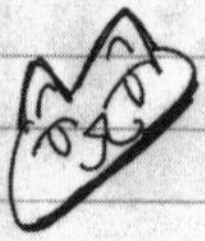

oh my god she just APPEARED!!!!! i woke up and she was there on my bed, i don't know where she came from!!! oh wow, I am so happy now. everything seems perfect now, i feel so relieved! i'm so excited i can hardly even write this! where could she have been? was she hiding out in Bowden House the whole time? is there a secret cat community she went to?? i wish she could talk or that I could understand cat language so i could know. or maybe she could write, she could use her paw in some dirt and write what happened. i guess maybe she would only write in cat language, though. meow meow mew meow mewmew mew.

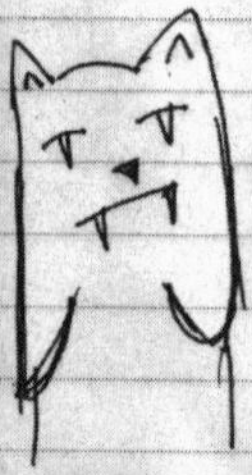

SO HAPPY!!

# 18

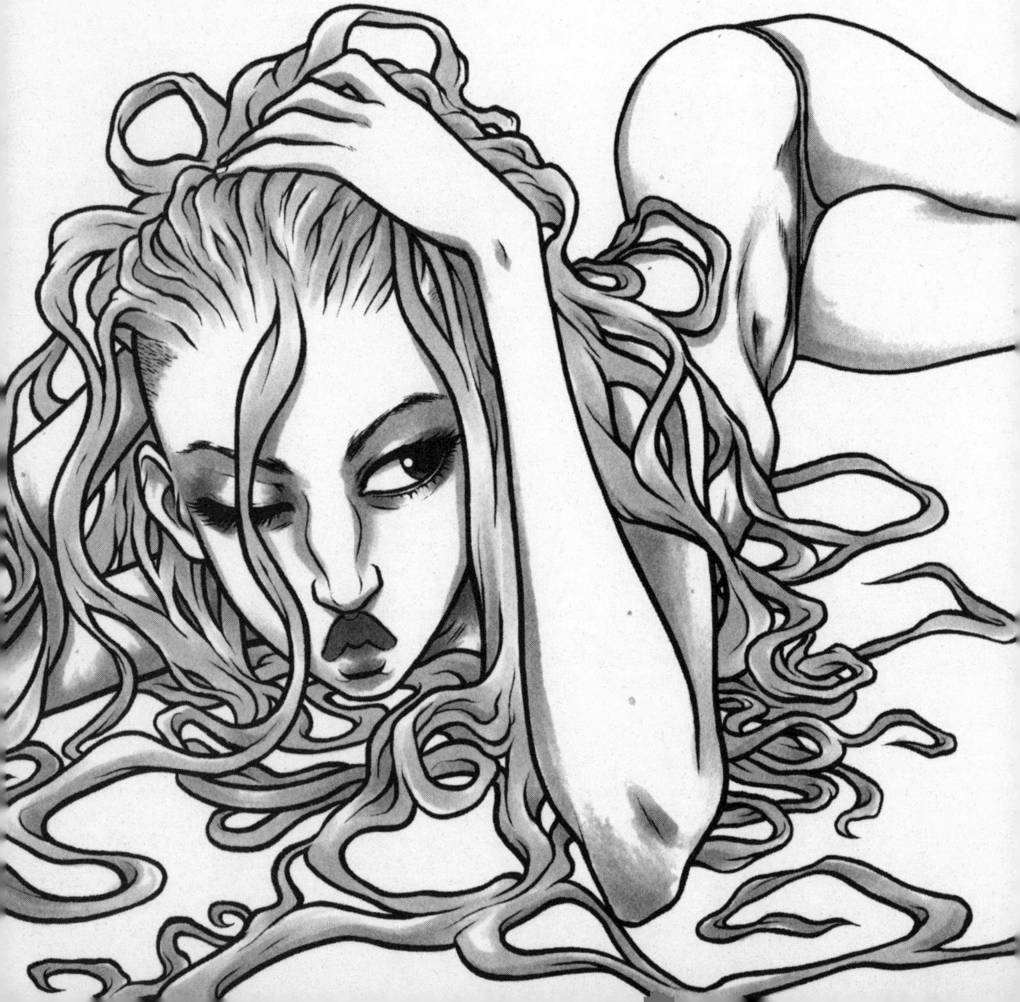

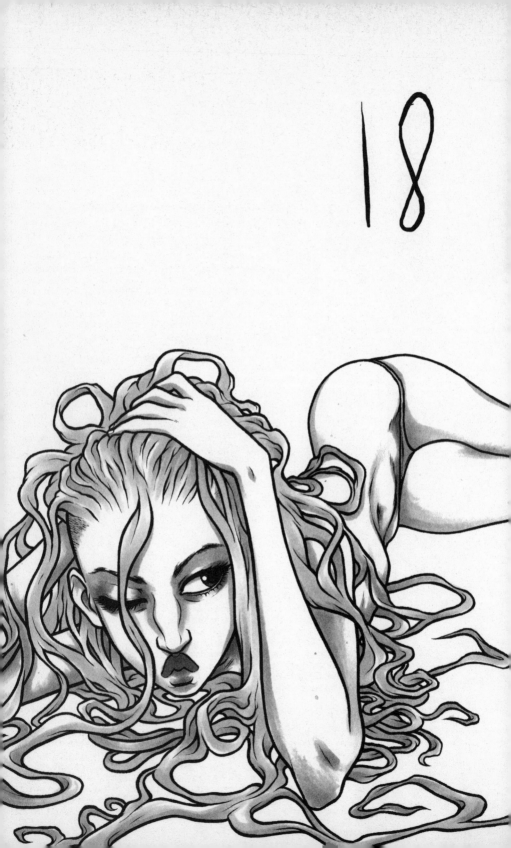

# The Wonders At Your Feet

[ friendtoroaches@gmail.com ]

Recent Entries Archive Friends User Info

## mara's journal

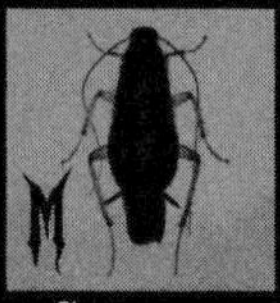

profile

## *October 28th, 1:31am*

### *CATHODE RAYS BLAST LIKE METEOR RAIN TO MY BRAIN.*

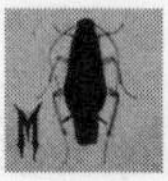

i think everythings good with Natalie now. we hung out today for a little while it was cool. but also weird because she lives in the same dorm as Cleo so i felt like i was sneaking around or something. i don't think Cleo was home like usual. Natalie is so skinny. she is so skinny it's painful. i wonder if she's anorexic or something. she wants me to be her model for her photo project, i don't know what i think about that. i'm real flattered on one hand, but totally nervous and weird on the other. why does she want me for the project? she could find a billion other girls who are prettier or hotter or whatever. i don't know. i hope it's not a nude photo shoot. i don't know what the fuck i'd do then. actually i guess it wouldn't be so bad. i'd probably get over it quick. at least i got a little bit of muscle now. anyway i'm glad it looks like we're friends now. i'll probably fuck it up later on though. maybe i should make this post friends-only.

softball is going great. i am excited for the Armadillo game but also scared, i don't know if we can win. i think pretty much everyone on our team smokes, me included, we won't be able to breathe out there. except Trilby. she used to smoke a little but one day she went "i'm quitting" and the next day she really did and she never smoked again. how did she do that. i haven't had any luck quitting so far but i'm really trying. i really want to be able to run really far.

i've been reseraching a lot about ancient Egypt recently. partly because it's cool and partly because i think i want my first film for class to have something to do with Egypt. i wish i could set it IN Egypt, but obviously i cant get over there. i thought at first something with a mummy, but not a super magic world domination wizard mummy like in those Mummy movies. like a fucking badass serious intense elder evil shambling mummy who comes out of a fucking tomb.

*mood: nervous*
*current music: sonic syndicate - only inhuman*

[ 0 comments | leave a comment ]

## *October 23rd, 11:12pm*

### *PEOPLE ARE BEING MURDERED RIGHT NOW.*

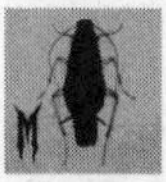

my serial killer screenplay is halfway finished. i thought about changing things a little and having TWO killers instead of one, since pretty much every killer story always seems to have only one. but i think i'll probably stick with that and keep the one like i have. i'm really excited to shoot this but i don't know when or if it will ever happen. i think the money part would be easy because there aren't any special effects except blood and no sets have to be built, it's all basic guerilla type filmmaking. i'm just worried about finding actors and a good camera and people willing to put effort in when they're not being paid much or at all. when it's not a job it's easy for people to blow it off.

i hate people who stomp insects and spiders. i read an article the other day about animals, insects too, having personalities. i think i've always thought that way but i guess it's a more scientific idea now with evidence and everything. i hate how people separate animals into the ones they like and they don't, like if an animal is cute they like it but if an animal is gross or loathsome they don't give two shits about it and will kill them without hesitation. but what is the difference? how is a "nice" bug like a ladybug that everyone likes any more threatening than a moth or housefly? or when somebody eats a cow it's okay, but if they eat a dog people flip out about it because dogs are "cute" and used as pets. i think part of it has to do with people projecting human traits onto animals and seeing themselves in a dog or cat, but it's hard for people to do that with more "alien" creatures like insects. but not

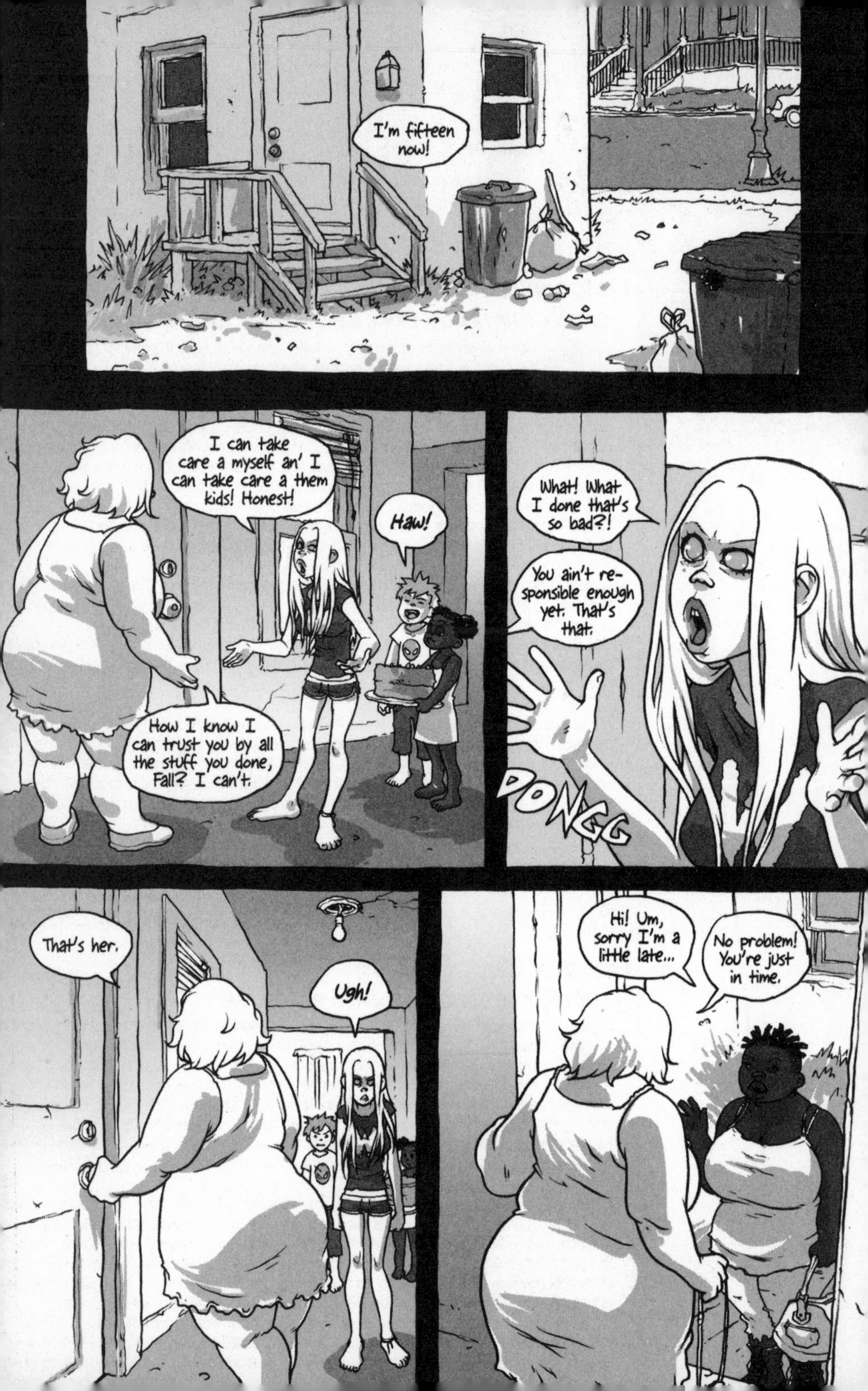
I'm fifteen now!
I can take care a myself an' I can take care a them kids! Honest!
Haw!
How I know I can trust you by all the stuff you done, Fall? I can't.
What! What I done that's so bad?!
You ain't re-sponsible enough yet. That's that.
DONGG
That's her.
Ugh!
Hi! Um, sorry I'm a little late...
No problem! You're just in time.

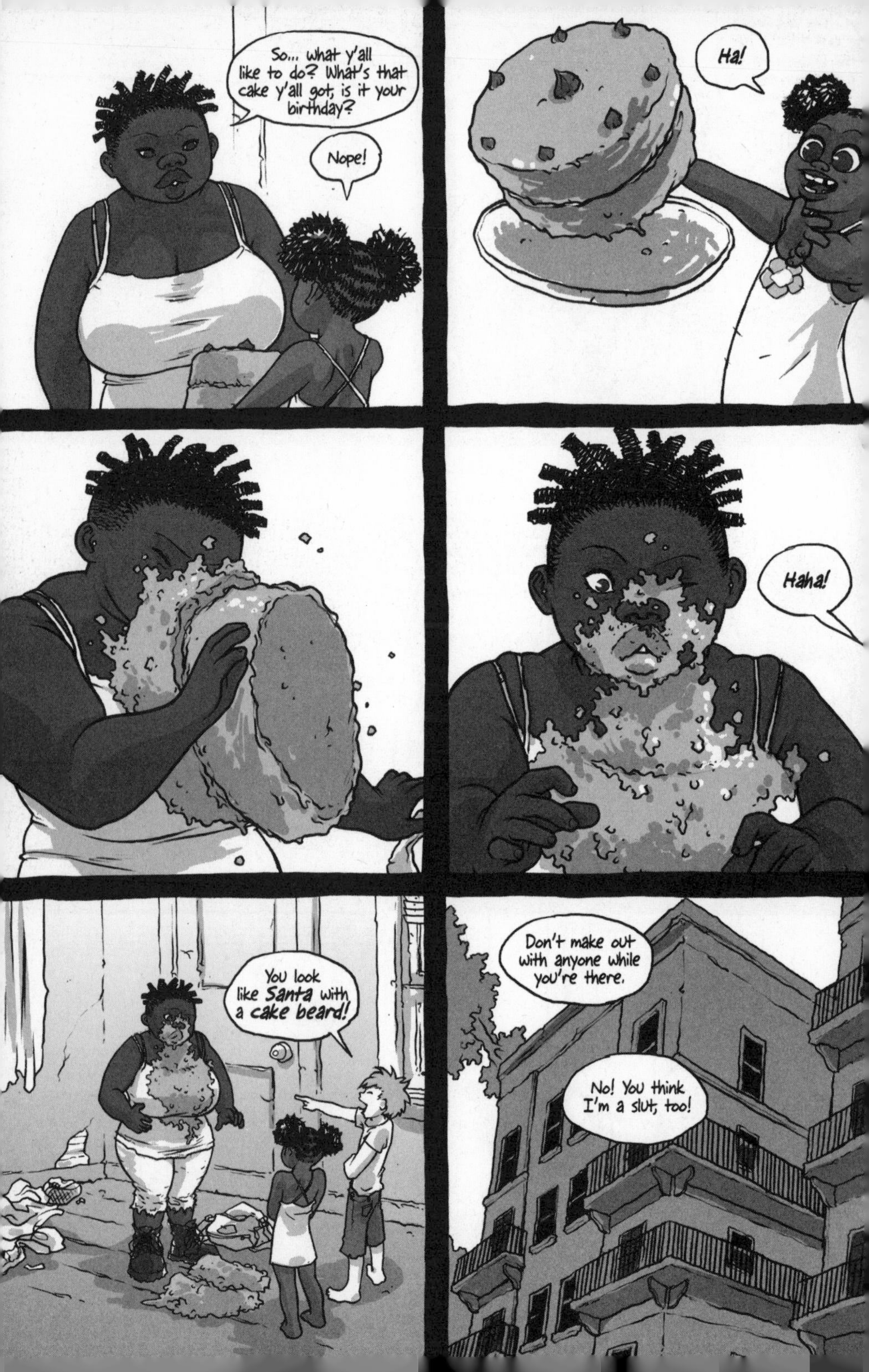
So... what y'all like to do? What's that cake y'all got, is it your birthday?
Nope!
Ha!
Haha!
You look like **Santa** with a **cake beard**!
Don't make out with anyone while you're there.
No! You think I'm a slut, too!

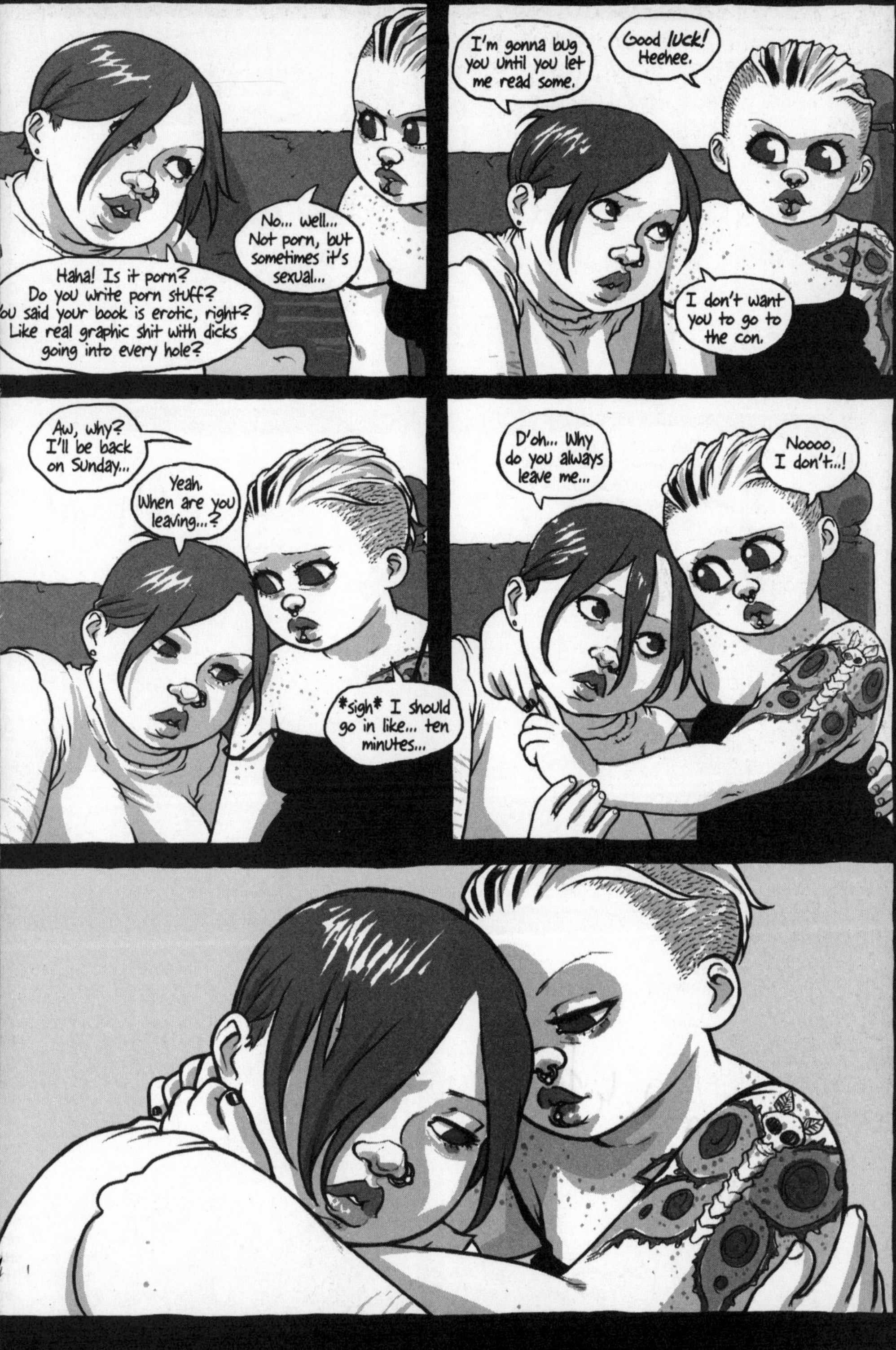
Haha! Is it porn? Do you write porn stuff? You said your book is erotic, right? Like real graphic shit with dicks going into every hole?
No... well... Not porn, but sometimes it's sexual...
I'm gonna bug you until you let me read some.
Good luck! Heehee.
I don't want you to go to the con.
Aw, why? I'll be back on Sunday...
Yeah. When are you leaving...?
*sigh* I should go in like... ten minutes...
D'oh... Why do you always leave me...
Noooo, I don't...!

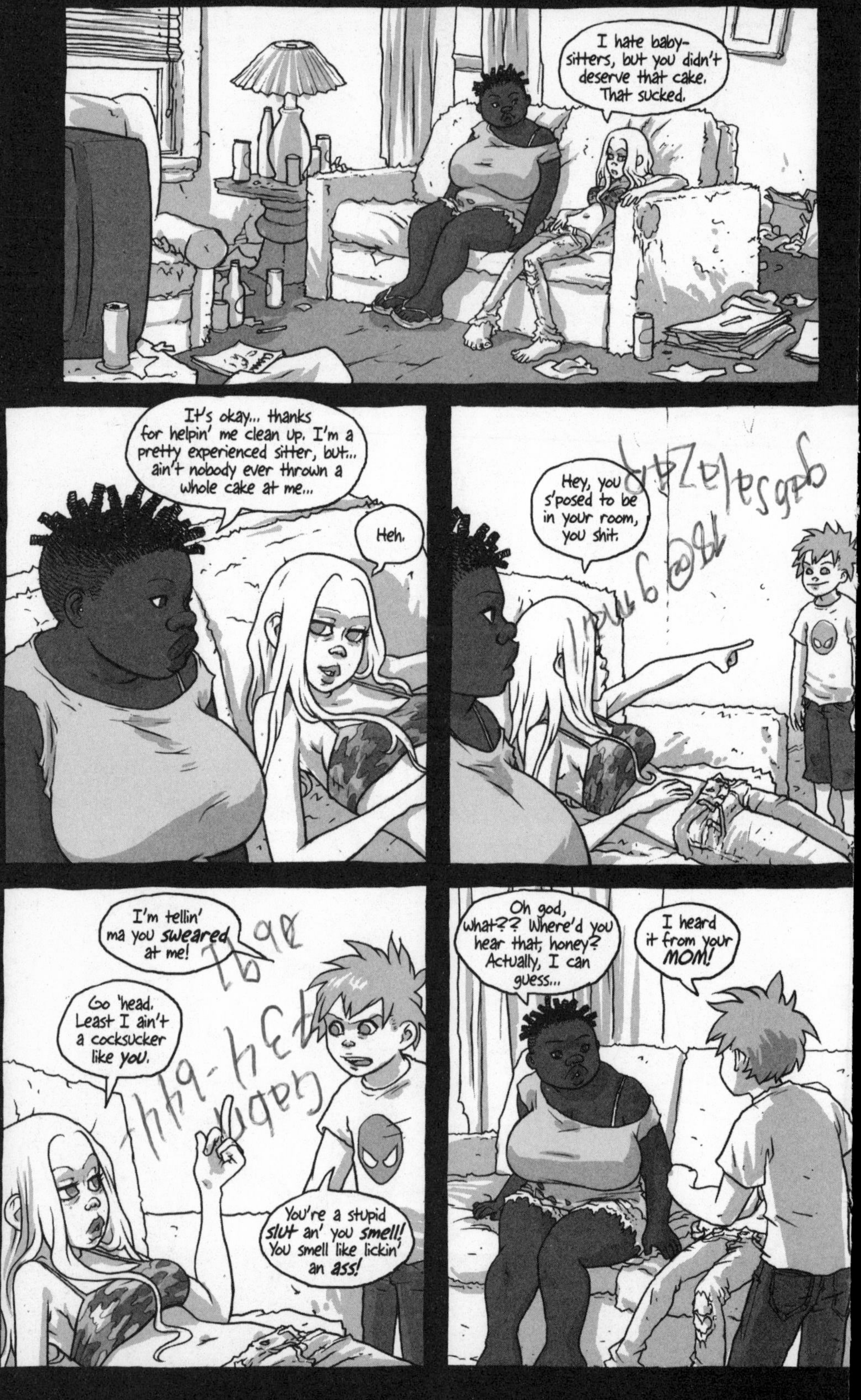

I hate baby-sitters, but you didn't deserve that cake. That sucked.
It's okay... thanks for helpin' me clean up. I'm a pretty experienced sitter, but... ain't nobody ever thrown a whole cake at me...
Heh.
Hey, you s'posed to be in your room, you shit.
I'm tellin' ma you **sweared** at me!
Go 'head. Least I ain't a cocksucker like **you**.
You're a stupid **slut** an' you **smell**! You smell like lickin' an **ass**!
Oh god, what?? Where'd you hear that, honey? Actually, I can guess...
I heard it from your **MOM**!

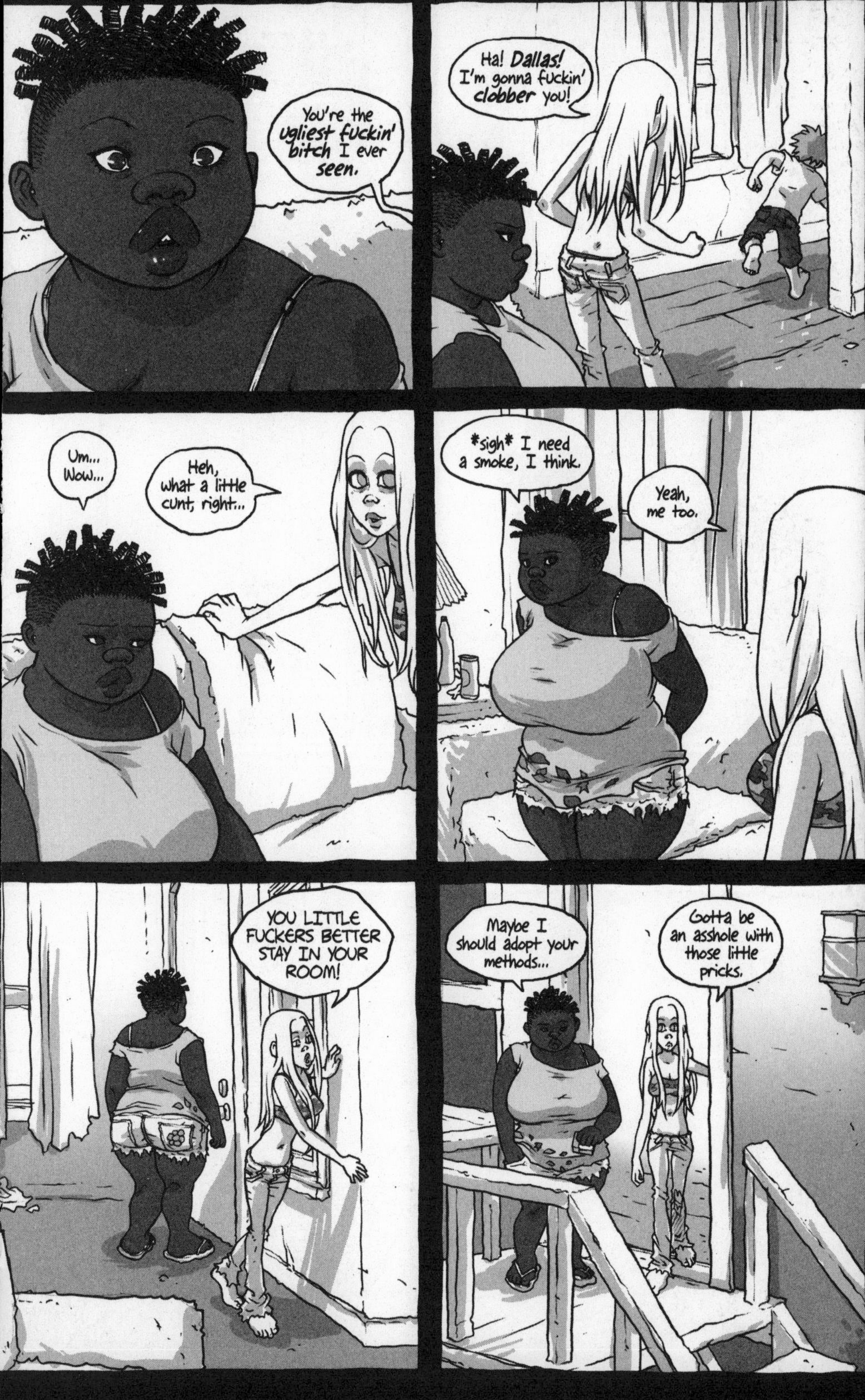

You're the ugliest fuckin' bitch I ever seen.
Ha! Dallas! I'm gonna fuckin' clobber you!
Um... Wow...
Heh, what a little cunt, right...
*sigh* I need a smoke, I think.
Yeah, me too.
YOU LITTLE FUCKERS BETTER STAY IN YOUR ROOM!
Maybe I should adopt your methods...
Gotta be an asshole with those little pricks.

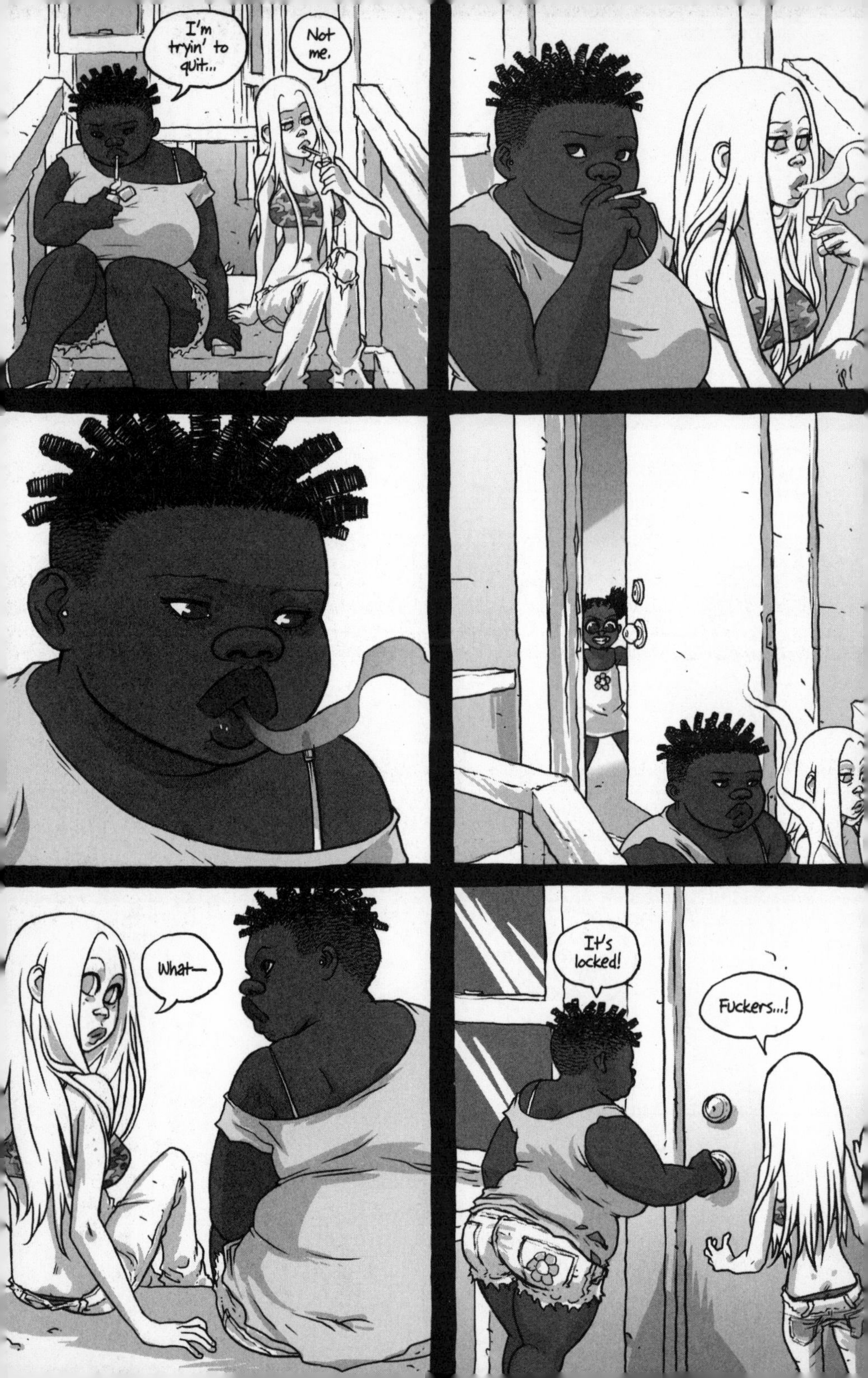
I'm tryin' to quit...
Not me.
What—
It's locked!
Fuckers...!

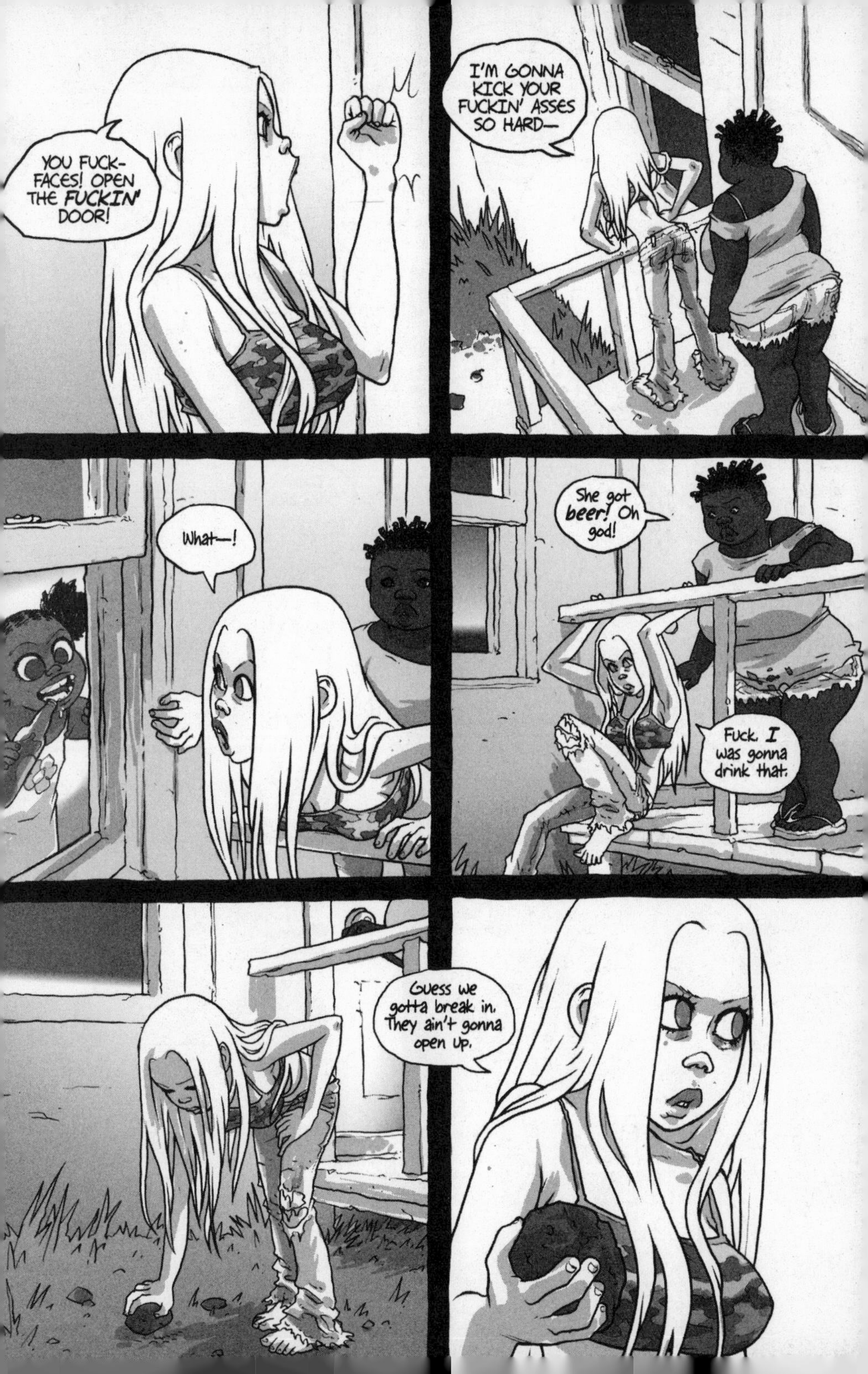
YOU FUCK-FACES! OPEN THE FUCKIN' DOOR!
I'M GONNA KICK YOUR FUCKIN' ASSES SO HARD—
What—!
She got beer! Oh god!
Fuck. I was gonna drink that.
Guess we gotta break in. They ain't gonna open up.

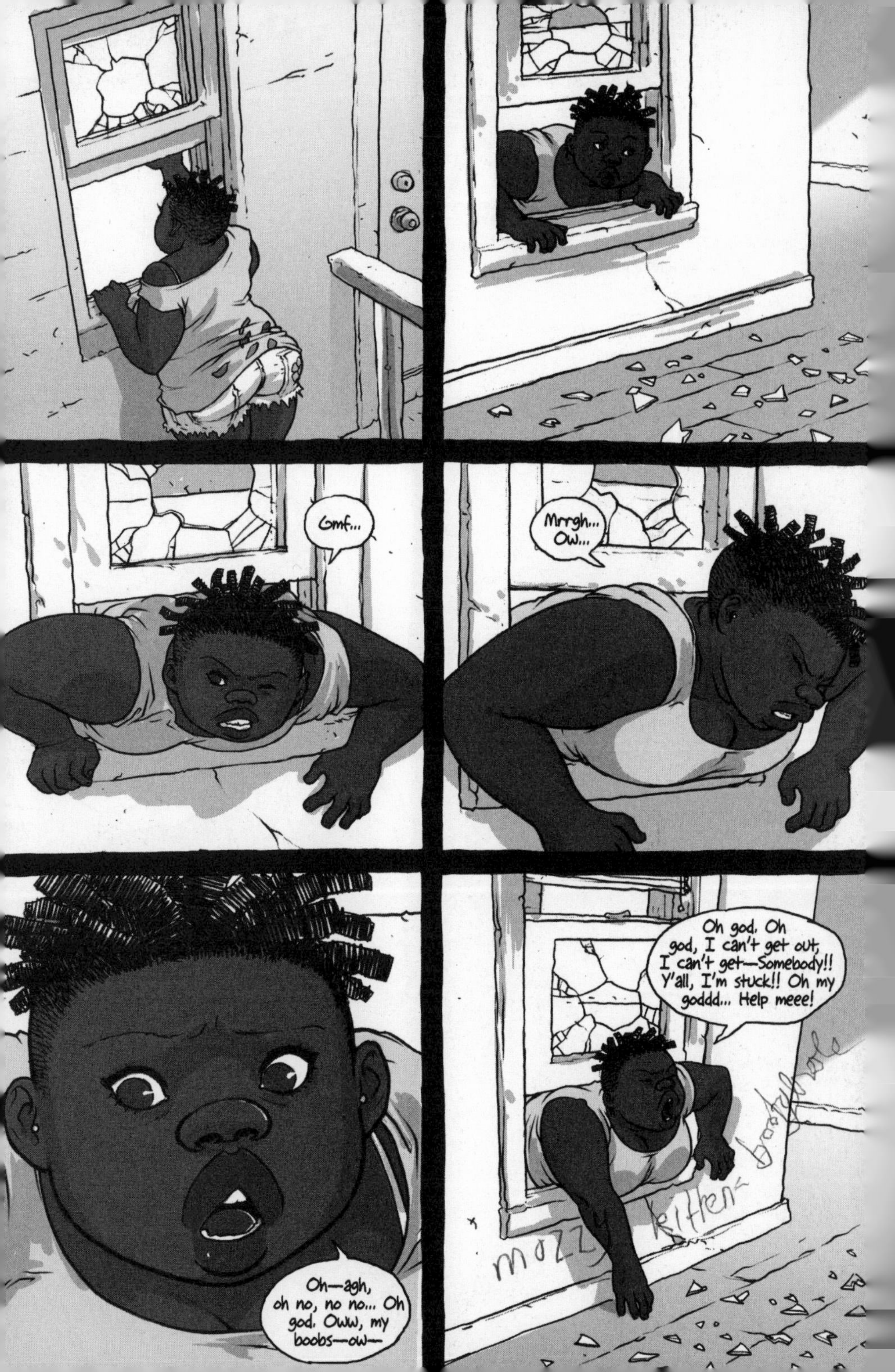
Gmf...
Mrrgh... Ow...
Oh—agh, oh no, no no... Oh god. Oww, my boobs—ow—
Oh god. Oh god, I can't get out, I can't get—Somebody!! Y'all, I'm stuck!! Oh my goddd... Help meee!
kitten
mozz

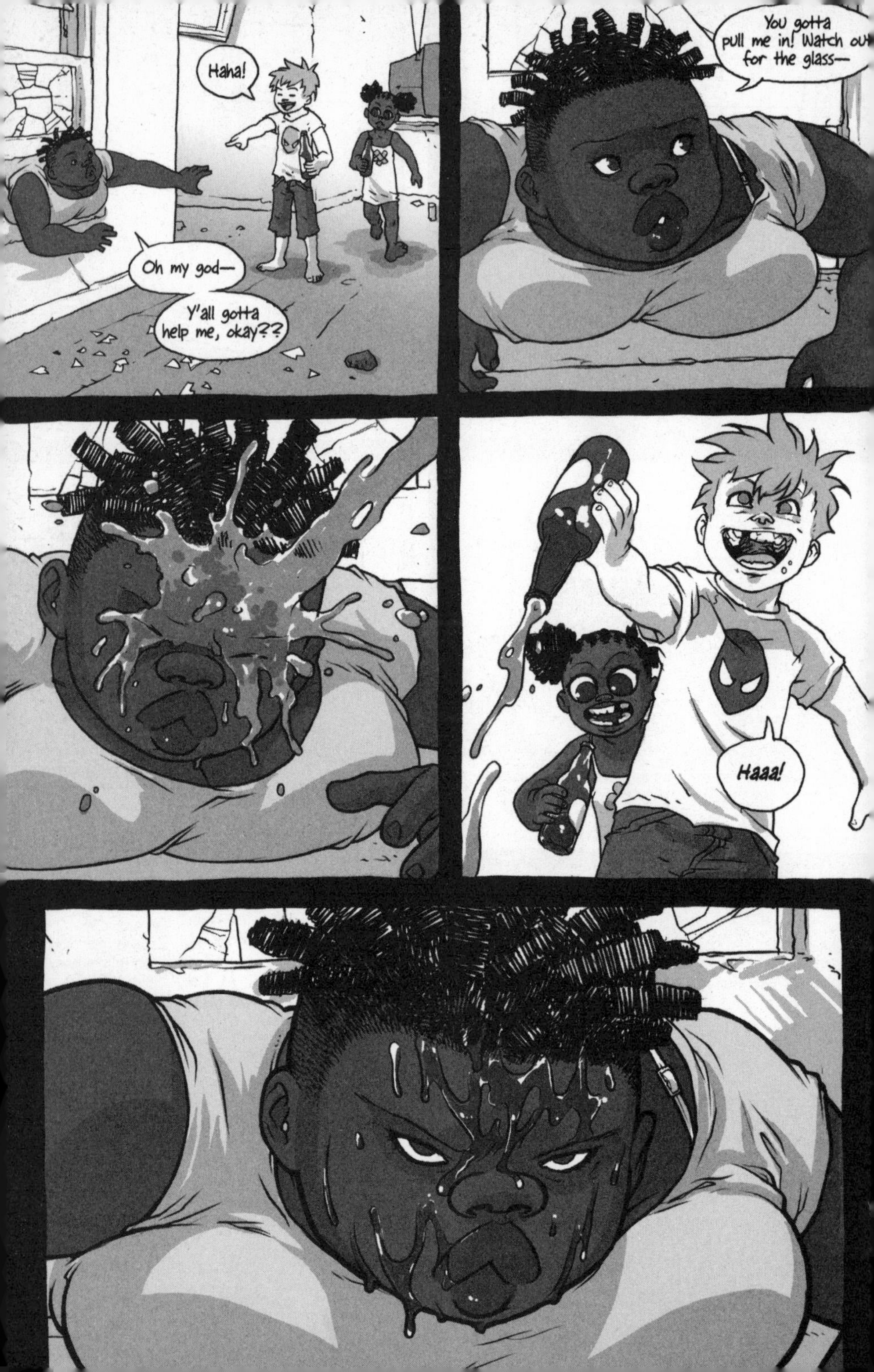

Haha!
Oh my god—
Y'all gotta help me, okay??
You gotta pull me in! Watch out for the glass—
Haaa!

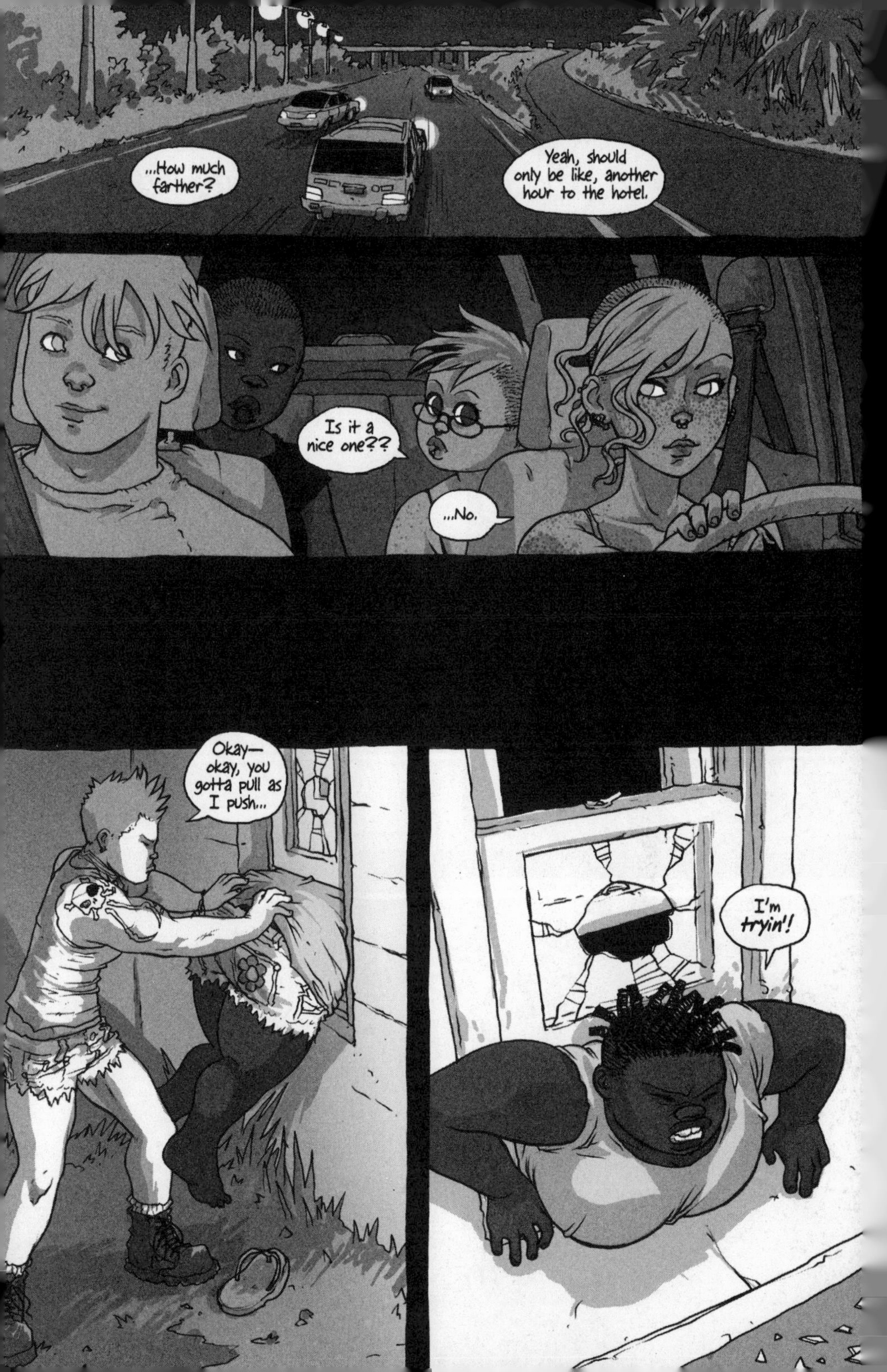
...How much farther?
Yeah, should only be like, another hour to the hotel.
Is it a nice one??
...No.
Okay— okay, you gotta pull as I push...
I'm *tryin'*!

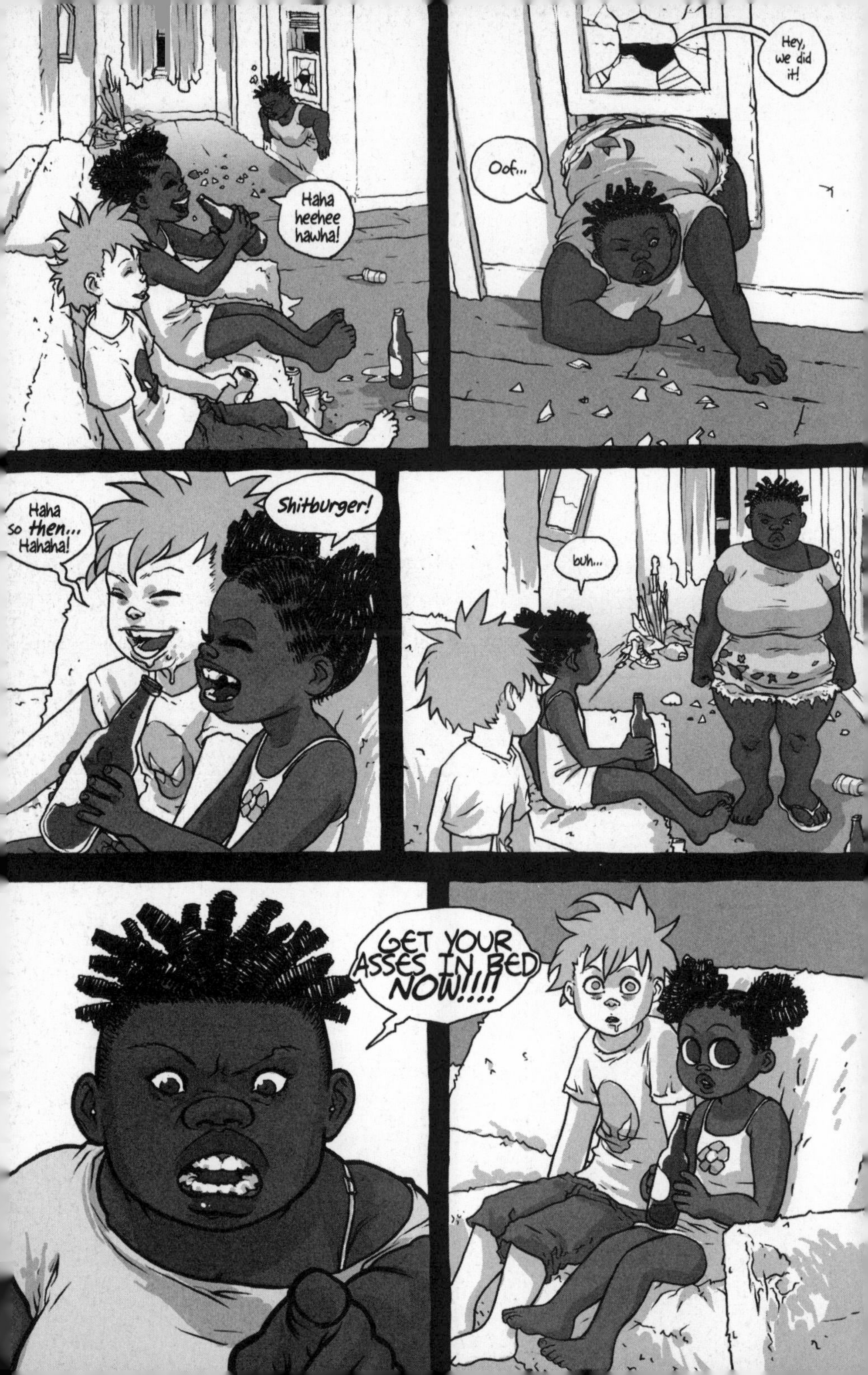
Haha heehee hawha!
Hey, we did it!
Oof...
Haha so *then*... Hahaha!
Shitburger!
buh...
GET YOUR ASSES IN BED NOW!!!!

# 19

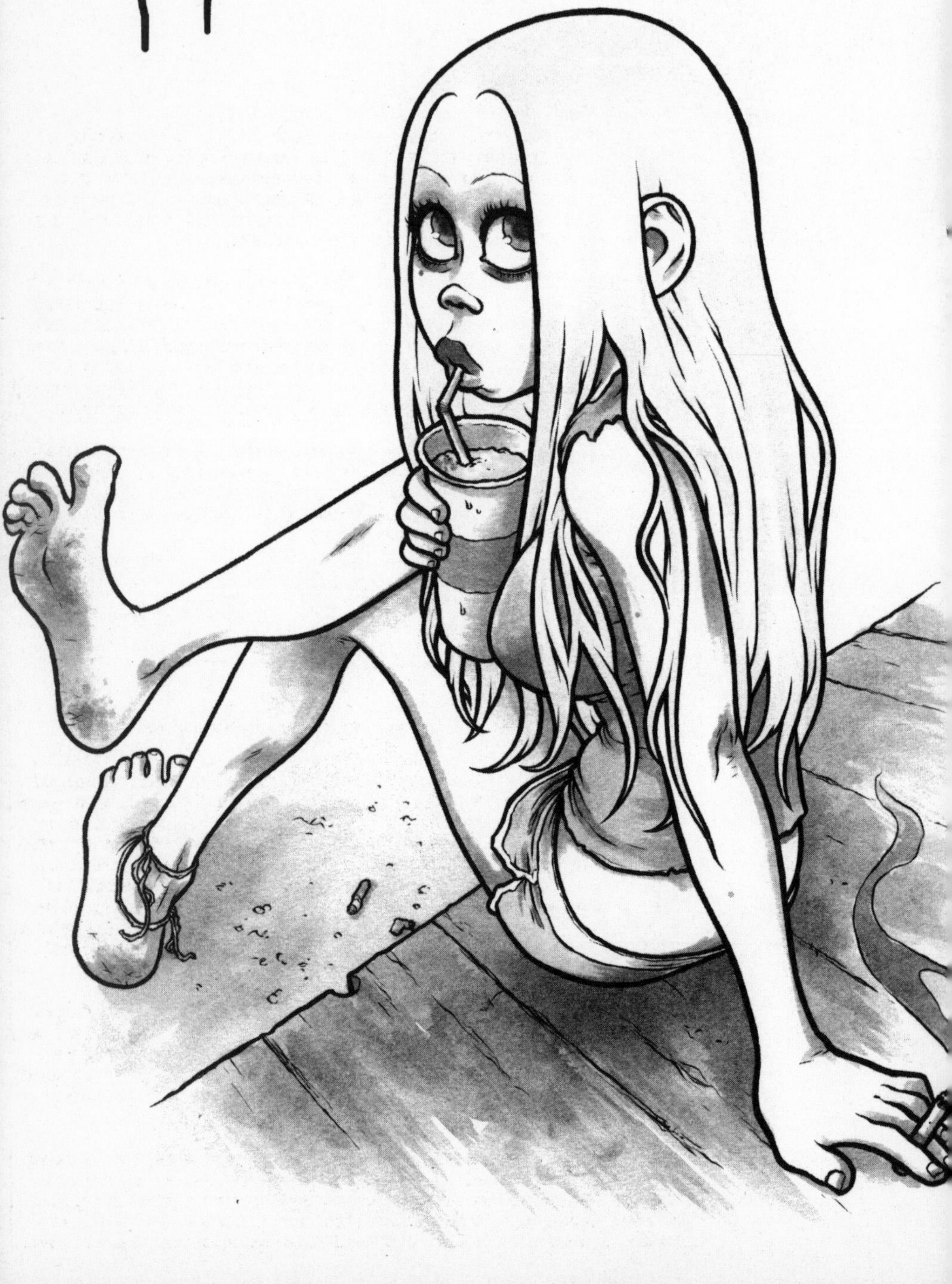

# The Wonders At Your Feet

[ friendtoroaches@gmail.com ]

Recent Entries   Archive   Friends   User Info

## mara's journal

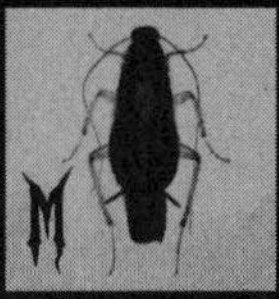

profile

## *October 31st, 2:22am*

### *OFFERING OF RED RAGE.*

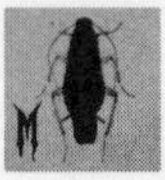

it's officially Halloween, and i have no costume. i'm very pleased about that, i think Halloween is overrated and i hate how people don't dress up in spooky or scary costumes anymore. i thought Halloween was supposed to be about monsters and ghosts and zombies, not nurses or video game characters or pirates. i guess nurses can be scary. but i'm rebelling against that and not dressing up at all. i'm scarier as my regular self than anything i could dress up as.

we finally made it to the hotel which is okay. it's kind of small and a little smelly and there's only one bed, but they actually have wireless internet. the drive down was okay. not too bad. we drove past a big car accident, though, and i saw a bloody guy laying on the road all twisted up like a red, wet pretzel. that's the first time i've ever seen a corpse and i have to say it wasn't that bad. maybe it would be worse if we werent driving by at 50 miles an hour. Cleo seems really upset by it though. she's very sensitive. right now Trilby is watching some alien show on the sci-fi channel, and Martin is taking a shower for some reason.

i can't believe i came to this con thing. it's going to be so stupid. we already saw a ton of nerds (Trilby says to call them con-goers, but i know they're just nerds) all around the hotel. every room must be filled up with con people and we're just four more. one girl was wearing stickers on her boobs and pants and nothing else. i don't get what this con is supposed to be about and it hasn't even started yet.

*mood: nervous*
*current music: sonic syndicate - only inhuman*

[ 0 comments | leave a comment ]

## *October 28th, 1:31am*

### *CATHODE RAYS BLAST LIKE METEOR RAIN TO MY BRAIN.*

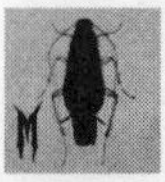

i think everythings good with Natalie now. we hung out today for a little while it was cool. but also weird because she lives in the same dorm as Cleo so i felt like i was sneaking around or something. i don't think Cleo was home like usual. Natalie is so skinny. she is so skinny it's painful. i wonder if she's anorexic or something. she wants me to be her model for her photo project, i don't know what i think about that. i'm real flattered on one hand, but totally nervous and weird on the other. why does she want me for the project? she could find a billion other girls who are prettier or hotter or whatever. i don't know. i hope it's not a nude photo shoot. i don't know what the fuck i'd do then. actually i guess it wouldn't be so bad. i'd probably get over it quick. at least i got a little bit of muscle now. anyway i'm glad it looks like we're friends now. i'll probably fuck it up later on though. maybe i should make this post friends-only.

softball is going great. i am excited for the Armadillo game but also scared, i don't know if we can win. i think pretty much everyone on our team smokes, me included, we won't be able to breathe out there. except Trilby. she used to smoke a little but one day she went "i'm quitting" and the next day she really did and she never smoked again. how did she do that. i haven't had any luck quitting so far but i'm really trying. i really want to be able to run really far.

i've been reseraching a lot about ancient Egypt recently. partly because it's cool and partly because i think i want my first film for class to have something to do with Egypt. i wish i could set it IN Egypt, but obviously i cant get over there. i thought at first something with a mummy, but not a super magic world domination wizard mummy like in those Mummy movies. like a fucking badass serious intense elder evil shambling mummy who comes

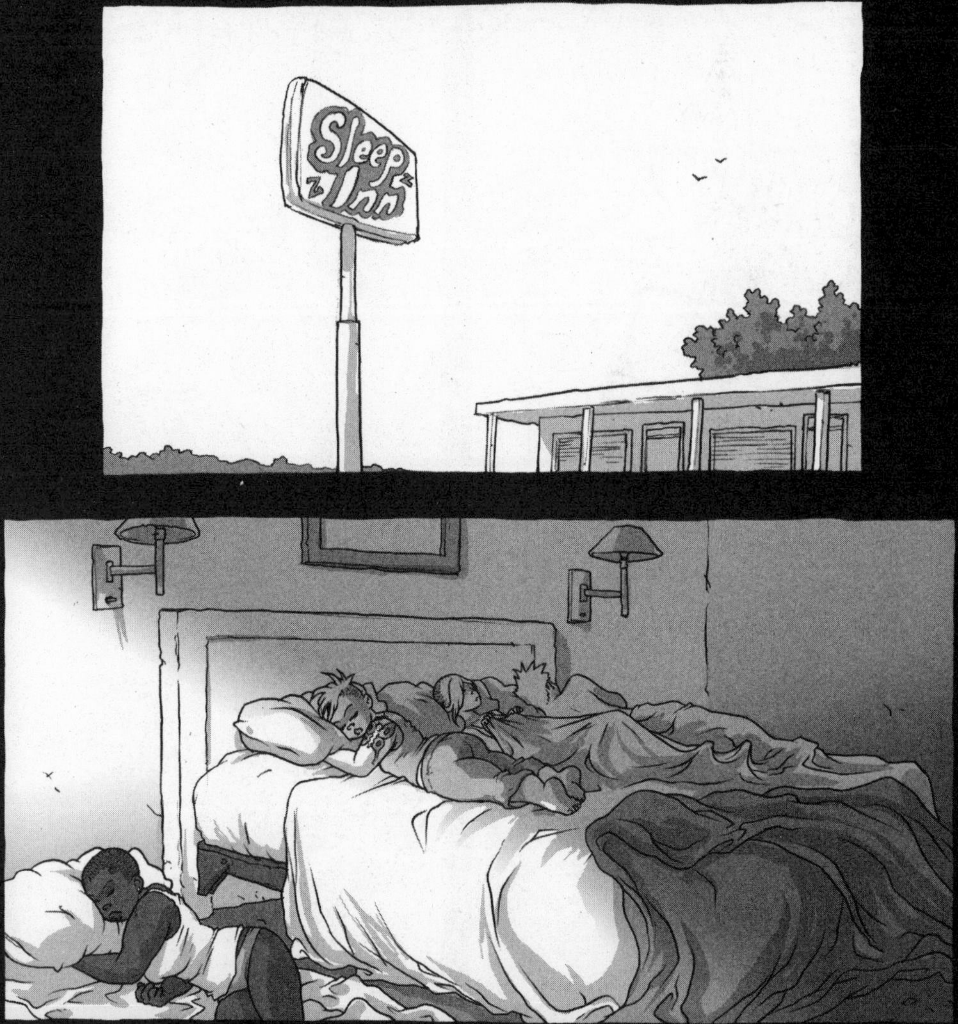
Sleep Inn

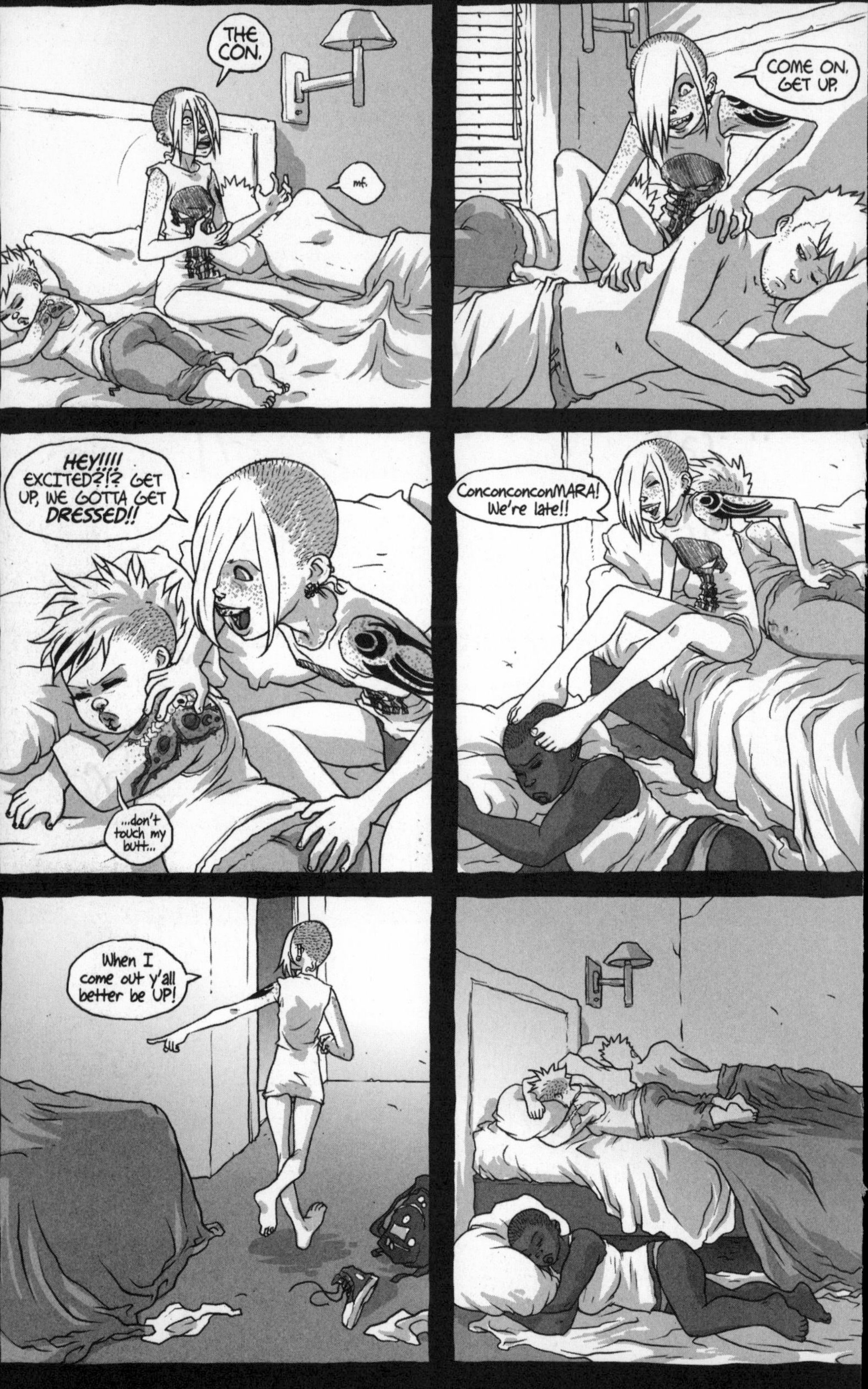
THE CON.
mf.
COME ON. GET UP.
HEY!!!! EXCITED?!? GET UP, WE GOTTA GET DRESSED!!
...don't touch my butt...
ConconconconMARA! We're late!!
When I come out y'all better be UP!

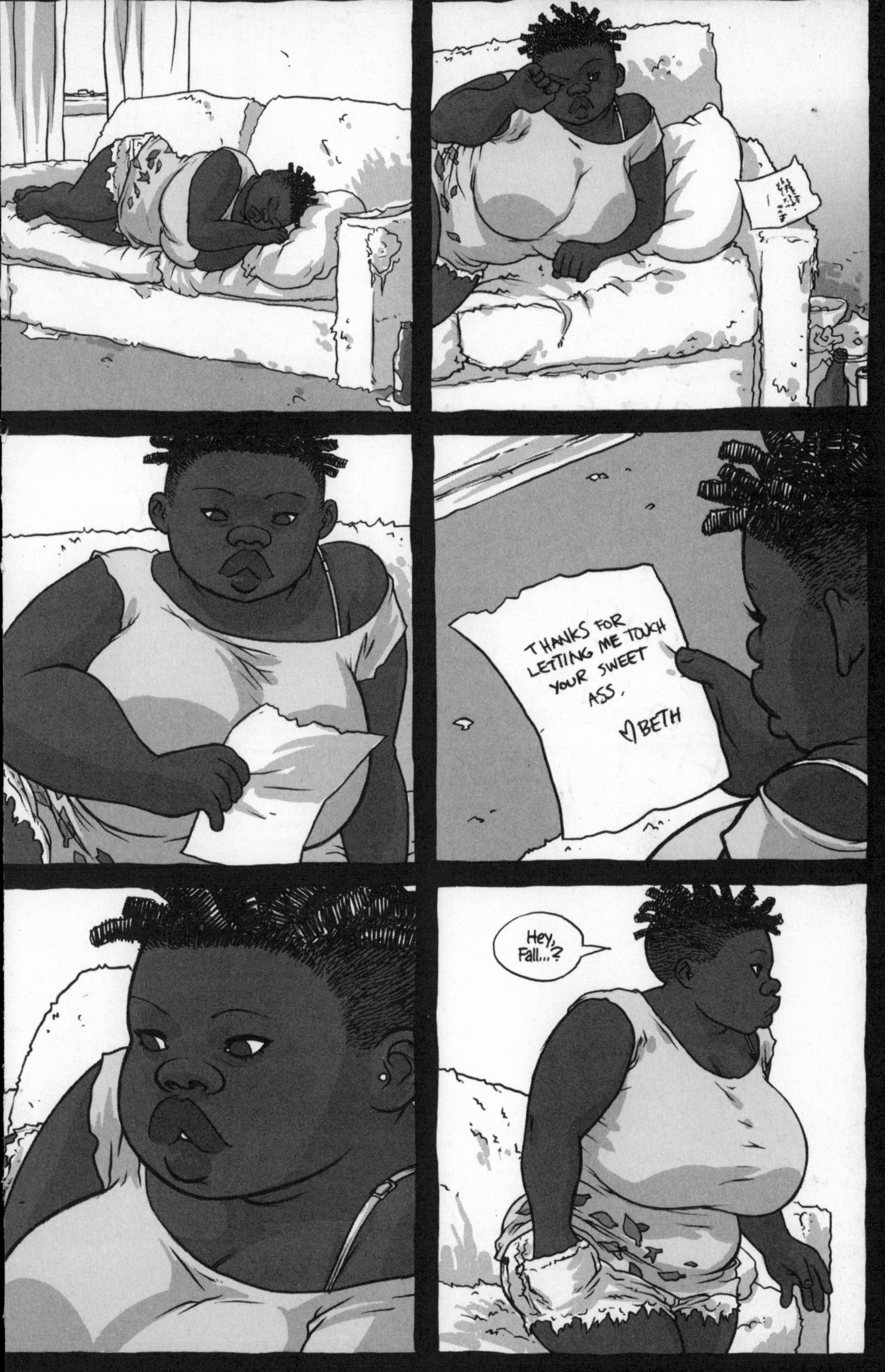
THANKS FOR LETTING ME TOUCH YOUR SWEET ASS.
♡BETH
Hey, Fall...?

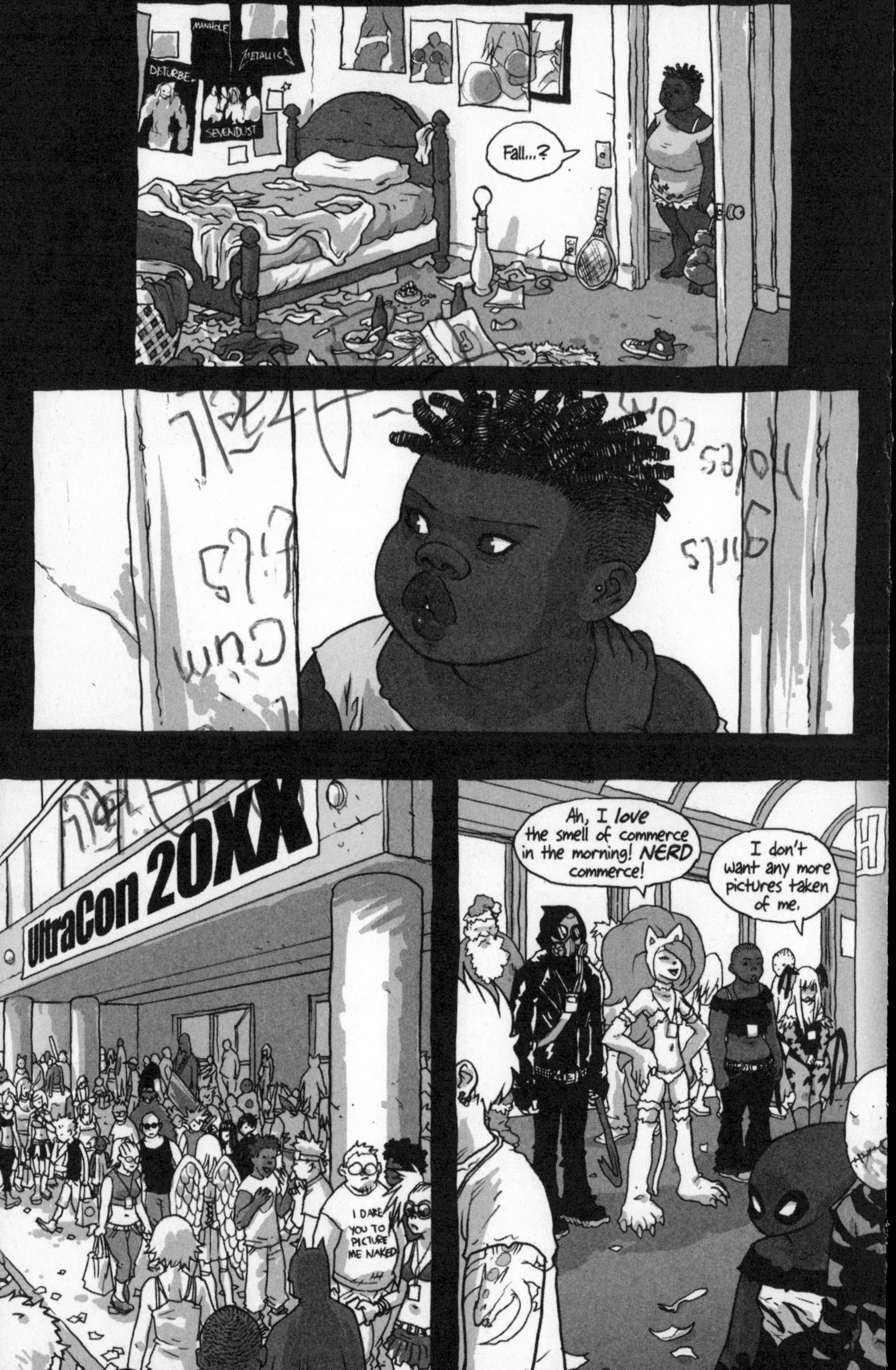
MANHOLE
METALLICA
SEVENDUST
Fall...?
UltraCon 20XX
I DARE YOU TO PICTURE ME NAKED
Ah, I *love* the smell of commerce in the morning! *NERD* commerce!
I don't want any more pictures taken of me.

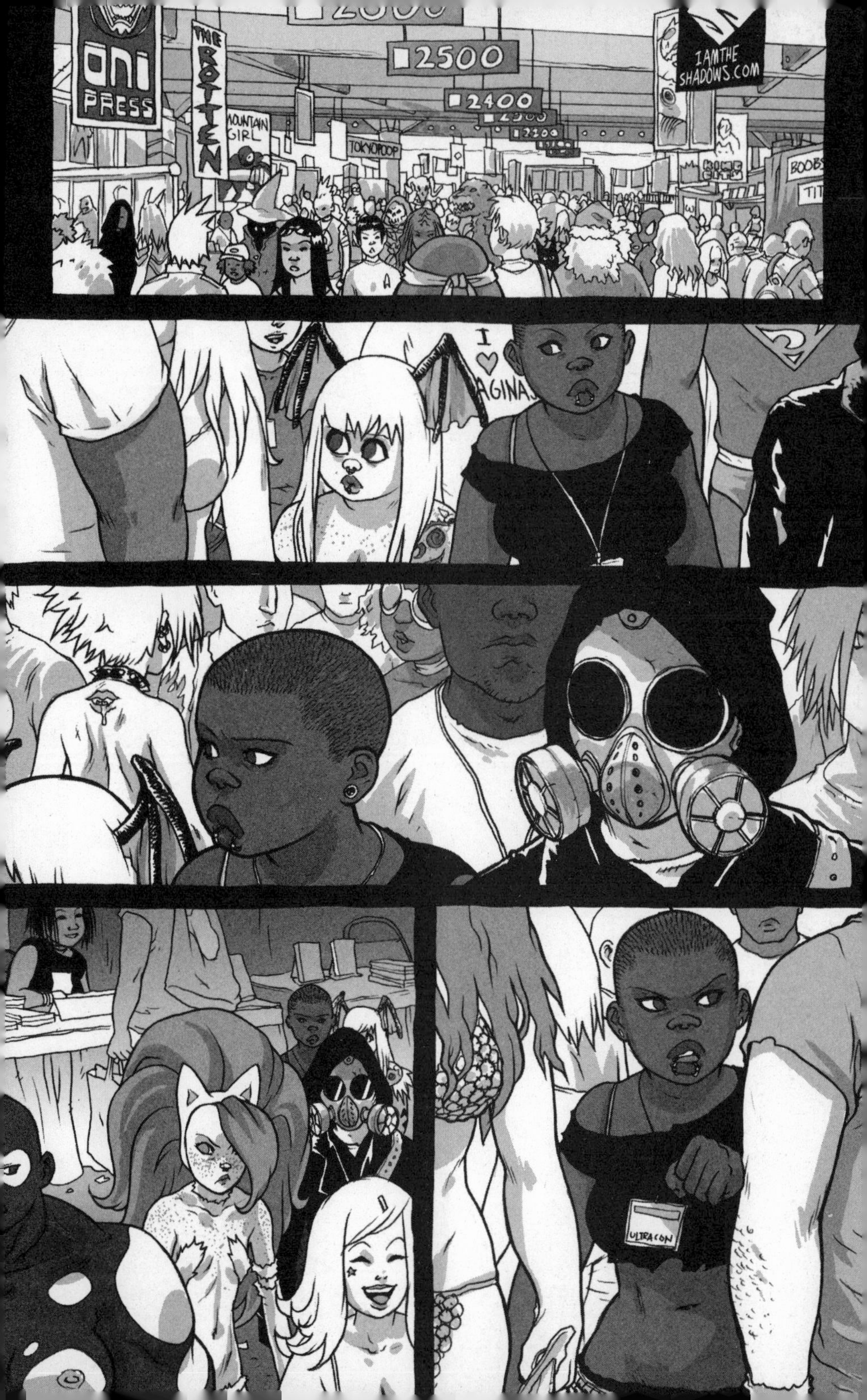
ONI PRESS
THE ROTTEN
2500
2400
IAMTHE SHADOWS.COM
MOUNTAIN GIRL
TOKYOPOP
BOOBS
ULTRACON

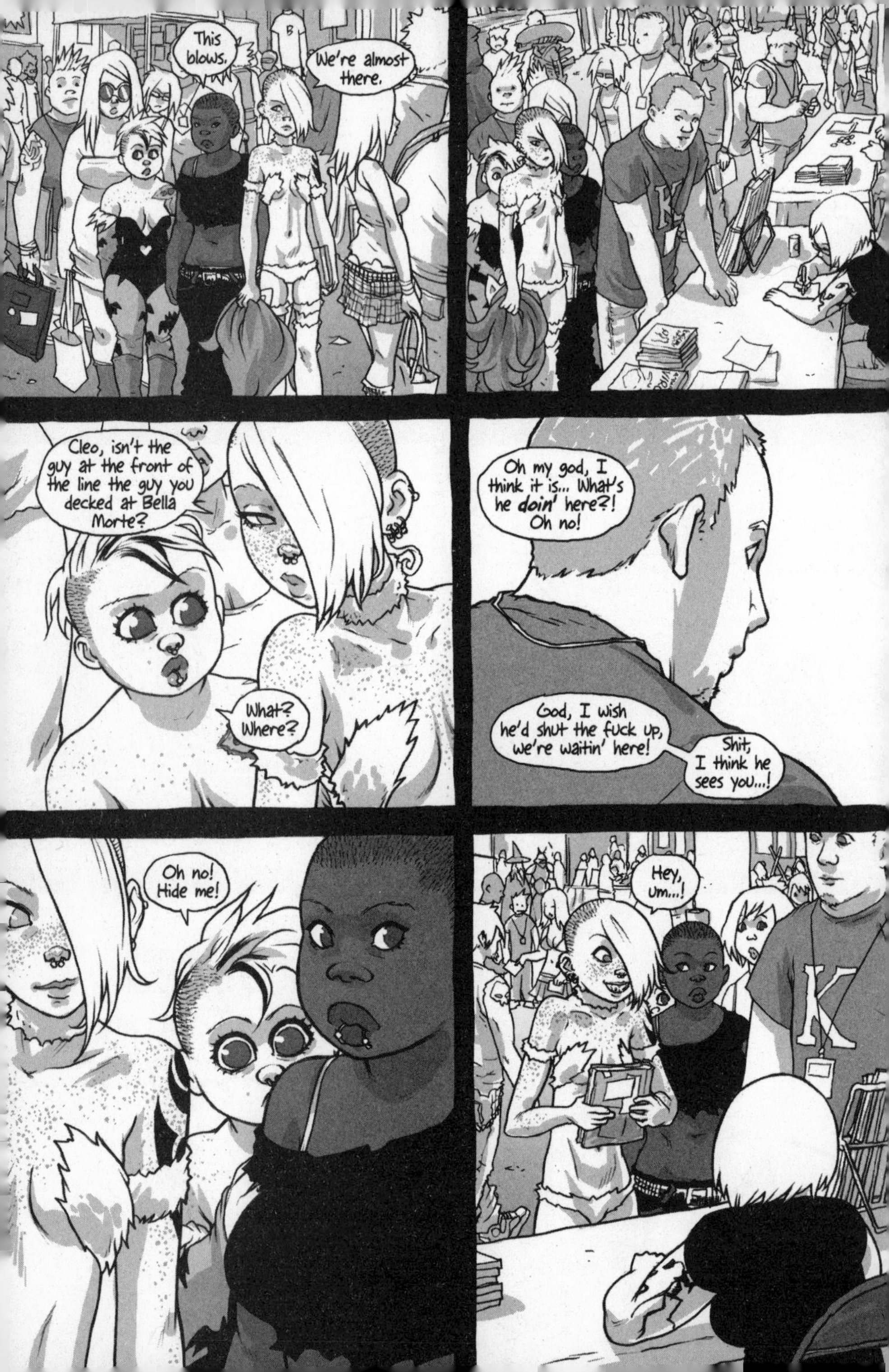
This blows.
We're almost there.
Cleo, isn't the guy at the front of the line the guy you decked at Bella Morte?
What? Where?
Oh my god, I think it is... What's he doin' here?! Oh no!
God, I wish he'd shut the fuck up, we're waitin' here!
Shit, I think he sees you...!
Oh no! Hide me!
Hey, um...!

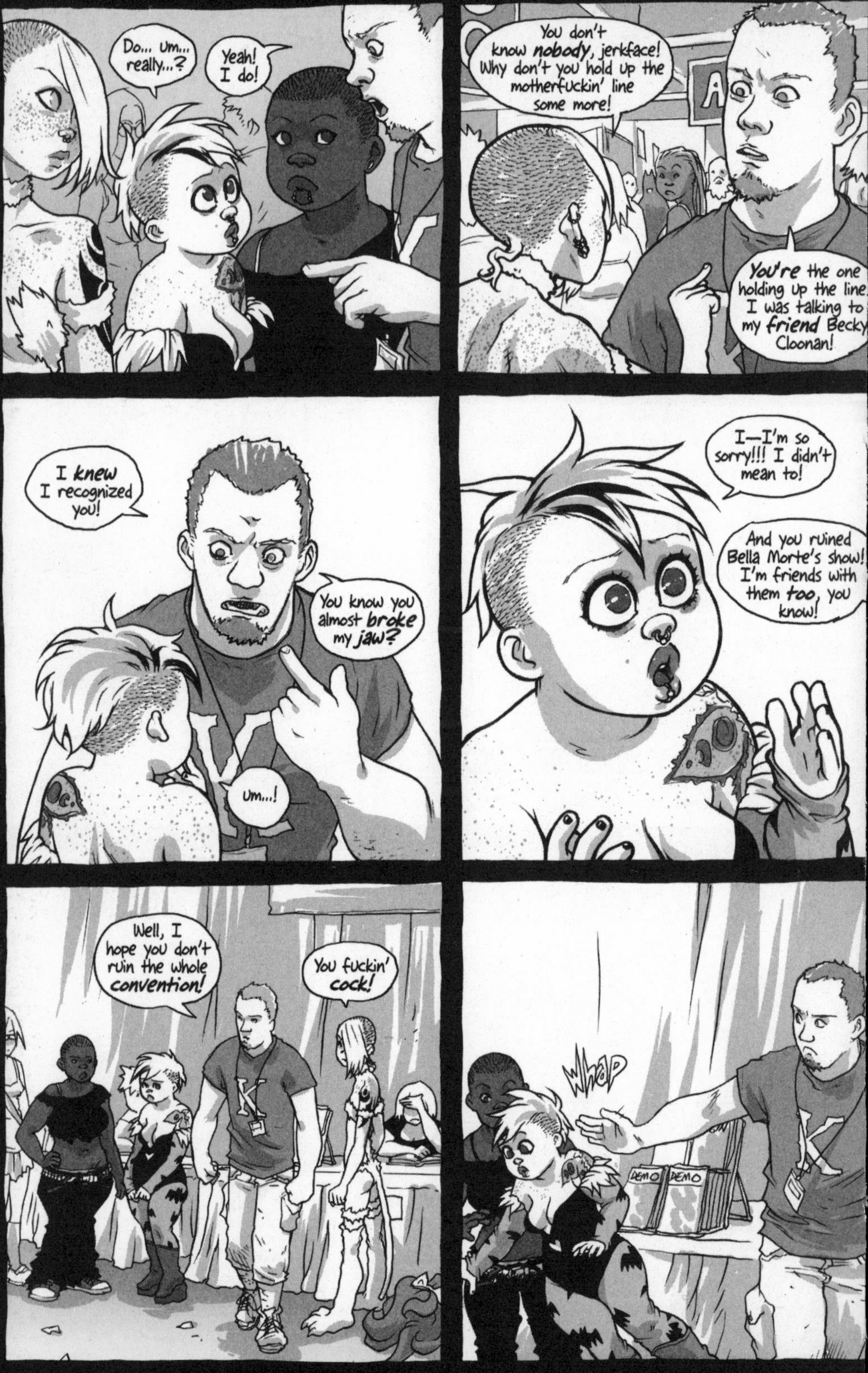
Do... um... really...?
Yeah! I do!
You don't know **nobody**, jerkface! Why don't you hold up the motherfuckin' line some more!
***You're*** the one holding up the line. I was talking to my ***friend*** Becky Cloonan!
I ***knew*** I recognized you!
You know you almost ***broke*** my ***jaw?***
Um...!
I—I'm so sorry!!! I didn't mean to!
And you ruined Bella Morte's show! I'm friends with them ***too***, you know!
Well, I hope you don't ruin the whole ***convention!***
You fuckin' ***cock!***
WHAP
DEMO
DEMO

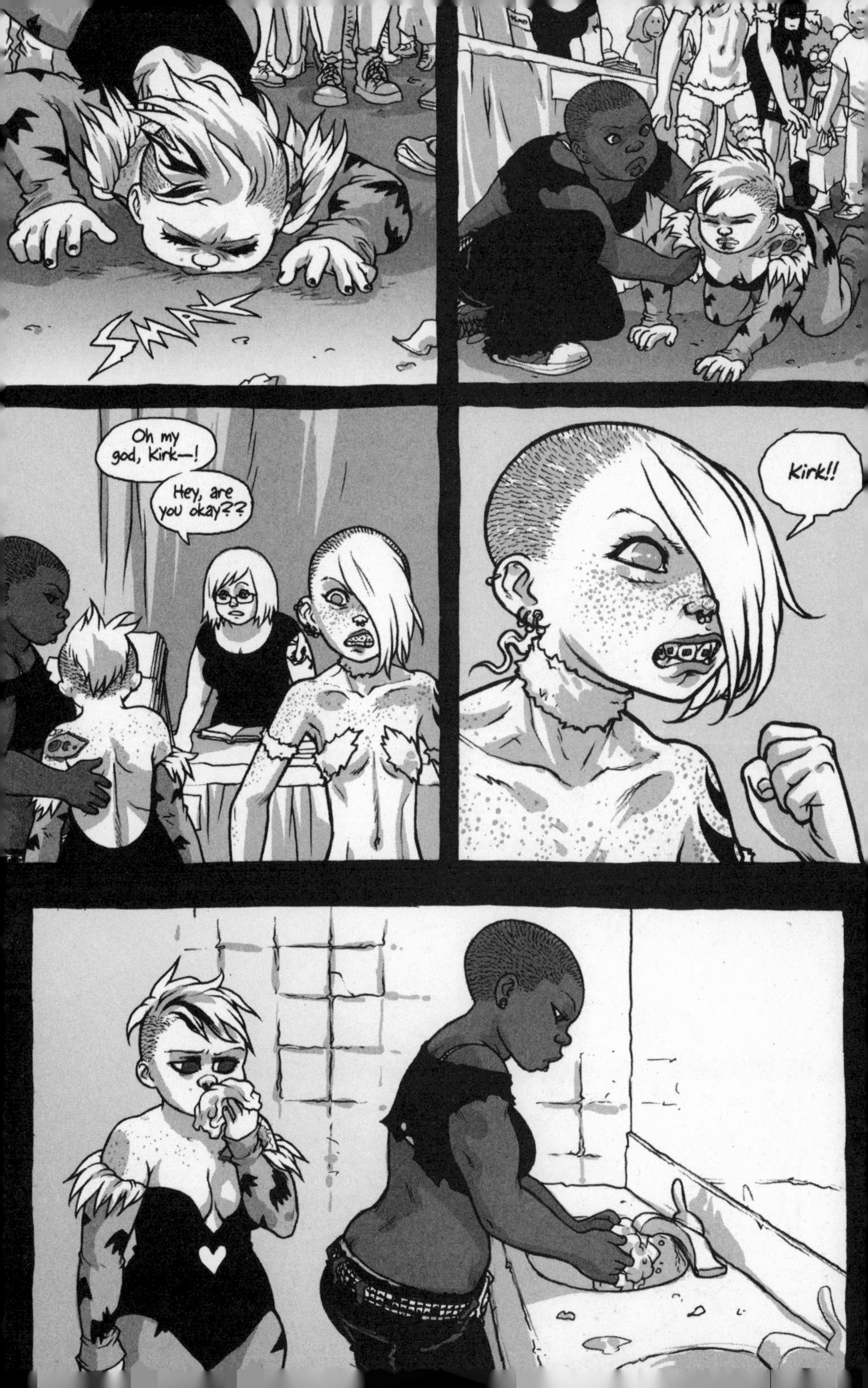
SMAK
Oh my god, Kirk—!
Hey, are you okay??
Kirk!!

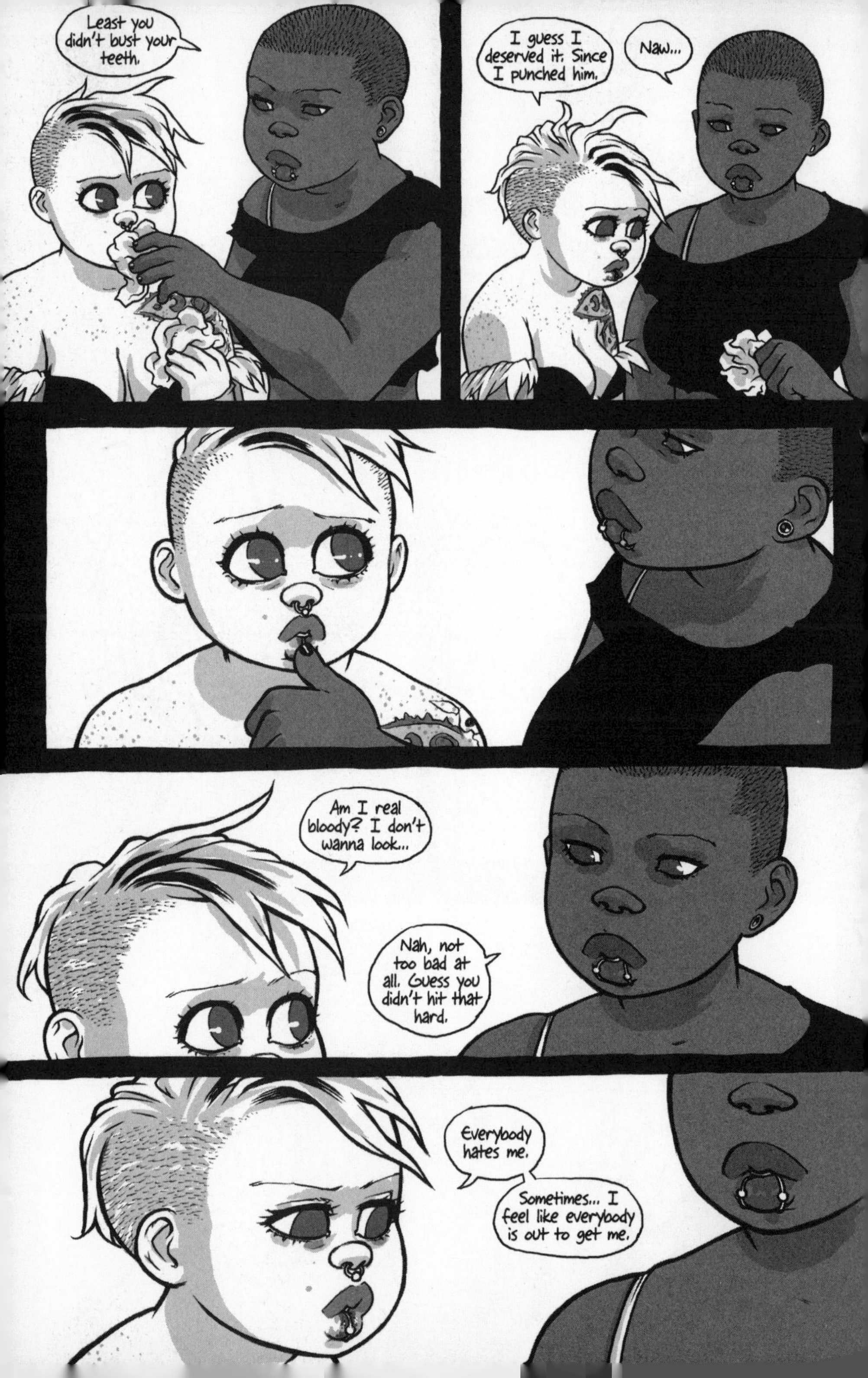
Least you didn't bust your teeth.
I guess I deserved it. Since I punched him.
Naw...
Am I real bloody? I don't wanna look...
Nah, not too bad at all. Guess you didn't hit that hard.
Everybody hates me.
Sometimes... I feel like everybody is out to get me.

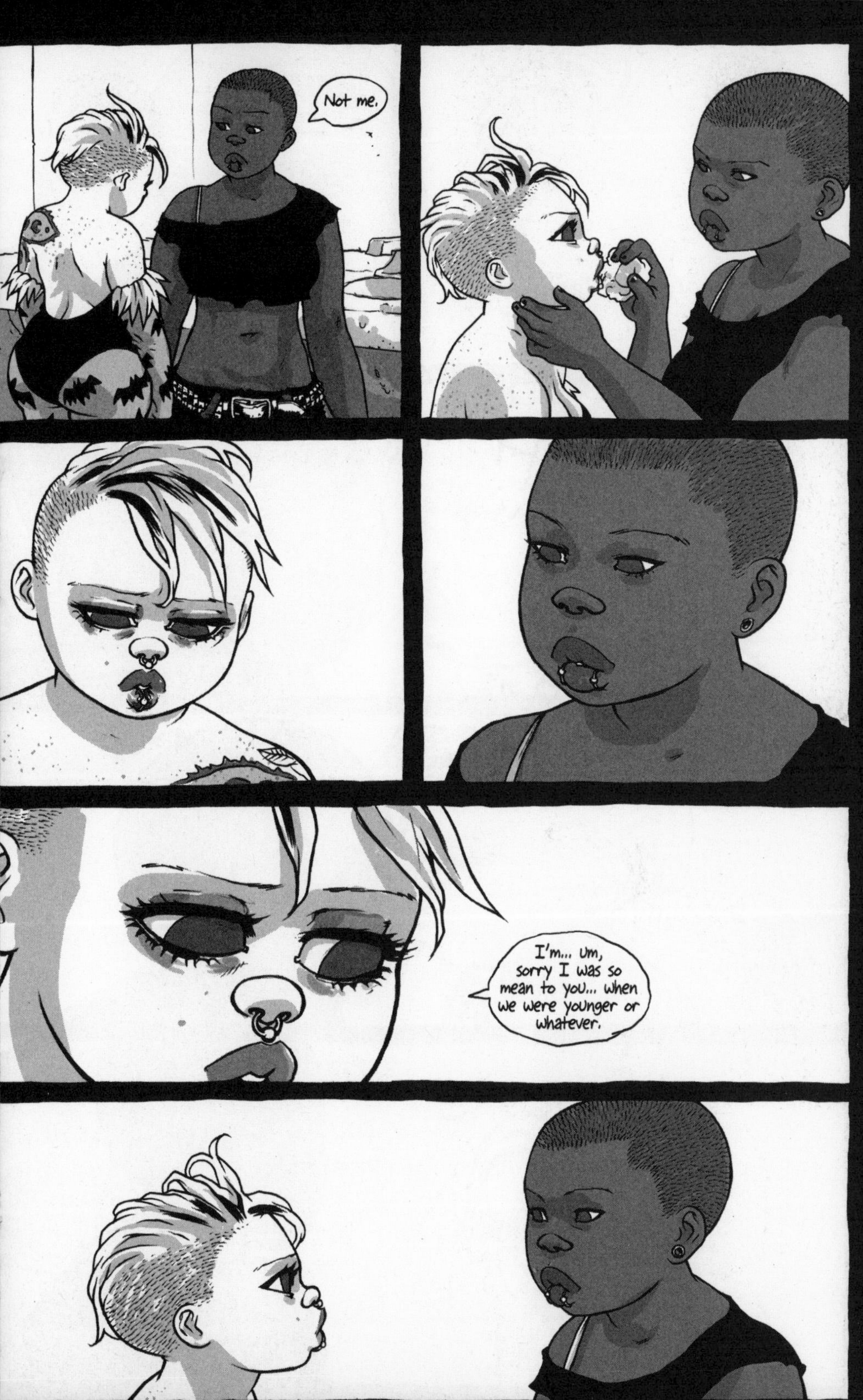
Not me.
I'm... um, sorry I was so mean to you... when we were younger or whatever.

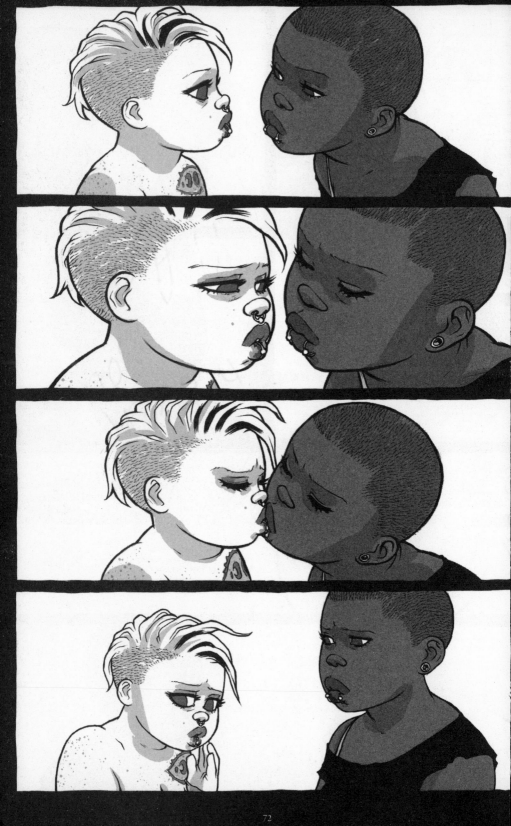

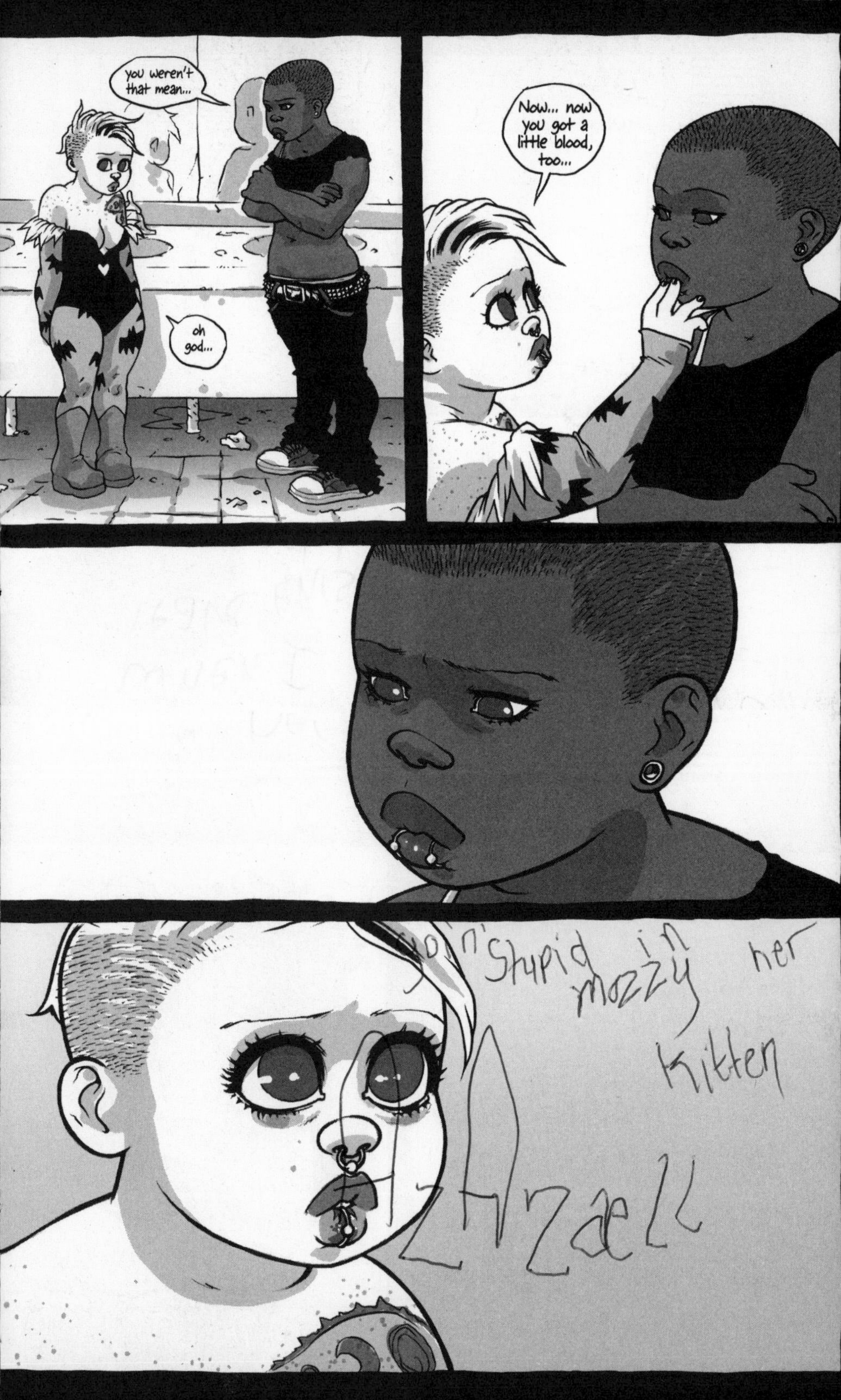
you weren't that mean...
oh god...
Now... now you got a little blood, too...
Stupid
mozzy
her
Kitten

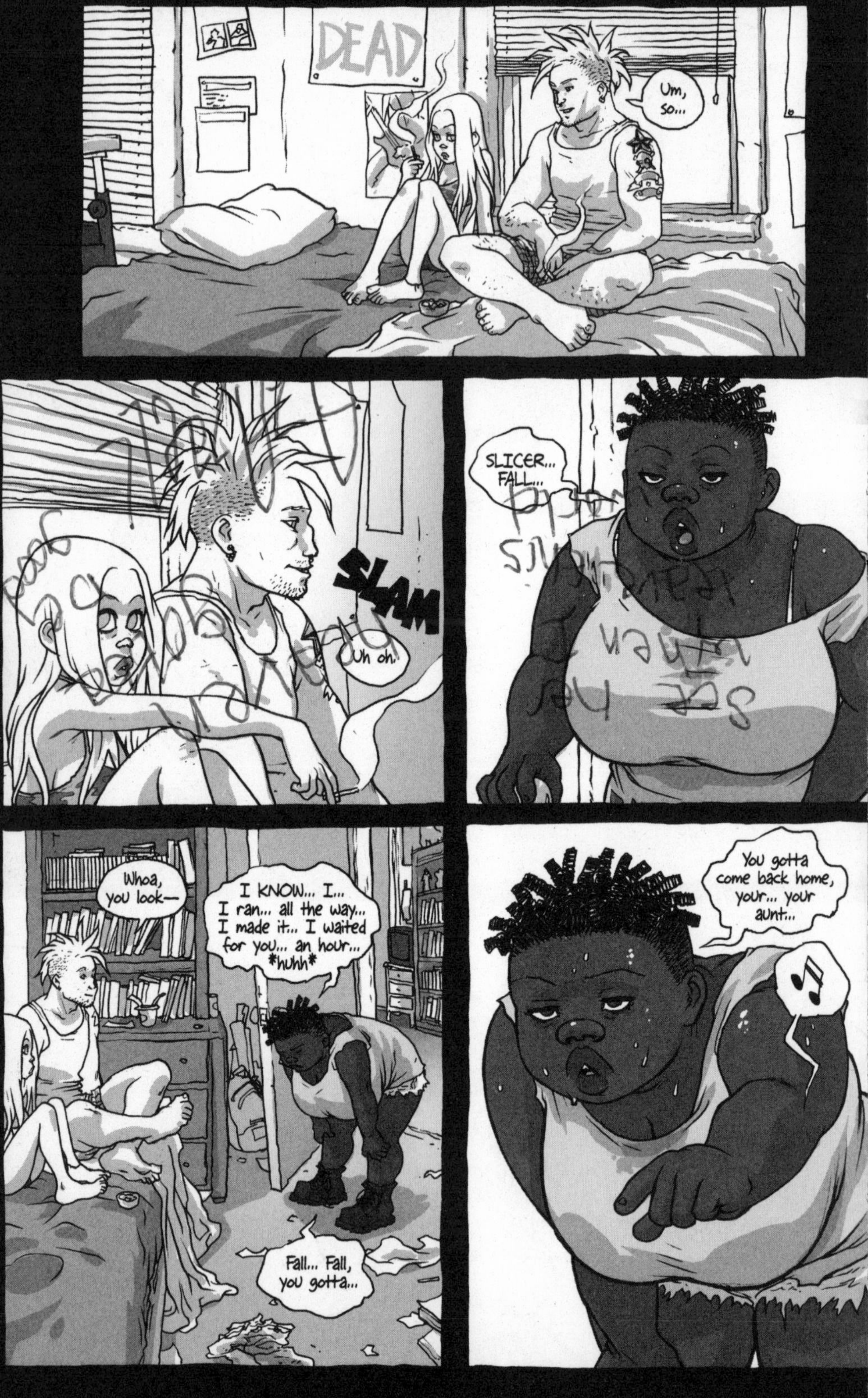
Um, so...
Uh oh.
SLAM
SLICER... FALL...
Whoa, you look—
I KNOW... I... I ran... all the way... I made it... I waited for you... an hour... *huhh*
Fall... Fall, you gotta...
You gotta come back home, your... your aunt...

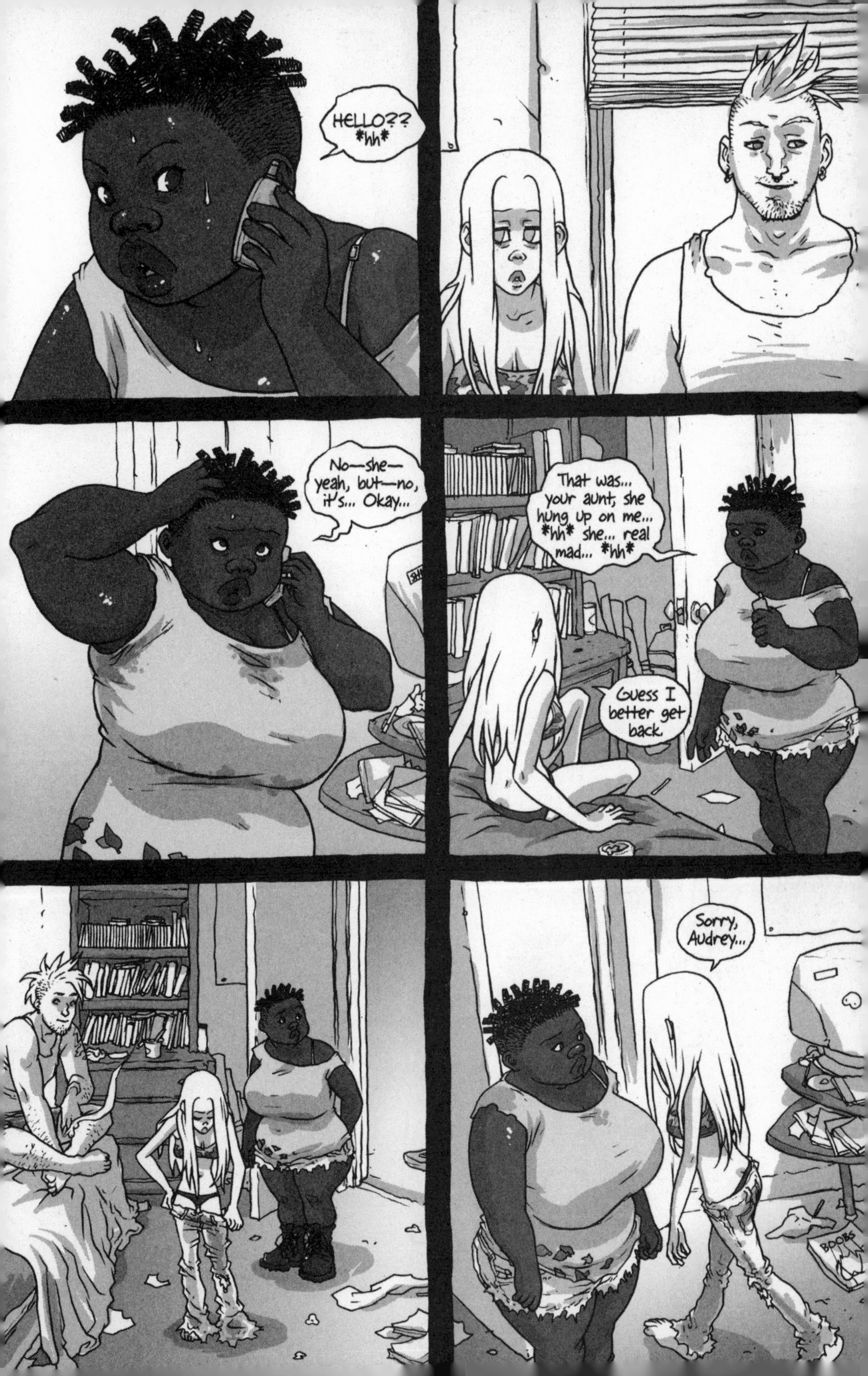
HELLO?? *hh*
No—she—yeah, but—no, it's... Okay...
That was... your aunt, she hung up on me... *hh* she... real mad... *hh*
Guess I better get back.
Sorry, Audrey...
BOOBS

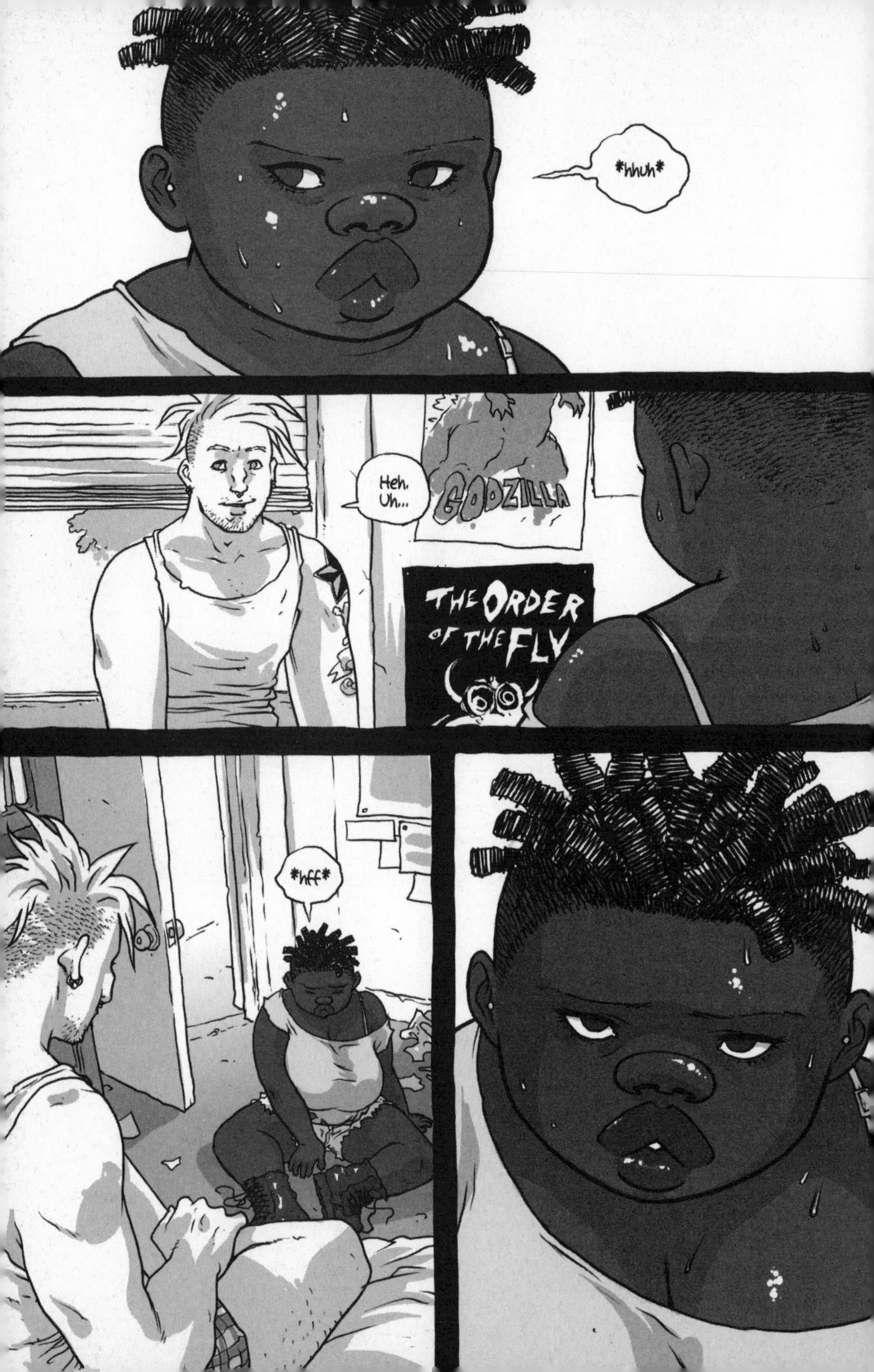
*hhuh*
Heh. Uh...
GODZILLA
THE ORDER OF THE FLY
*hff*

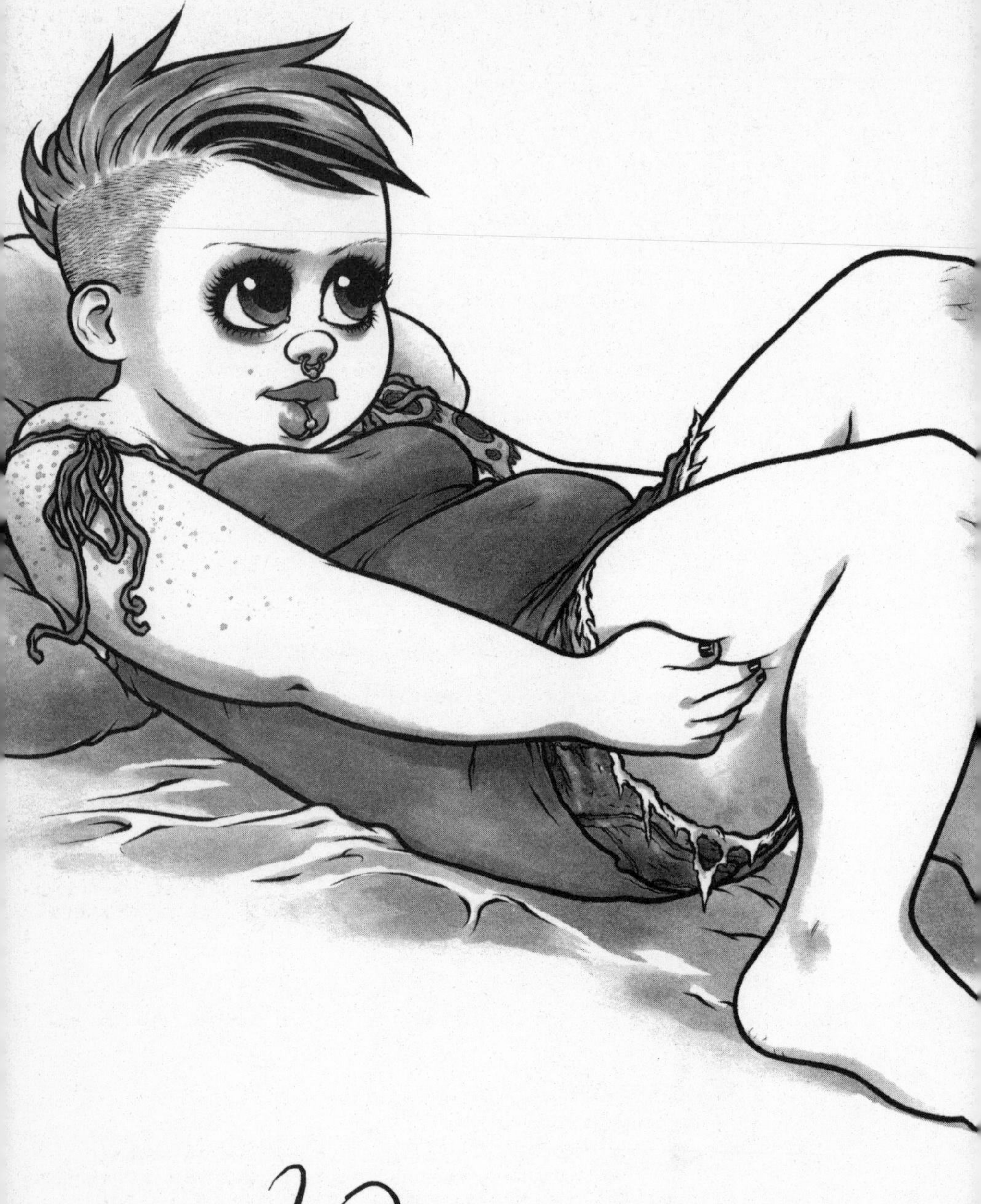

# 20

# The Wonders At Your Feet

[ friendtoroaches@gmail.com ]

Recent Entries Archive Friends User Info

## mara's journal

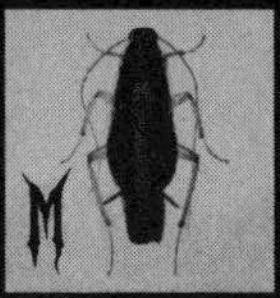

profile

## *October 31st, 10:38pm*

***SPEAR MY HEART.***

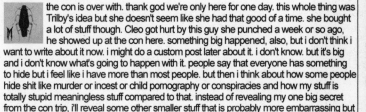

the con is over with. thank god we're only here for one day. this whole thing was Trilby's idea but she doesn't seem like she had that good of a time. she bought a lot of stuff though. Cleo got hurt by this guy she punched a week or so ago, he showed up at the con here. something big happened, also, but i don't think i want to write about it now. i might do a custom post later about it. i don't know. but it's big and i don't know what's going to happen with it. people say that everyone has something to hide but i feel like i have more than most people. but then i think about how some people hide shit like murder or incest or child pornography or conspiracies and how my stuff is totally stupid meaningless stuff compared to that. instead of revealing my one big secret from the con trip, i'll reveal some other smaller stuff that is probably more embarrassing but won't get me in trouble.

- i used to have lots of piercings because i thought they would make me pretty. didn't work.

- i masturbate a lot but i can't orgasm.

- i lie about what i've done with boys (which is pretty much nothing) to sound experienced.

- i bite myself when shit gets too stressful.

- i write stories besides my screenplay stuff but none of my friends know i do.

- i think this one probably goes for everyone, but sometimes i get real freaked out that nobody likes being around me but won't tell me.

- i have a secret tattoo on my left buttcheek that i've never shown anyone except obviously the tattooist who did it. i never wear thongs or change in front of people because of it. it's kind of a stupid tattoo and i won't say what it is here. i guess that'll be for another "secrets" post. i don't know why i keep it so secret, but it's really private to me. maybe Natalie will have to see it for the photoshoot. oh no.

*mood: honest*
*current music: none*

[ 0 comments | leave a comment ]

## *October 31st, 2:22am*

***OFFERING OF RED RAGE.***

it's officially Halloween, and i have no costume. i'm very pleased about that, i think Halloween is overrated and i hate how people don't dress up in spooky or scary costumes anymore. i thought Halloween was supposed to be about monsters and ghosts and zombies, not nurses or video game characters or pirates. i guess nurses can be scary. but i'm rebelling against that and not dressing up at all. i'm scarier as my regular self than anything i could dress up as.

we finally made it to the hotel which is okay. it's kind of small and a little smelly and there's only one bed, but they actually have wireless internet. the drive down was okay. not too bad. we drove past a big car accident, though, and i saw a bloody guy laying on the road all twisted up like a red, wet pretzel. that's the first time i've ever seen a corpse and i have to say it wasn't that bad. maybe it would be worse if we werent driving by at 50 miles an hour. Cleo seems really upset by it though. she's very sensitive. right now Trilby is watching some alien show on the sci-fi channel, and Martin is taking a shower for some reason.

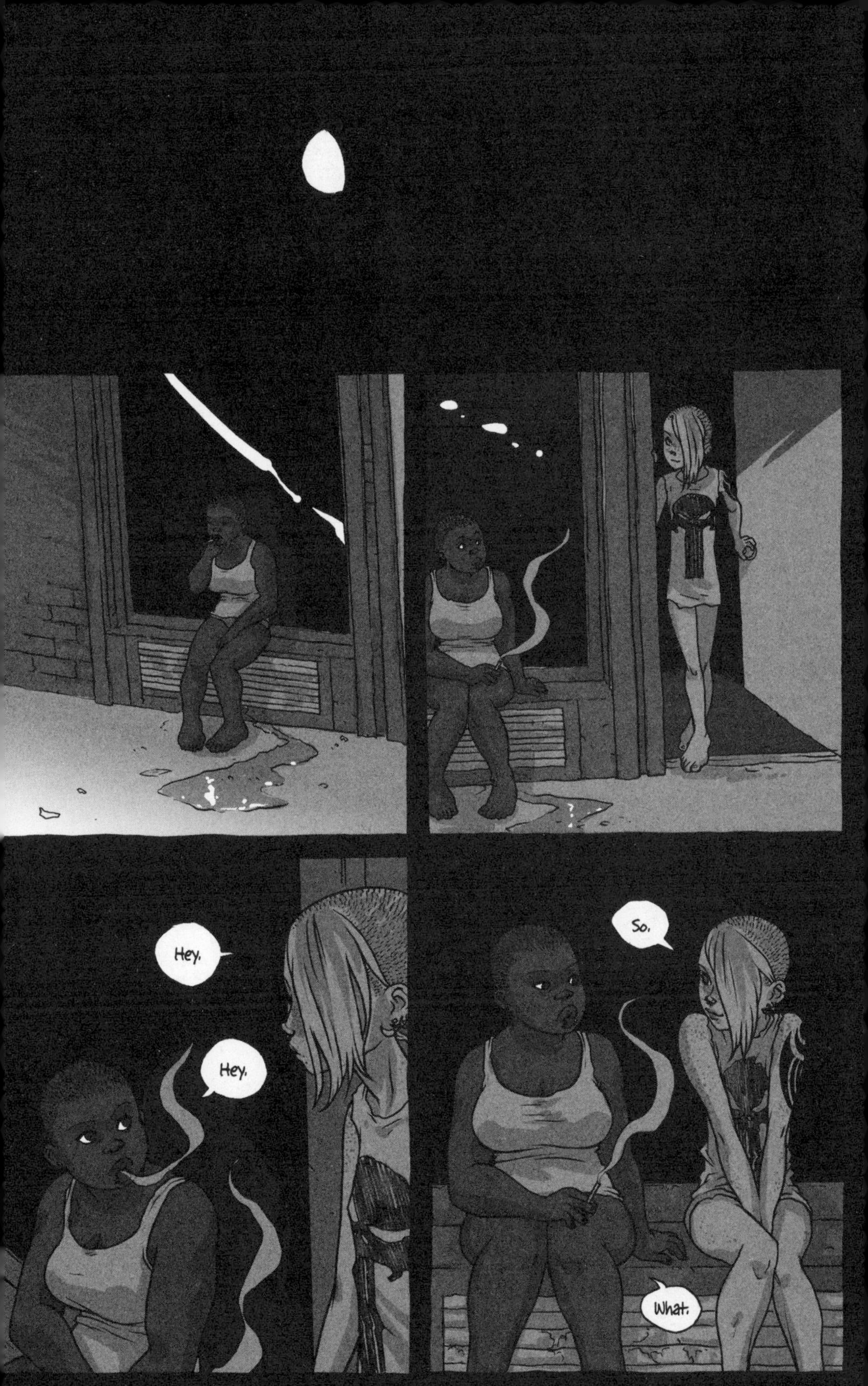
Hey.
Hey.
So.
What.

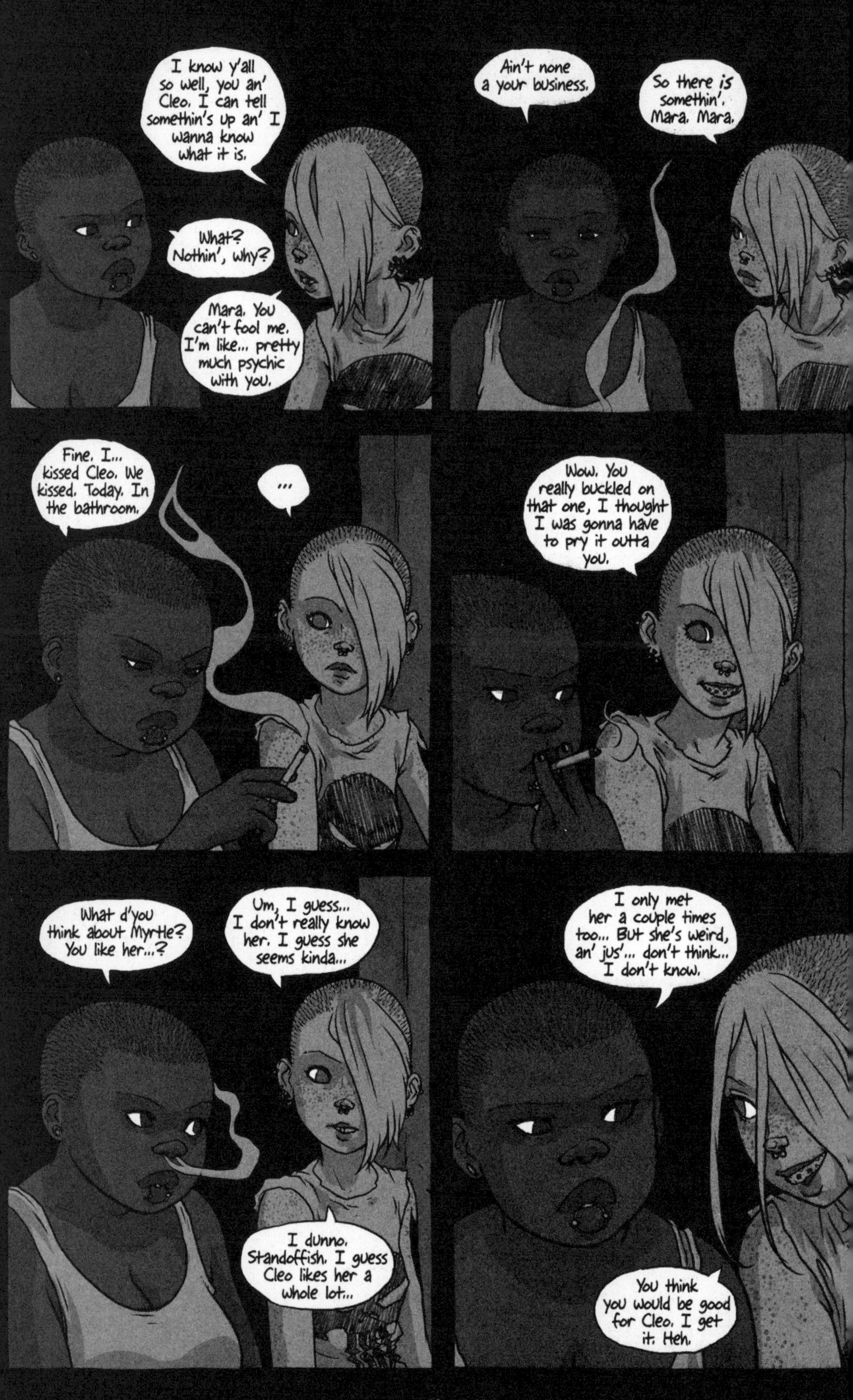
I know y'all so well, you an' Cleo. I can tell somethin's up an' I wanna know what it is.
What? Nothin', why?
Mara. You can't fool me. I'm like... pretty much psychic with you.
Ain't none a your business.
So there *is* somethin'. Mara. Mara.
Fine. I... kissed Cleo. We kissed. Today. In the bathroom.
...
Wow. You really buckled on that one, I thought I was gonna have to pry it outta you.
What d'you think about Myrtle? You like her...?
Um, I guess... I don't really know her. I guess she seems kinda...
I dunno. Standoffish. I guess Cleo likes her a whole lot...
I only met her a couple times too... But she's weird, an' jus'... don't think... I don't know.
You think you would be good for Cleo. I get it. Heh.

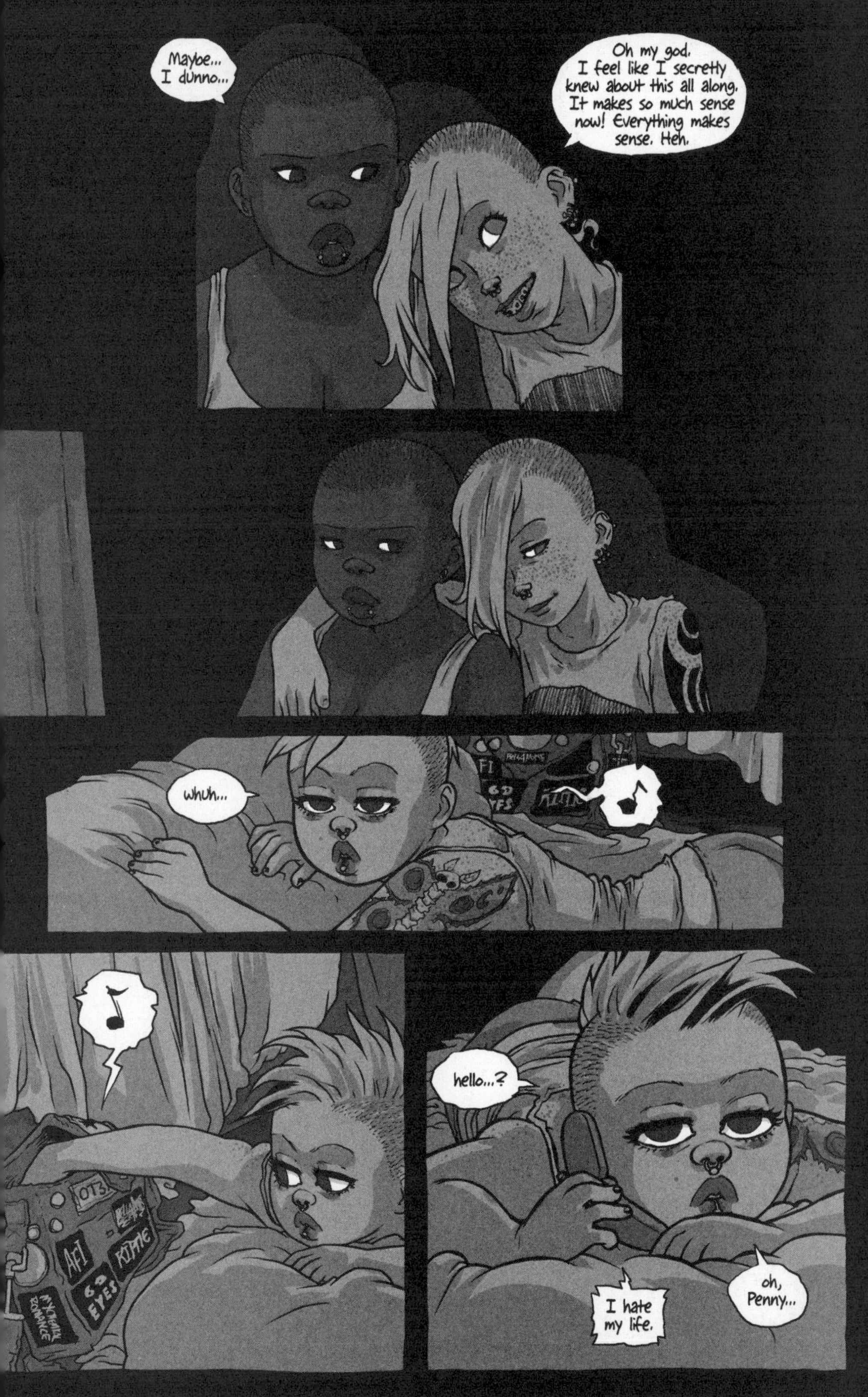
Maybe... I dunno...
Oh my god. I feel like I secretly knew about this all along. It makes so much sense now! Everything makes sense. Heh.
whuh...
AFI
AFI
60 EYES
hello...?
I hate my life.
oh, Penny...

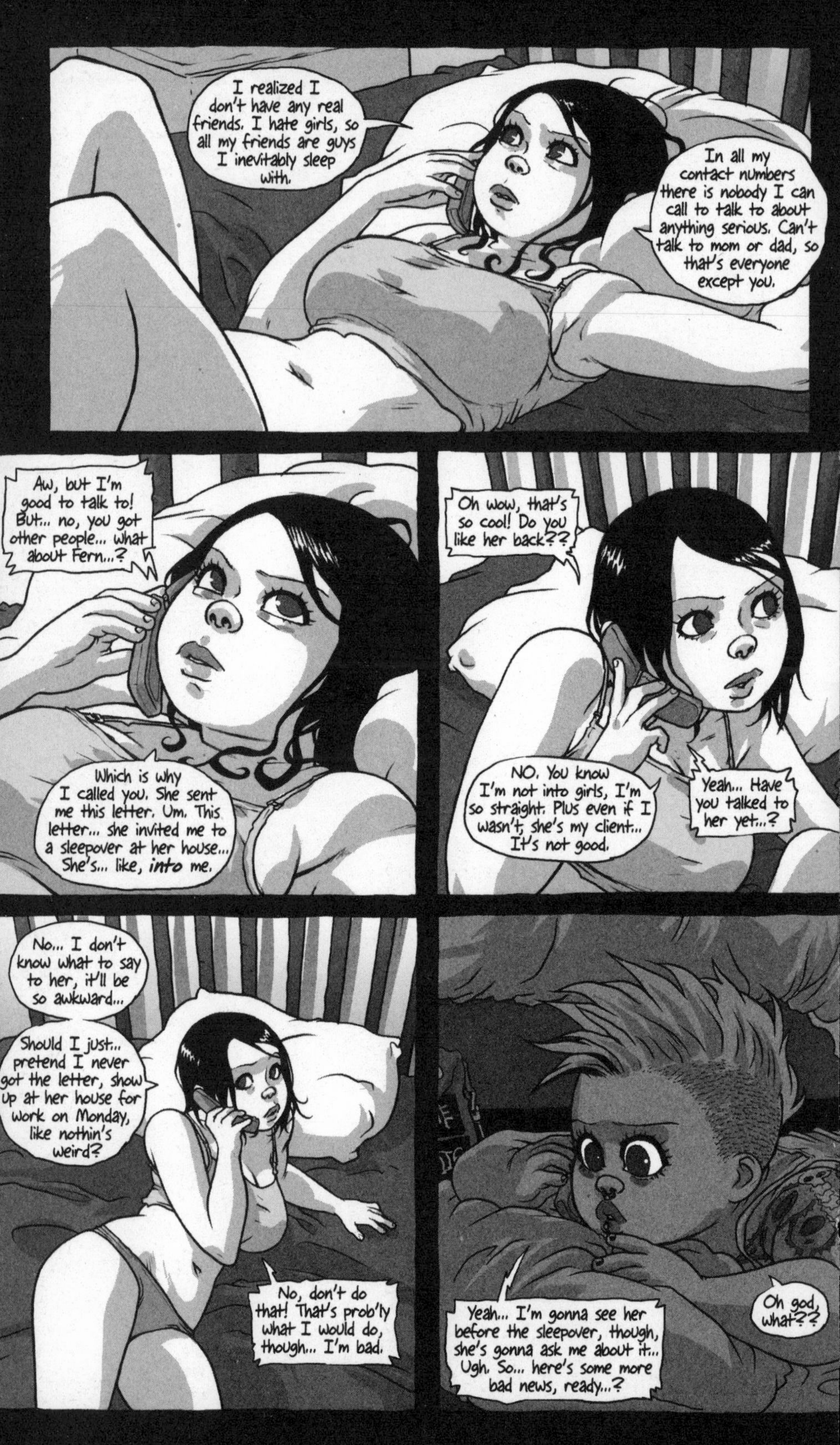
I realized I don't have any real friends. I hate girls, so all my friends are guys I inevitably sleep with.
In all my contact numbers there is nobody I can call to talk to about anything serious. Can't talk to mom or dad, so that's everyone except you.
Aw, but I'm good to talk to! But... no, you got other people... what about Fern...?
Which is why I called you. She sent me this letter. Um. This letter... she invited me to a sleepover at her house... She's... like, *into* me.
Oh wow, that's so cool! Do you like her back??
NO. You know I'm not into girls, I'm so straight. Plus even if I wasn't, she's my client... It's not good.
Yeah... Have you talked to her yet...?
No... I don't know what to say to her, it'll be so awkward...
Should I just... pretend I never got the letter, show up at her house for work on Monday, like nothin's weird?
No, don't do that! That's prob'ly what I would do, though... I'm bad.
Yeah... I'm gonna see her before the sleepover, though, she's gonna ask me about it... Ugh. So... here's some more bad news, ready...?
Oh god, what??

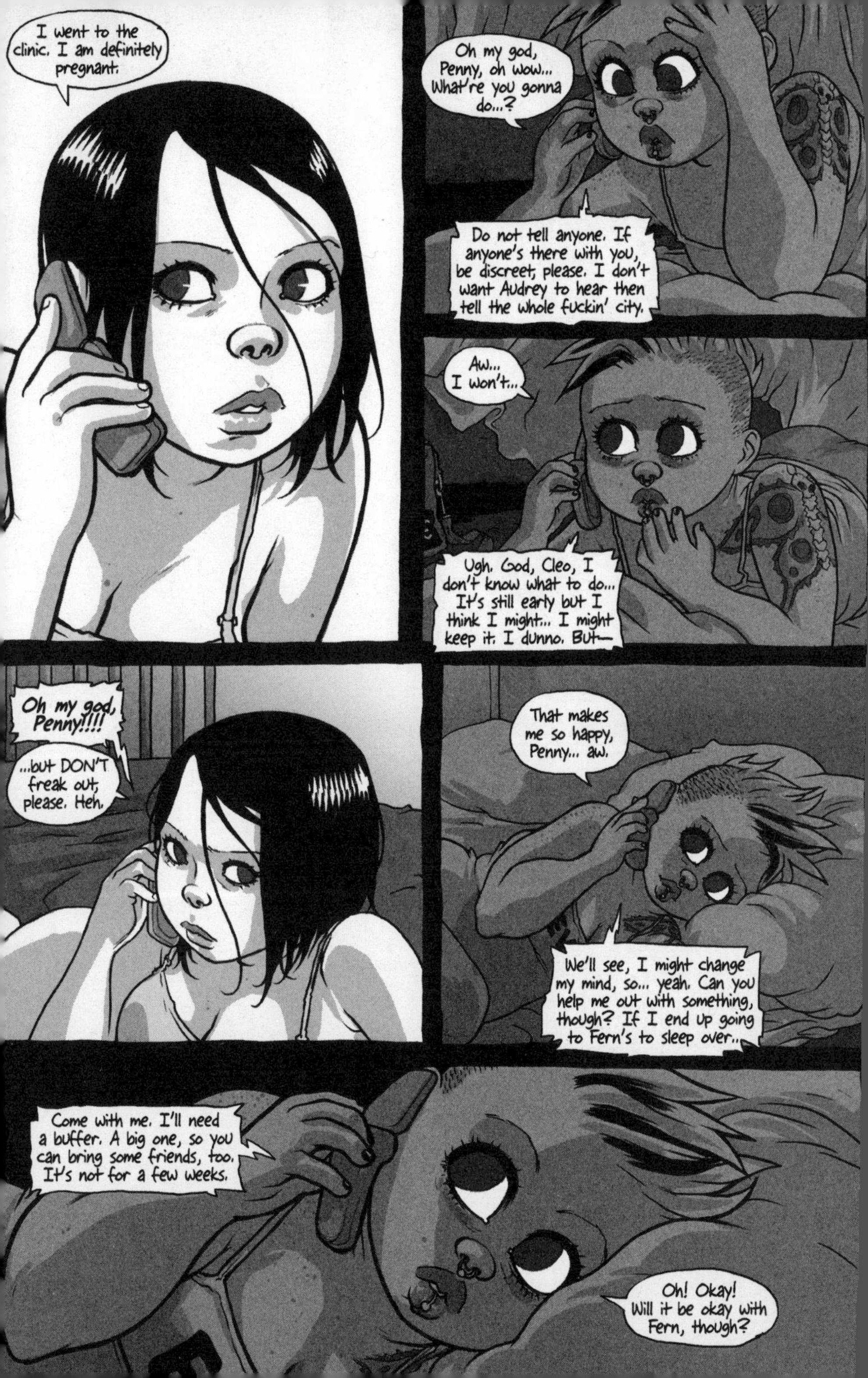
I went to the clinic. I am definitely pregnant.
Oh my god, Penny, oh wow... What're you gonna do...?
Do not tell anyone. If anyone's there with you, be discreet, please. I don't want Audrey to hear then tell the whole fuckin' city.
Aw... I won't...
Ugh. God, Cleo, I don't know what to do... It's still early but I think I might... I might keep it. I dunno. But—
Oh my god, Penny!!!!
...but DON'T freak out, please. Heh.
That makes me so happy, Penny... aw.
We'll see, I might change my mind, so... yeah. Can you help me out with something, though? If I end up going to Fern's to sleep over...
Come with me. I'll need a buffer. A big one, so you can bring some friends, too. It's not for a few weeks.
Oh! Okay! Will it be okay with Fern, though?

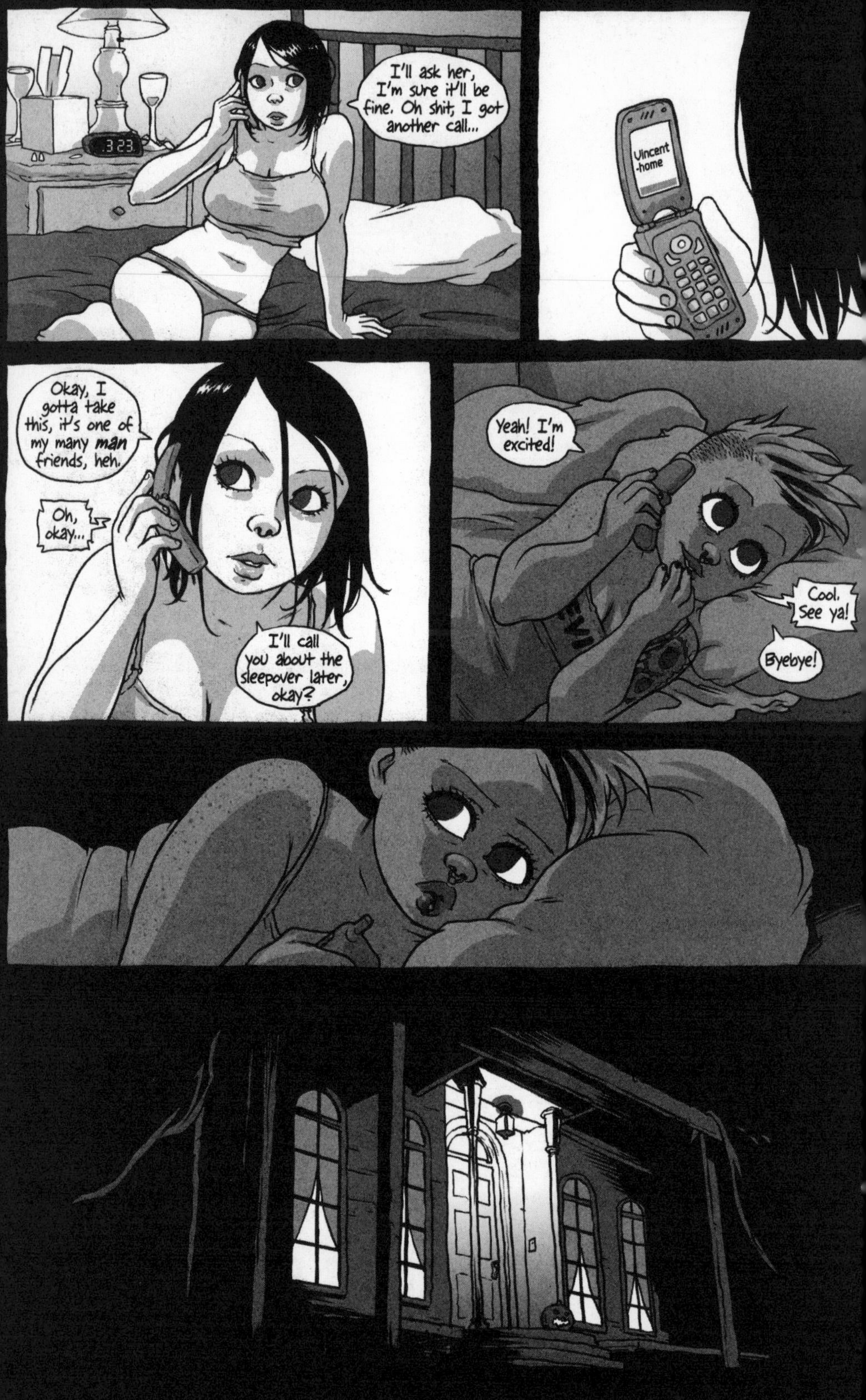
3:23
I'll ask her, I'm sure it'll be fine. Oh shit, I got another call...
Vincent -home
Okay, I gotta take this, it's one of my many man friends, heh.
Oh, okay...
I'll call you about the sleepover later, okay?
Yeah! I'm excited!
Cool. See ya!
Byebye!

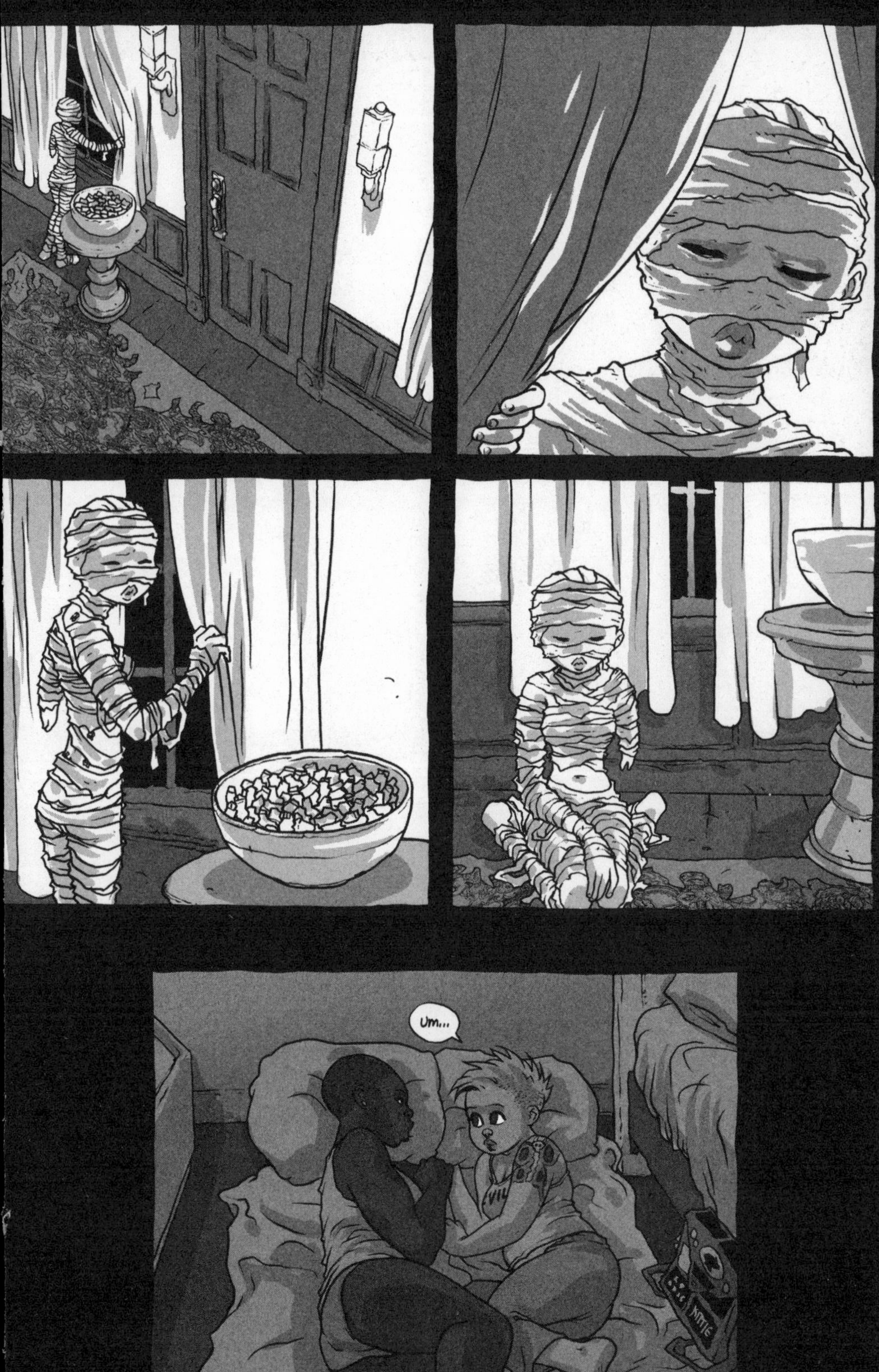
Um...

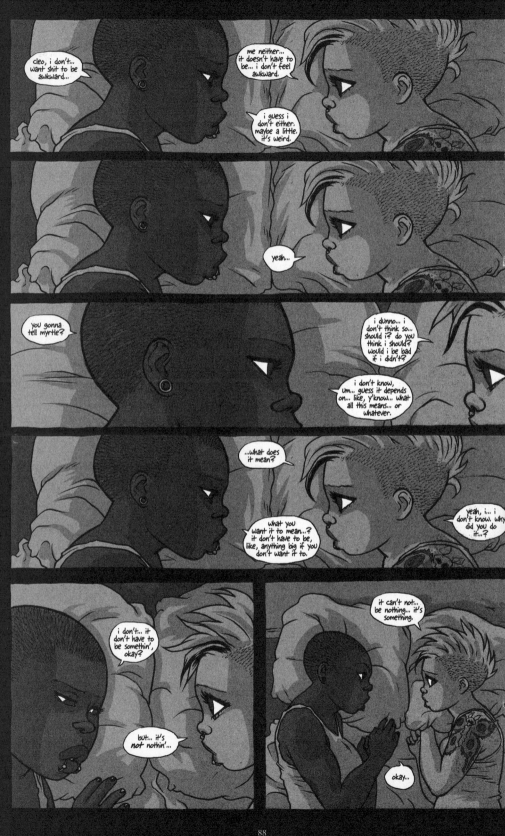

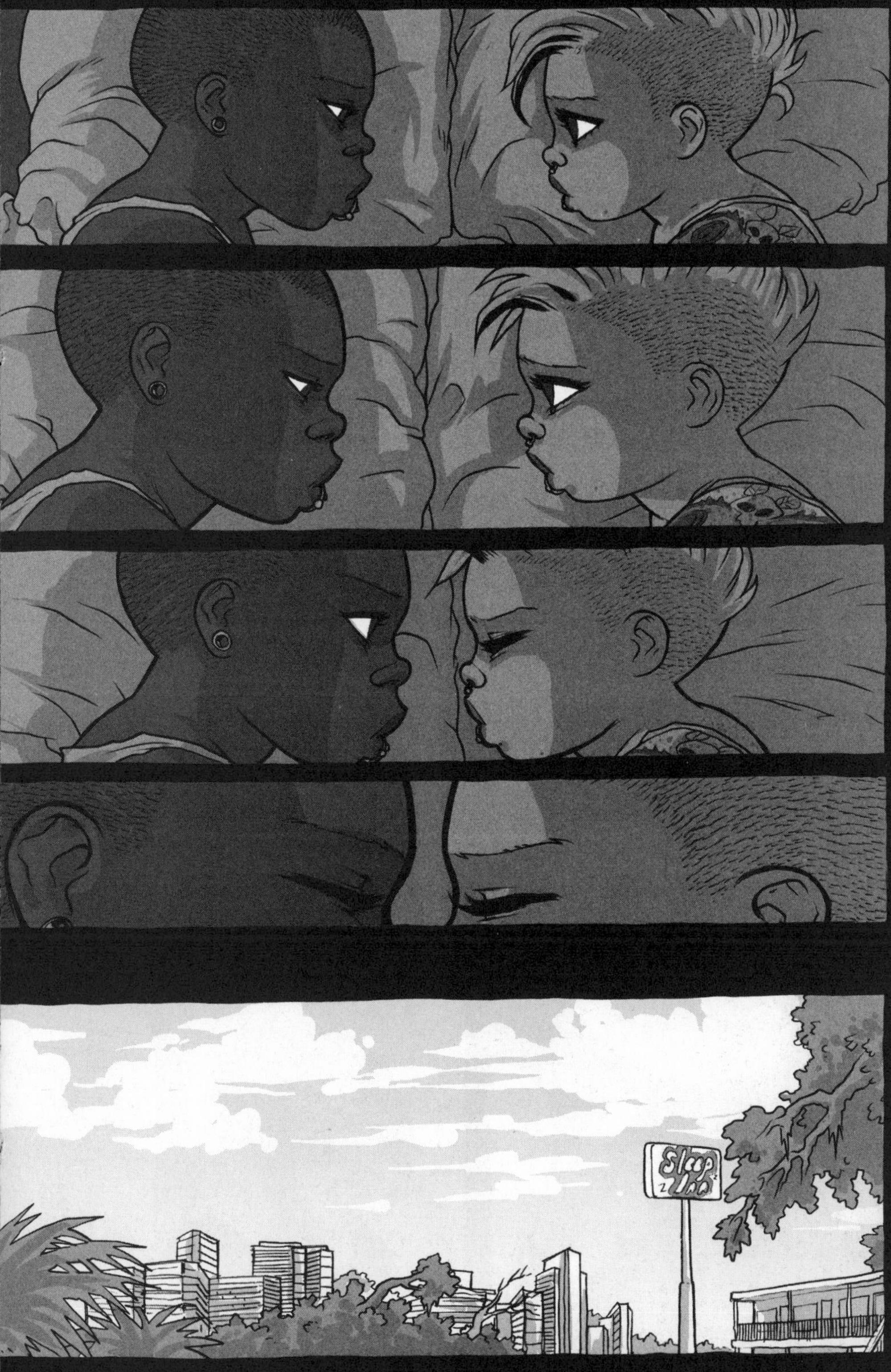
Sleep Inn

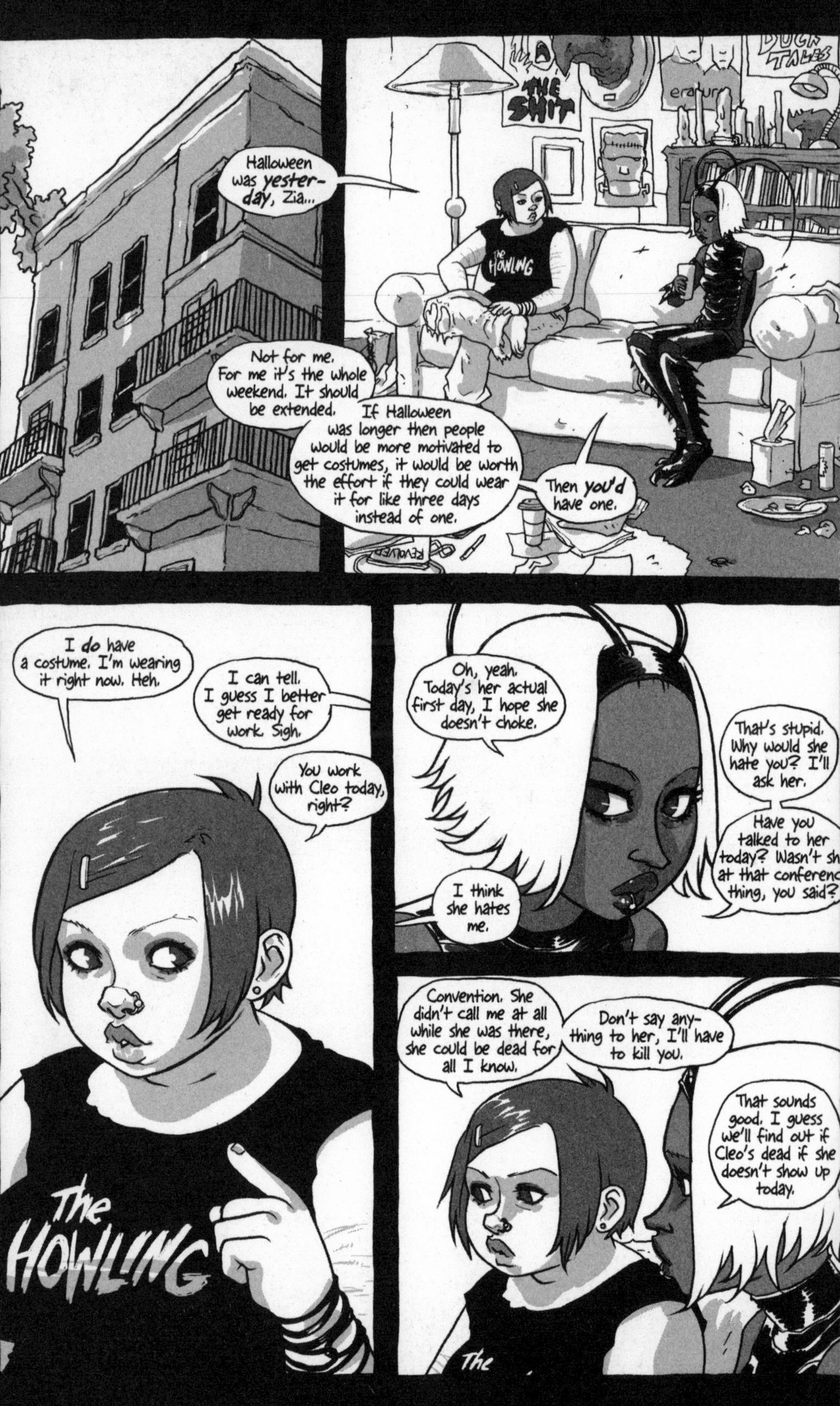
THE SHIT
DUCK TALES
Halloween was yester-day, Zia...
Not for me. For me it's the whole weekend. It should be extended.
If Halloween was longer then people would be more motivated to get costumes, it would be worth the effort if they could wear it for like three days instead of one.
Then you'd have one.
THE HOWLING
REVOLVER
I do have a costume. I'm wearing it right now. Heh.
I can tell. I guess I better get ready for work. Sigh.
You work with Cleo today, right?
Oh, yeah. Today's her actual first day, I hope she doesn't choke.
I think she hates me.
That's stupid. Why would she hate you? I'll ask her.
Have you talked to her today? Wasn't sh at that conferenc thing, you said?
The HOWLING
Convention. She didn't call me at all while she was there, she could be dead for all I know.
Don't say any-thing to her, I'll have to kill you.
That sounds good. I guess we'll find out if Cleo's dead if she doesn't show up today.

November 1

i'm writing this before my first day at work! oh my god, I am actually going to work, a real job, I'm so nervous! I don't even know what to wear, they don't have a uniform or any dress code really, so anything goes! I'd almost rather them have a uniform, then I wouldn't have to think so much about it! thank god my lip isn't bad or swollen. its a little yucky on the inside where i bit it but that's okay.

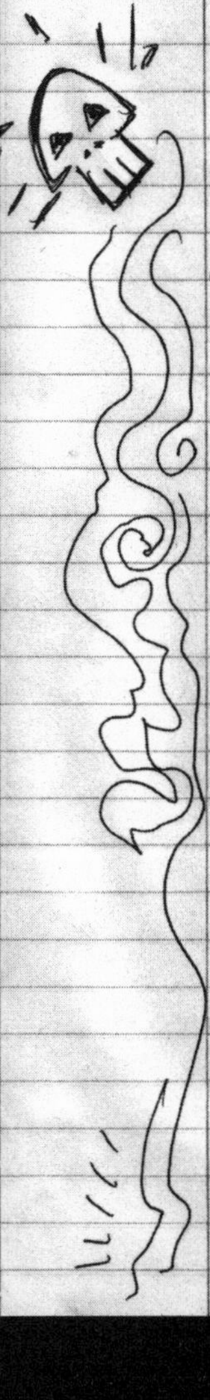

the slutty angels are performing in a couple of weeks, I'm so excited. i wish they had more gigs but they're such a small band (so far!). it's also going to be weird because they're going to play the song myrtle's writing for me! i know its a really sweet and amazing gesture but i still feel kind of pressured by it... i think i was saying before how much of an undertaking creating a song is, since it requires writing so many different parts and takes the whole band to perform... all for me. i don't know. i feel

so great about it but at the same time it's still scary in some ways. and... something happened with ~~the~~ mara that makes it even scarier. i ran afoul of that guy from the Bella Morte show who I punched, there was violence, mara took me into the bathroom to clean up and...

we kissed. i feel like... totally alien writing that, but it happened and can't be denied. it just came out of nowhere. and I think normally i'd be freaking out or grossed out because she's my friend and i've known her for so long but on the other hand i don't feel that weird about it, at least not the kiss itself or what it might mean. but i do feel confused about it. does it **HAVE** to mean anything? can two friends do something like this and just be normal about it? i know some girls can can do that. but mara also is like sort of into me in some extrafriend way, so does she want this to mean something more? we haven't really talked about it much ~~yet~~ yet, but i hope it isn't glossed

over even though i'd feel weird
bringing it up now. and what if
it does turn out to mean something?
do i have to choose, will it come
down to me having to choose one
girl over the other? myrtle's
writing me a song, but mara...
she's my best friend pretty much,
what would a romance be like
with that sort of foundation?
but then a romance would WRECK
a best friendship, too... and what
if it did happen, i can't even
bear thinking about us telling our
families... at least we know each
other's families so that wouldn't
be weird. i can't believe i'm even
on this train of thought, i can't
believe any of this is happening.
it's so crazy.

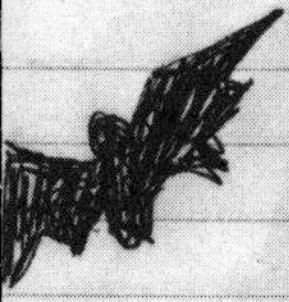

it's really scary liking girls now.
I find myself noticing things
about random girls that i didn't
before and then i start questioning
it and myself. I keep thinking
about telling everyone, that
maybe that's the best and easiest
thing to do, but then i think i
have to keep everything inside
because it might not be okay
if everyone knew, i don't know

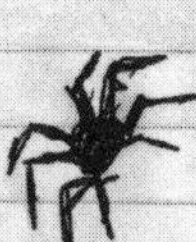

how they would react, and i don't think i'm even comfortable yet coming out., am i even IN?? i don't know!! and like even if all ~~my~~ my friends and family knew, is it okay to go out to like a restaurant or something and hold Myrtle's hand? what would people do? i think ~~about~~ a lot about Audrey, how, besides in our friend group she's still in the closet, and how terrifying being in there is AND how terrifying being out could be. i don't know how she lives everyday with this gigantic secret plus the knowledge that if it wasn't a secret anymore, things might be ~~better~~ WORSE for her. her parents could disown her, everyone ~~could~~ could shun her and throw things at her even, or be all prejudiced all the time. or i read about in the news how gay people get attacked and stuff like that. what if Audrey committed suicide because things got so bad? could i get to that point if i came out of the closet? i just said i was in the closet. am i? i don't know. i don't know where I am.

time for my first day at Burial Grounds!!! i'm excited about working with that girl Zia, she is super cool.

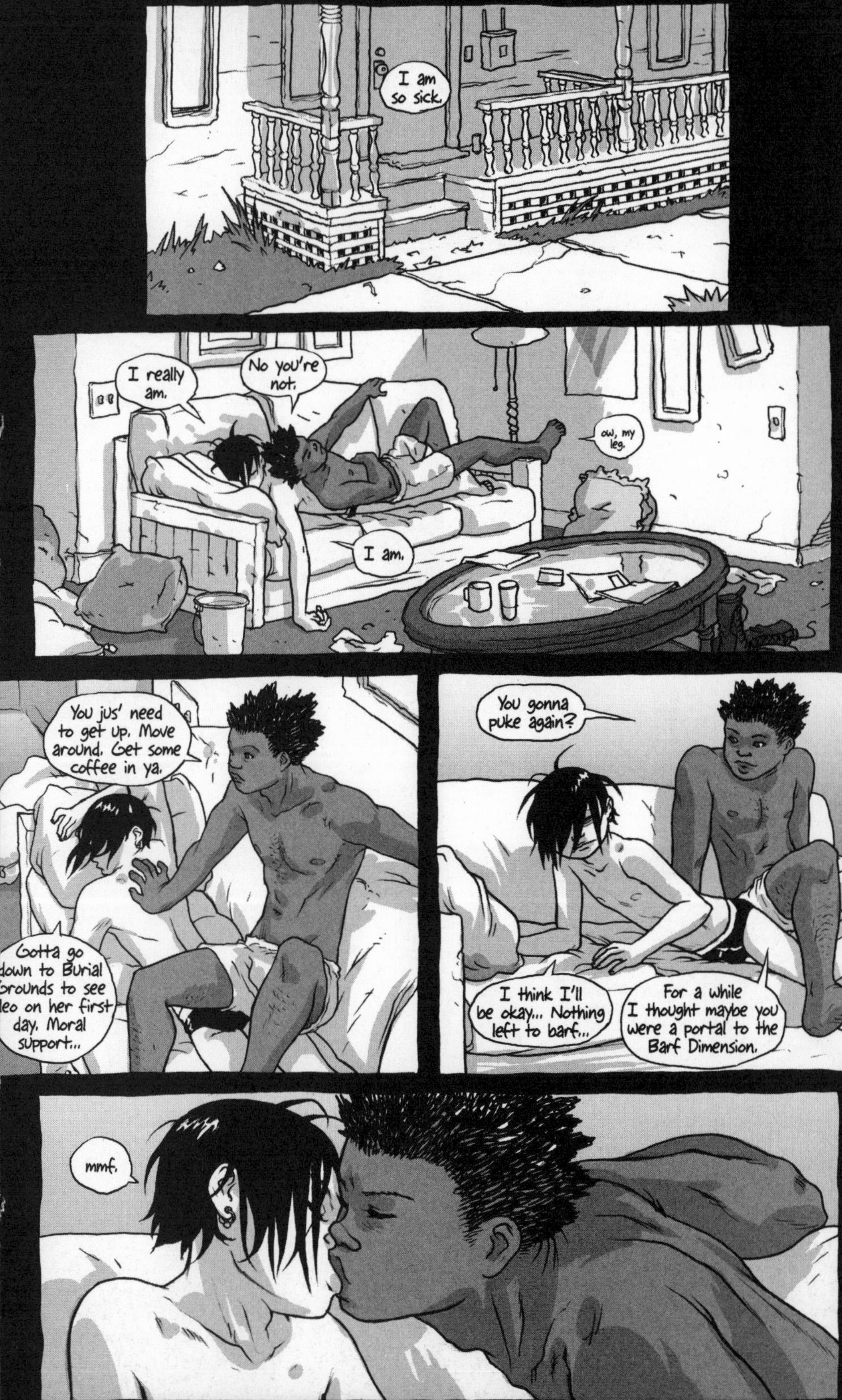
I am so sick.
I really am.
No you're not.
ow, my leg.
I am.
You jus' need to get up. Move around. Get some coffee in ya.
Gotta go down to Burial Grounds to see Cleo on her first day. Moral support...
You gonna puke again?
I think I'll be okay... Nothing left to barf...
For a while I thought maybe you were a portal to the Barf Dimension.
mmf.

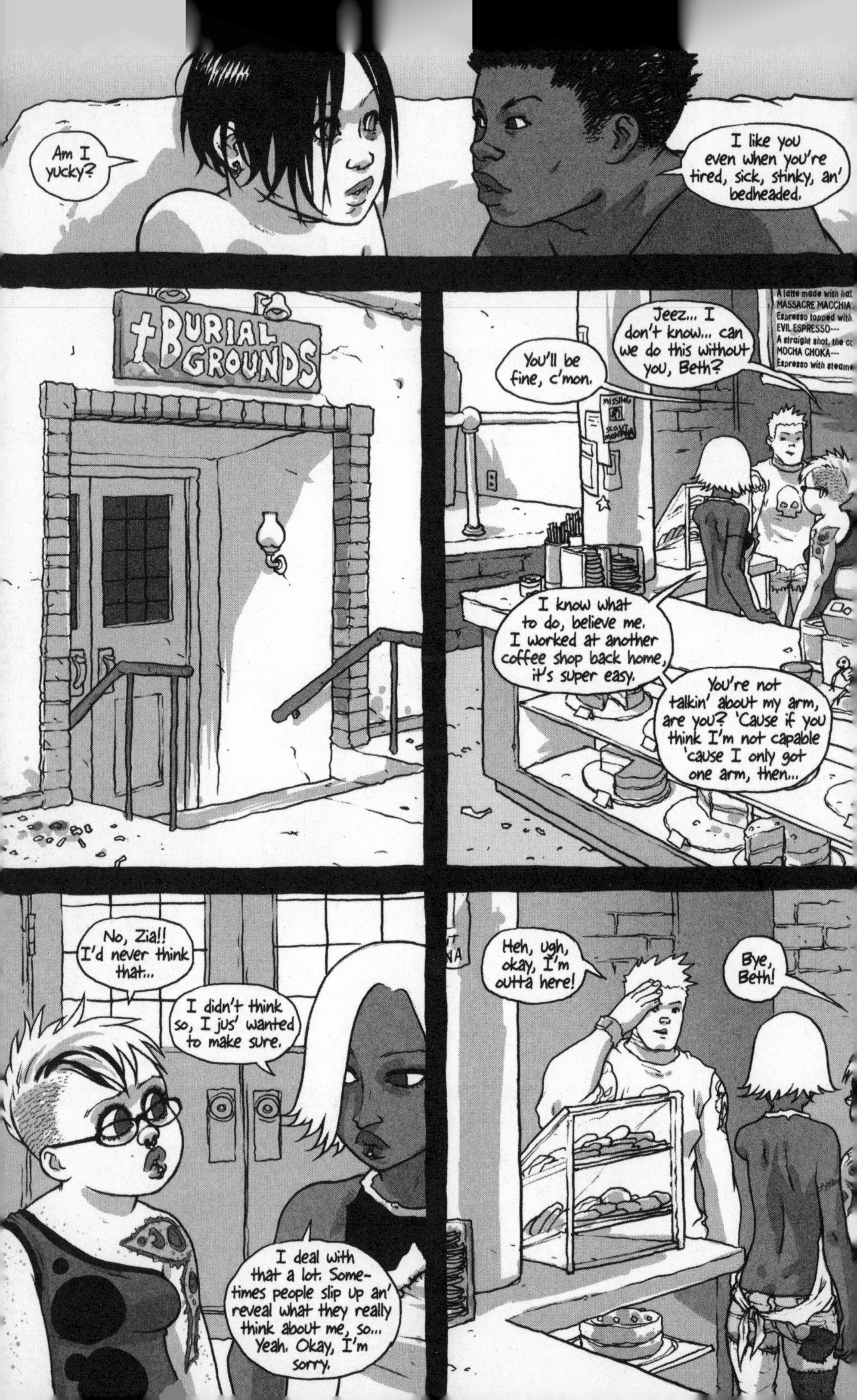

Am I yucky?
I like you even when you're tired, sick, stinky, an' bedheaded.
BURIAL GROUNDS
A latte made with hat
MASSACRE MACCHIA
Espresso topped with
EVIL ESPRESSO---
A straight shot, the co
MOCHA CHOKA---
Espresso with steame
Jeez... I don't know... can we do this without you, Beth?
You'll be fine, c'mon.
MISSING
I know what to do, believe me. I worked at another coffee shop back home, it's super easy.
You're not talkin' about my arm, are you? 'Cause if you think I'm not capable 'cause I only got one arm, then...
No, Zia!! I'd never think that...
I didn't think so, I jus' wanted to make sure.
I deal with that a lot. Sometimes people slip up an' reveal what they really think about me, so... Yeah. Okay, I'm sorry.
Heh, ugh, okay, I'm outta here!
Bye, Beth!

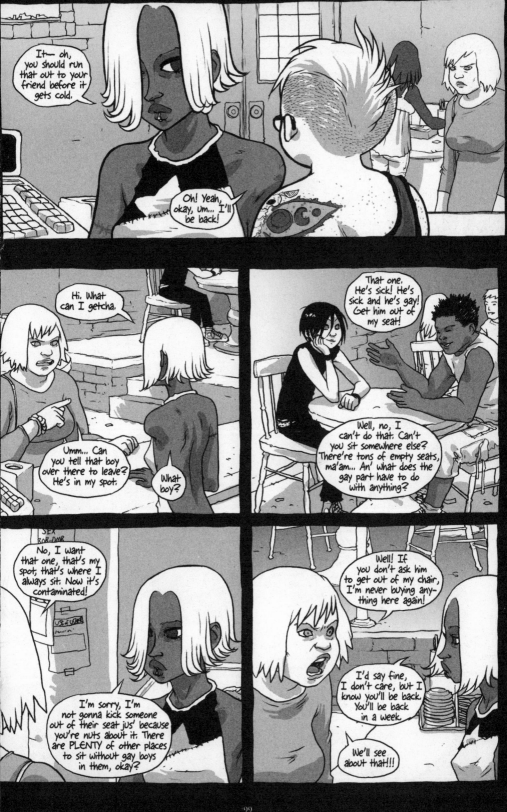

It— oh, you should run that out to your friend before it gets cold.

Oh! Yeah, okay, um... I'll be back!

Hi. What can I getcha.

Umm... Can you tell that boy over there to leave? He's in my spot.

What boy?

That one. He's sick! He's sick and he's gay! Get him out of my seat!

Well, no, I can't do that. Can't you sit somewhere else? There're tons of empty seats, ma'am... An' what does the gay part have to do with anything?

No, I want that one, that's my spot; that's where I always sit. Now it's contaminated!

I'm sorry, I'm not gonna kick someone out of their seat jus' because you're nuts about it. There are PLENTY of other places to sit without gay boys in them, okay?

Well! If you don't ask him to get out of my chair, I'm never buying anything here again!

I'd say fine, I don't care, but I know you'll be back. You'll be back in a week.

We'll see about that!!!

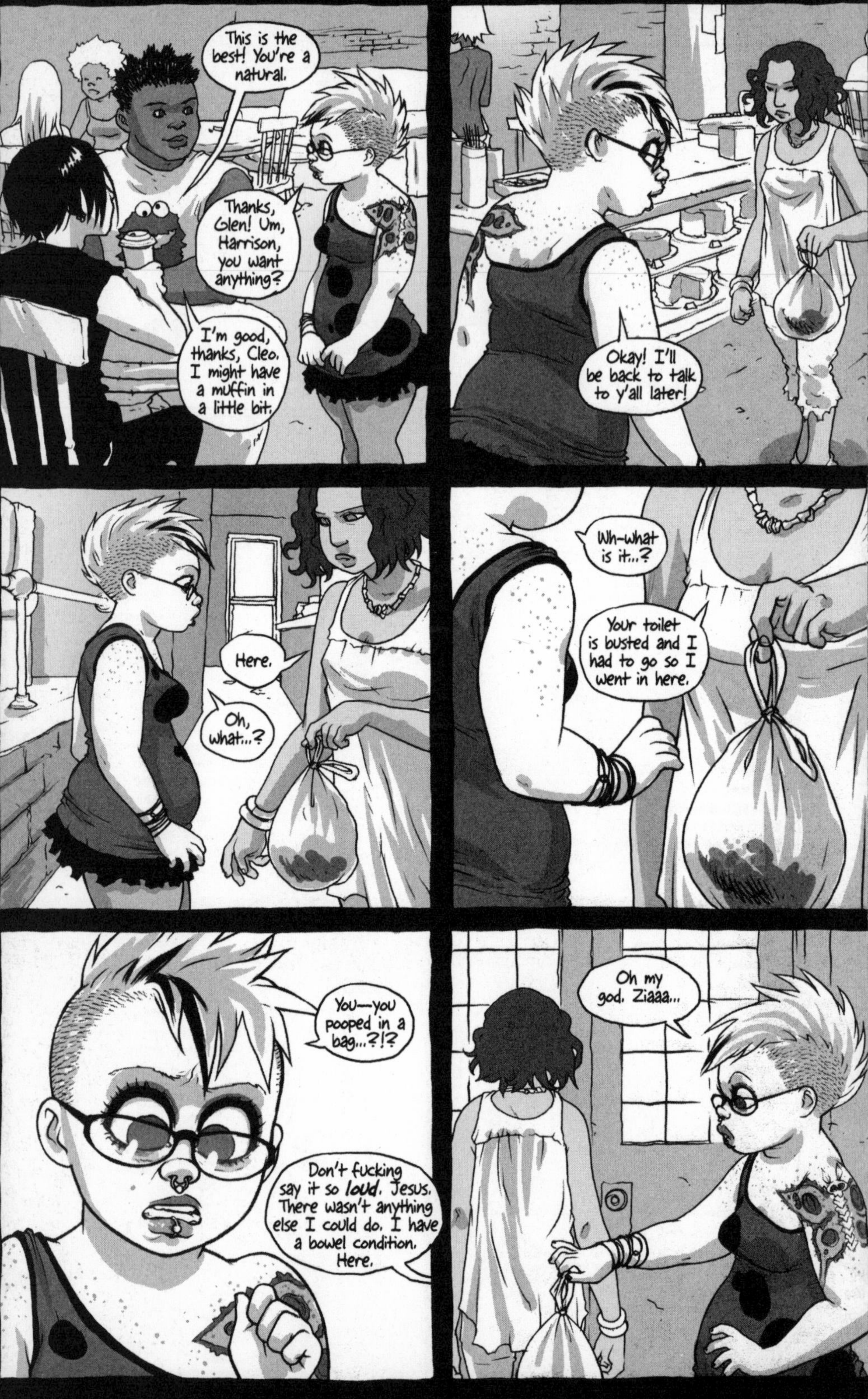
This is the best! You're a natural.
Thanks, Glen! Um, Harrison, you want anything?
I'm good, thanks, Cleo. I might have a muffin in a little bit.
Okay! I'll be back to talk to y'all later!
Here.
Oh, what...?
Wh-what is it...?
Your toilet is busted and I had to go so I went in here.
You—you pooped in a bag...?!?
Don't fucking say it so loud. Jesus. There wasn't anything else I could do. I have a bowel condition. Here.
Oh my god. Ziaaa...

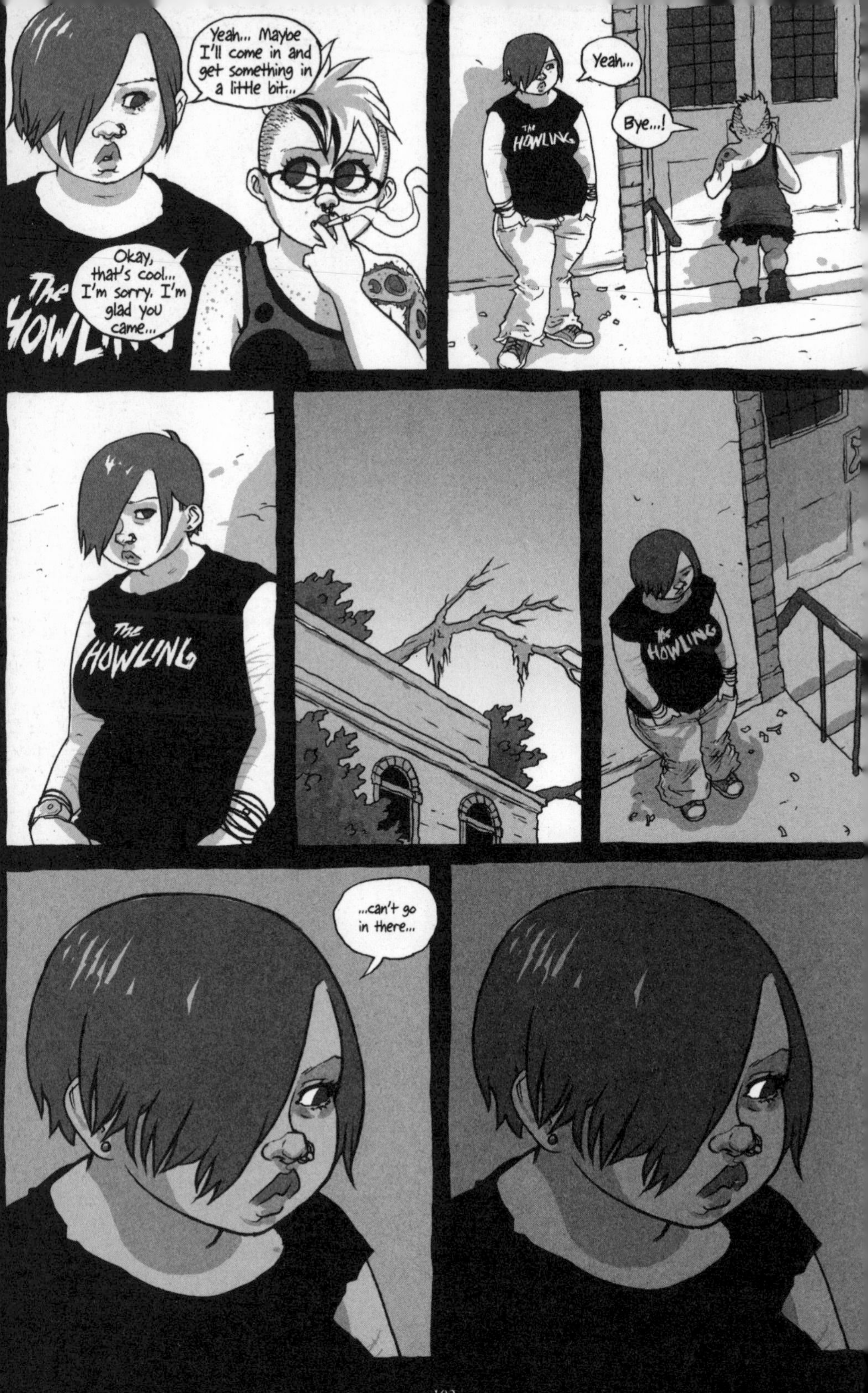
Yeah... Maybe I'll come in and get something in a little bit...
Okay, that's cool... I'm sorry, I'm glad you came...
Yeah...
Bye...!
...can't go in there...

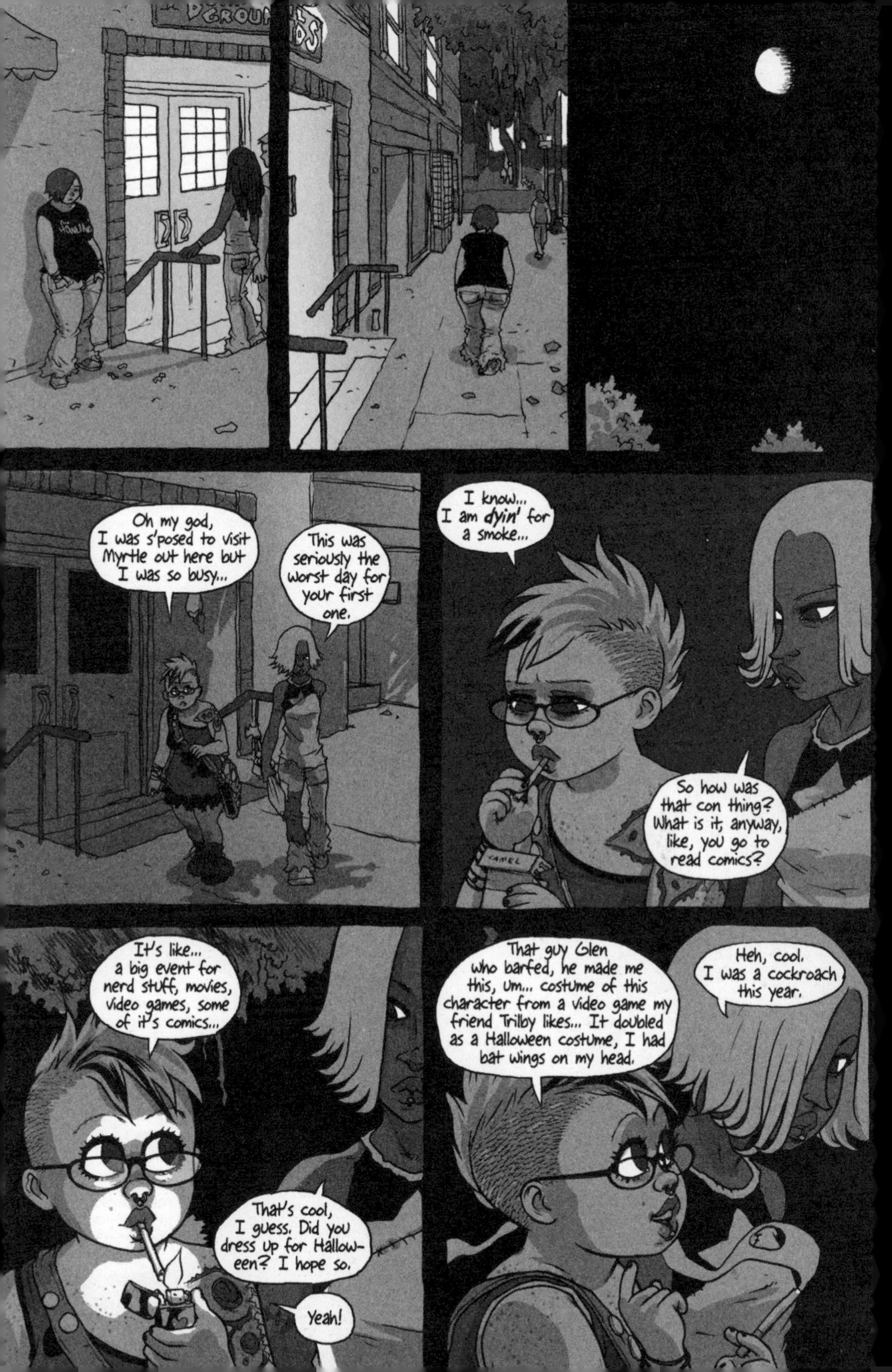
Oh my god, I was s'posed to visit Myrtle out here but I was so busy...
This was seriously the worst day for your first one.
I know... I am *dyin'* for a smoke...
So how was that con thing? What is it, anyway, like, you go to read comics?
It's like... a big event for nerd stuff, movies, video games, some of it's comics...
That's cool, I guess. Did you dress up for Hallow-een? I hope so.
Yeah!
That guy Glen who barfed, he made me this, um... costume of this character from a video game my friend Trilby likes... It doubled as a Halloween costume, I had bat wings on my head.
Heh, cool. I was a cockroach this year.

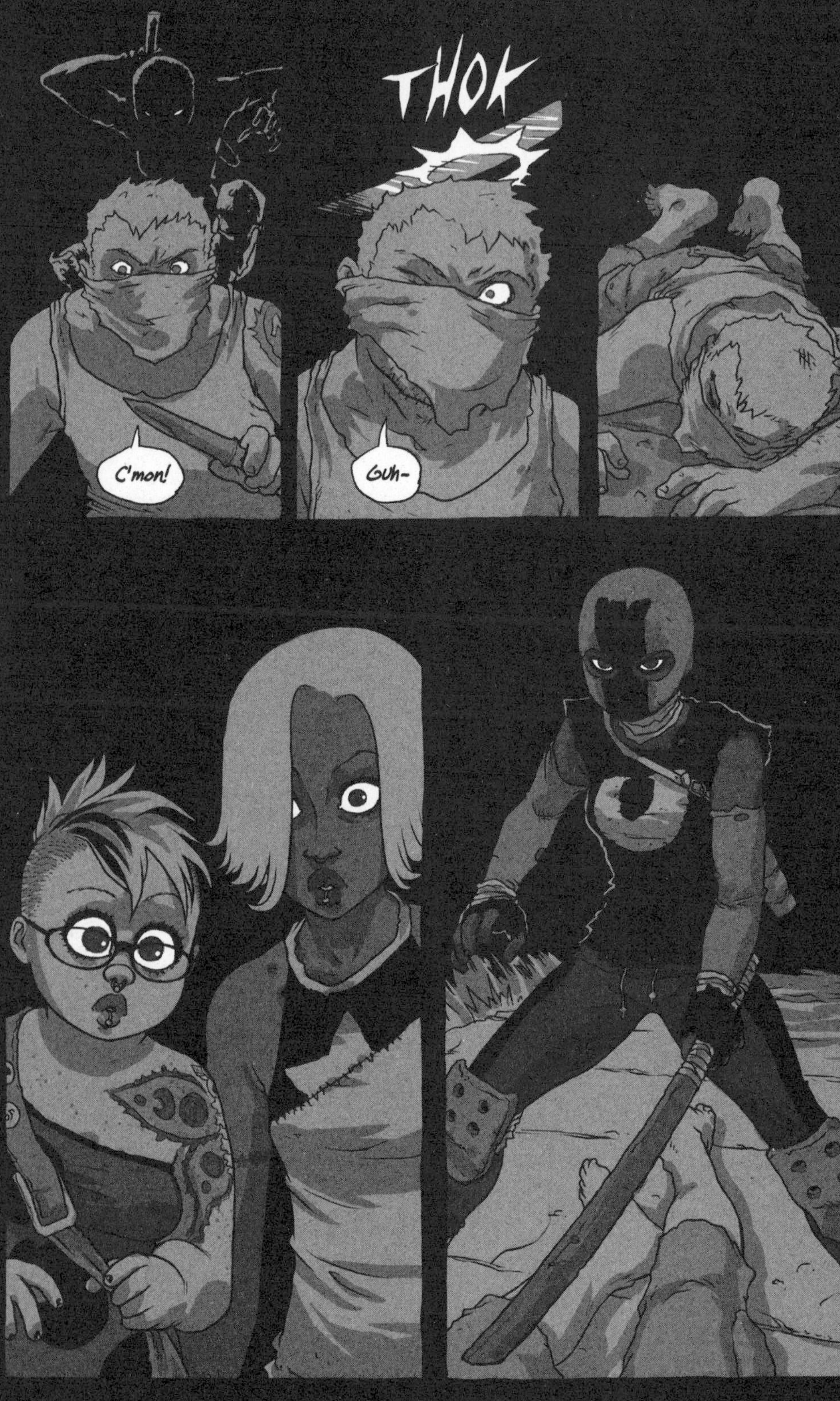
C'mon!
THOK
Guh-

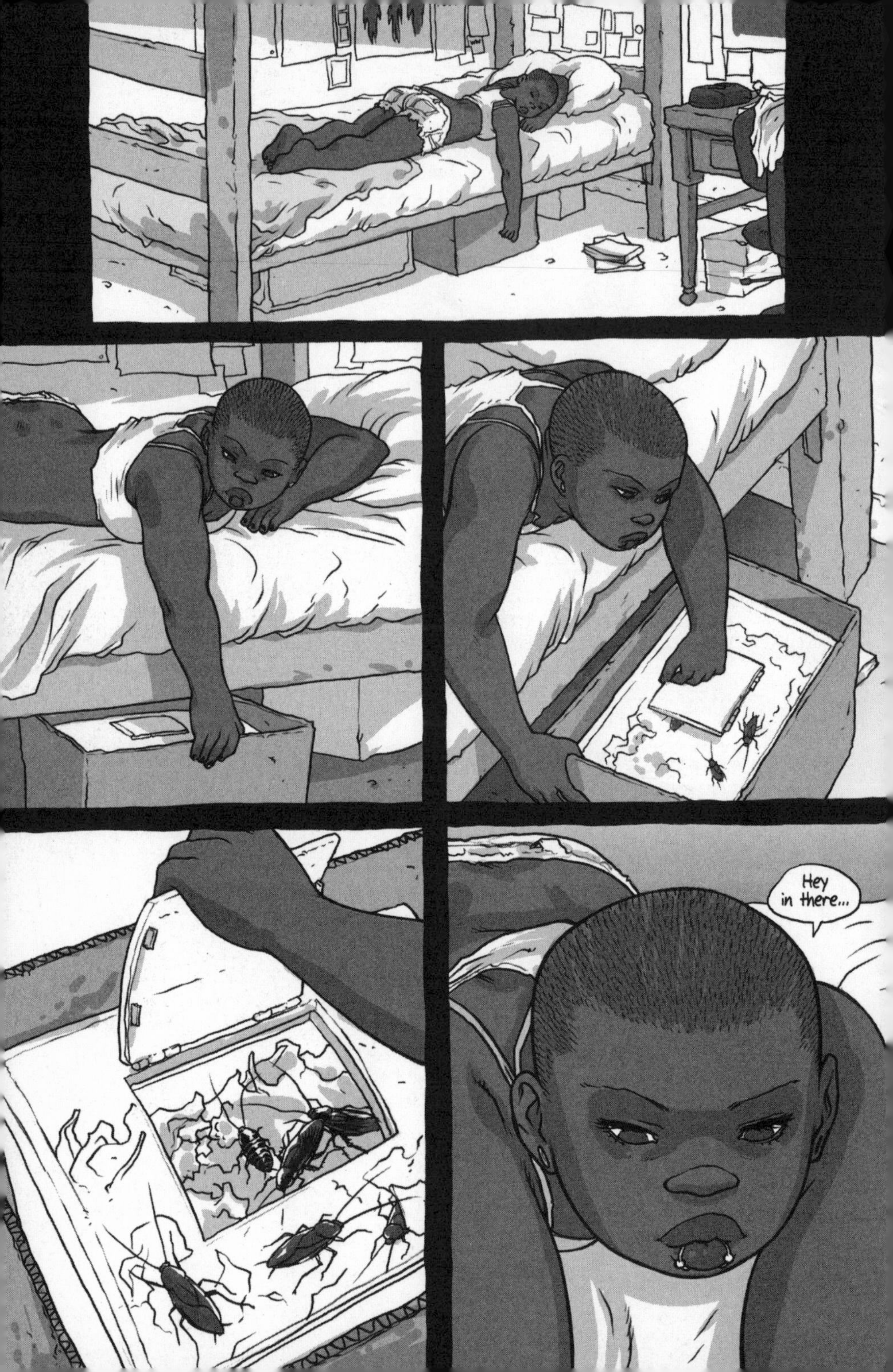
Hey
in there...

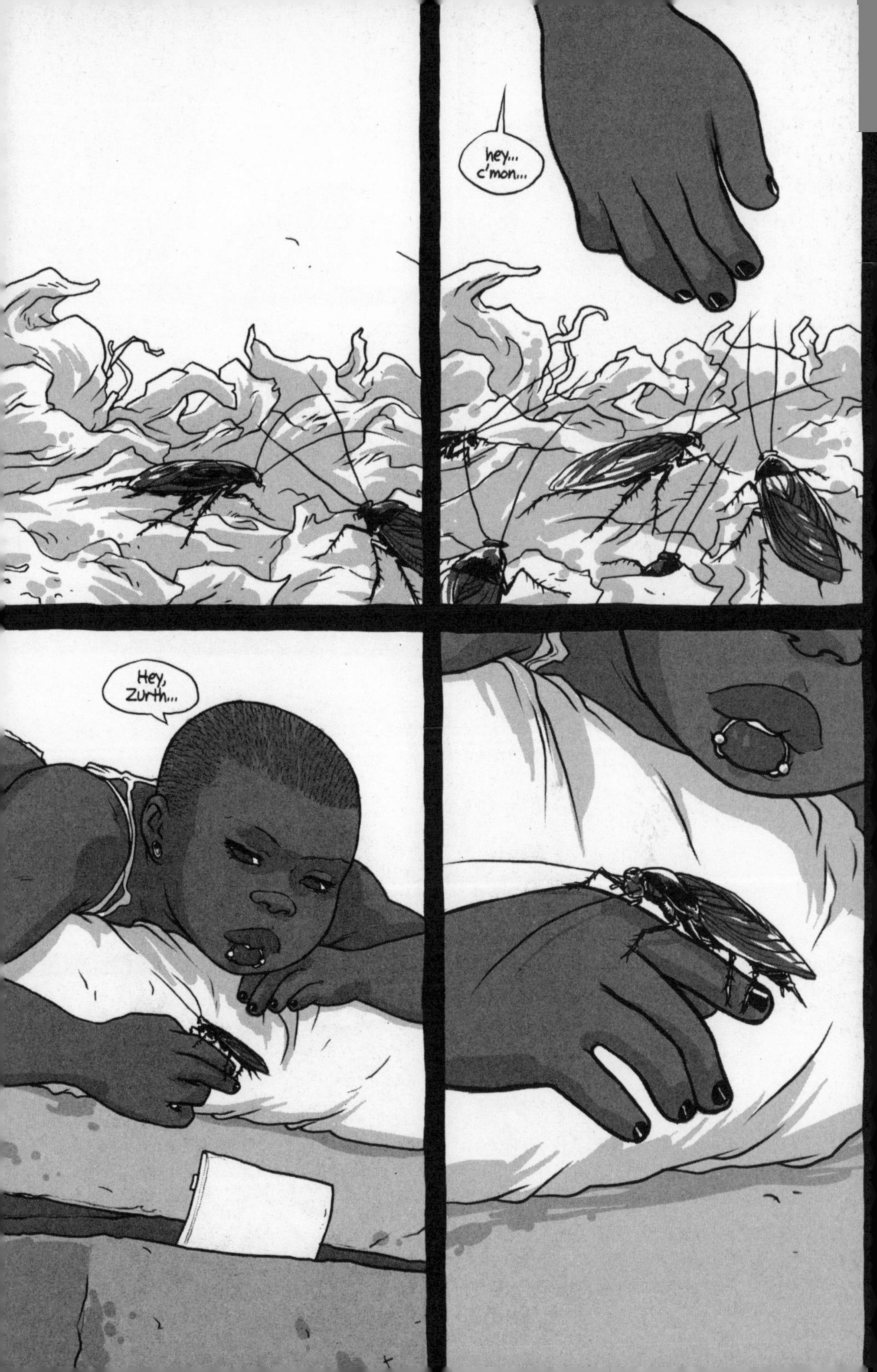
hey... c'mon...
Hey, Zurth...

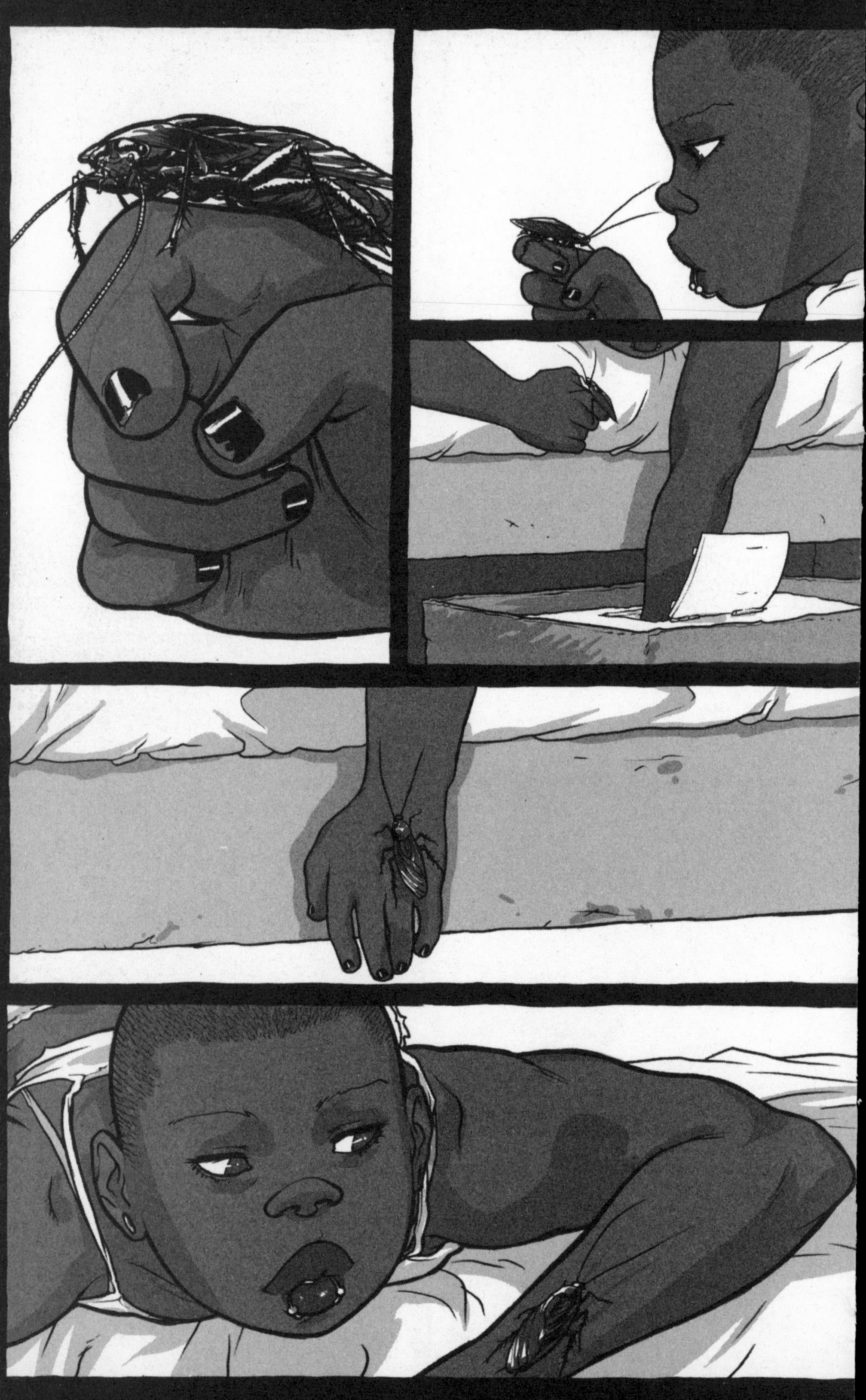

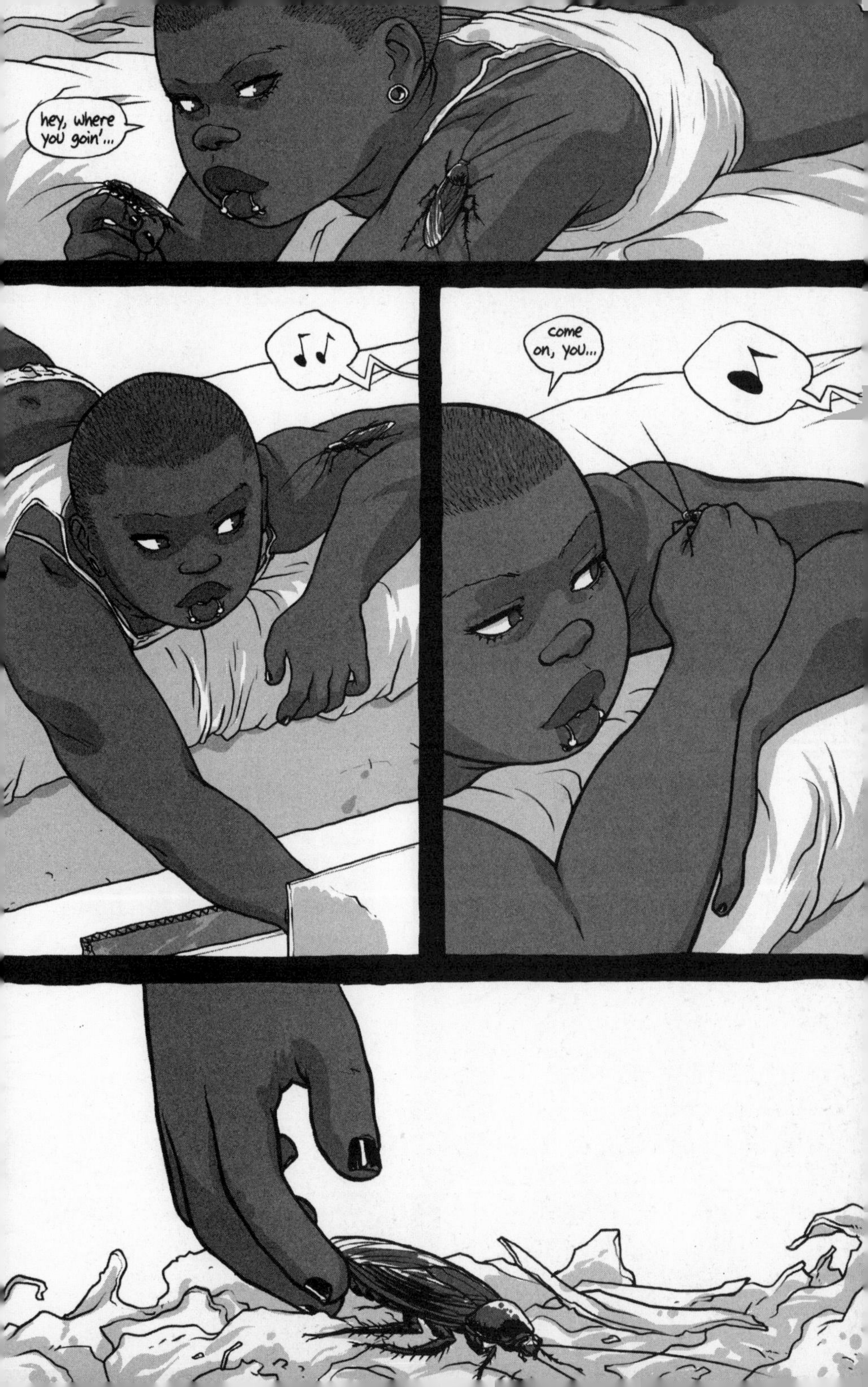
hey, where you goin'...
come on, you...

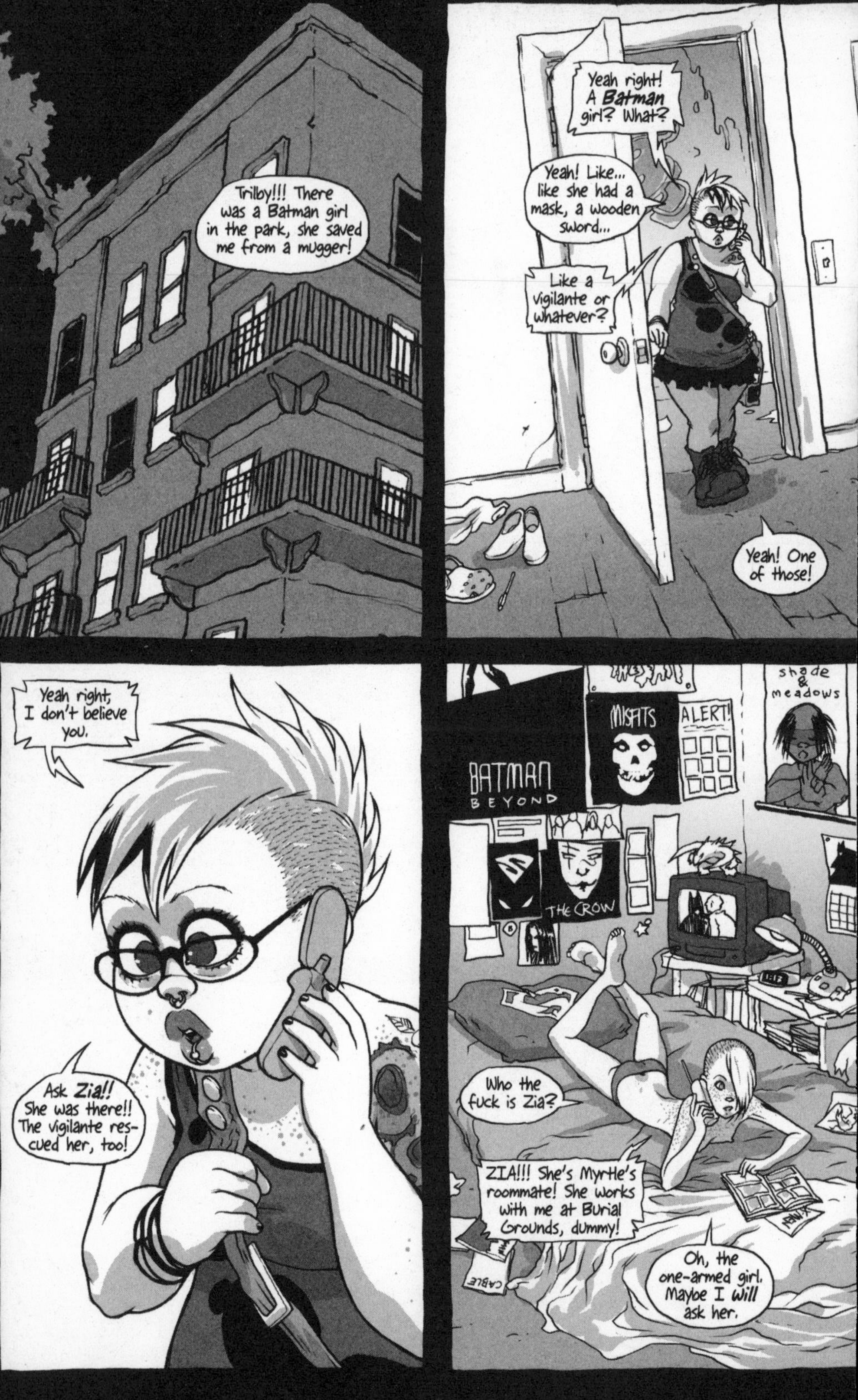
Trilby!!! There was a Batman girl in the park, she saved me from a mugger!
Yeah right! A **Batman** girl? What?
Yeah! Like... like she had a mask, a wooden sword...
Like a vigilante or whatever?
Yeah! One of those!
Yeah right, I don't believe you.
Ask **Zia!!** She was there!! The vigilante rescued her, too!
shade & meadows
MISFITS
ALERT!
BATMAN BEYOND
THE CROW
Who the fuck is Zia?
ZIA!!! She's Myrtle's roommate! She works with me at Burial Grounds, dummy!
Oh, the one-armed girl. Maybe I **will** ask her.
CABLE

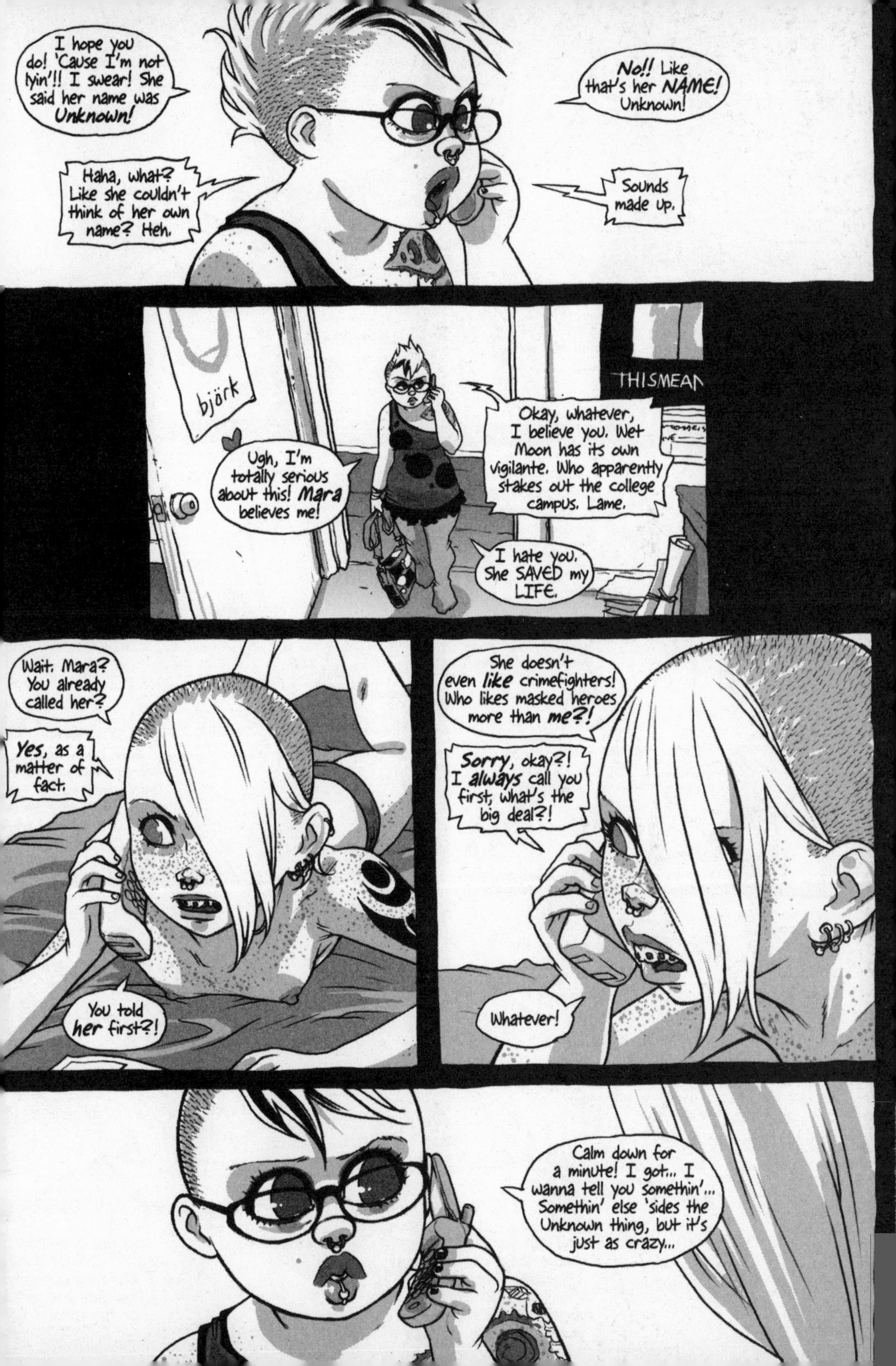
I hope you do! 'Cause I'm not lyin'!! I swear! She said her name was **Unknown!**
**No!!** Like that's her **NAME!** Unknown!
Haha, what? Like she couldn't think of her own name? Heh.
Sounds made up.
björk
THISMEAN
Okay, whatever, I believe you. Wet Moon has its own vigilante. Who apparently stakes out the college campus. Lame.
Ugh, I'm totally serious about this! **Mara** believes me!
I hate you. She SAVED my LIFE.
Wait. Mara? You already called her?
**Yes**, as a matter of fact.
You told **her** first?!
She doesn't even **like** crimefighters! Who likes masked heroes more than **me?!**
**Sorry**, okay?! I **always** call you first, what's the big deal?!
Whatever!
Calm down for a minute! I got... I wanna tell you somethin'... Somethin' else 'sides the Unknown thing, but it's just as crazy...

# 21

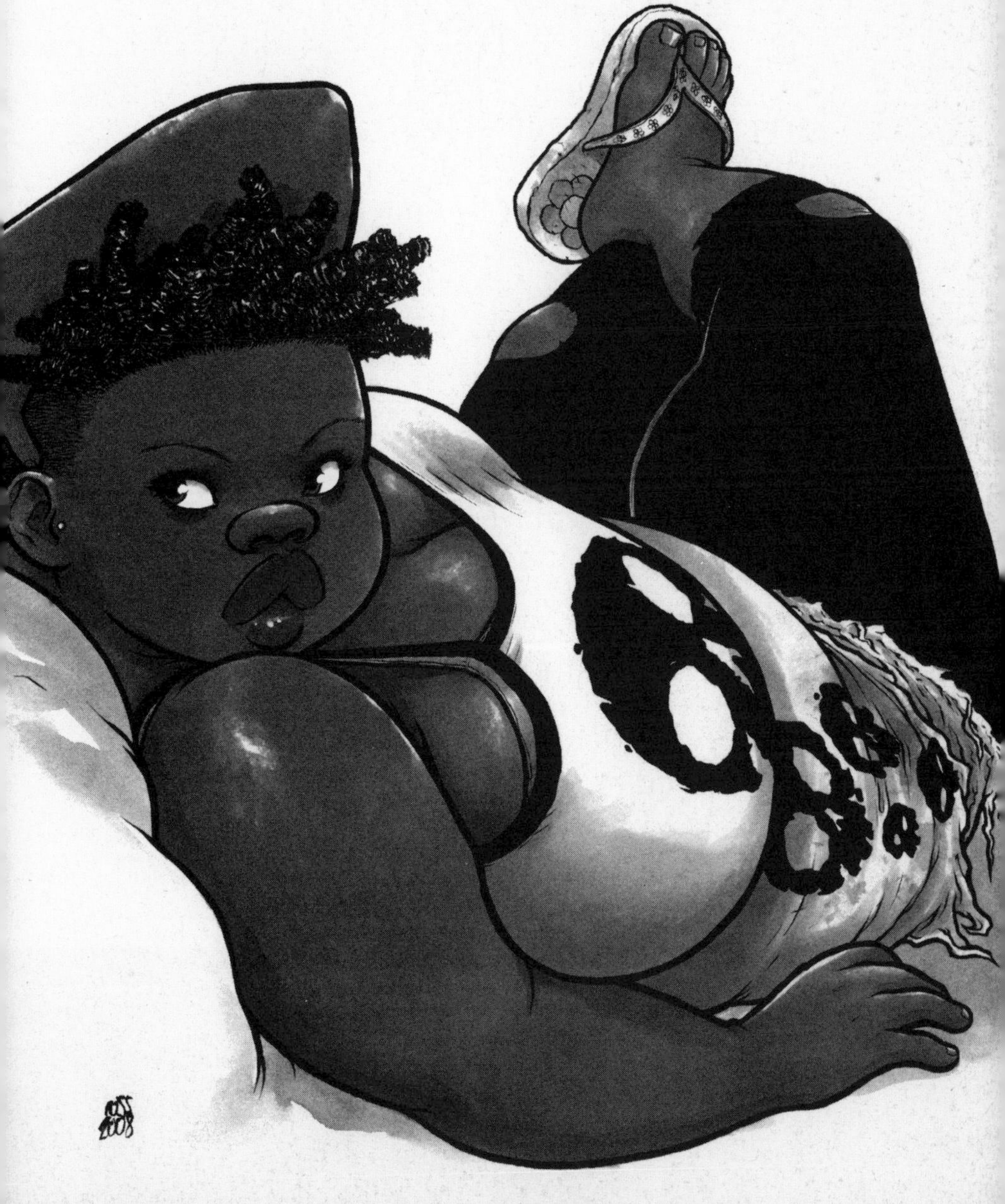

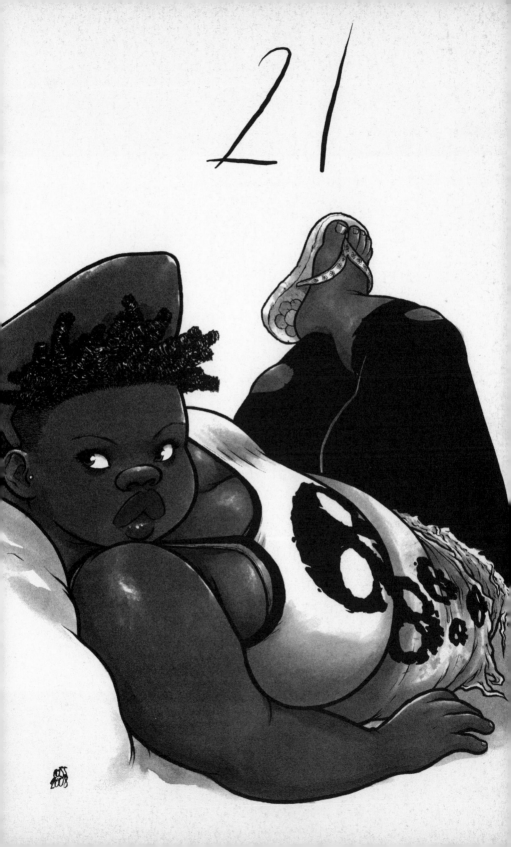

November 2

Burial Grounds kind of sucks.
it's so hectic and crazy and the
most fucked up people come in there,
and i only get three smoke
breaks for like seven hours of
work, i was freaking out. i just
can't make it that long but i guess
i'm going to have to learn how.
i'm up to about two packs a day,
i need a cigarette like every 20
minutes, it's so awful, i have got
to cut down. i guess this job will
help regulate it. i like smoking
most of the time but i still wish
i could quit. a girl actually gave
me a bag of her own shit at
work because the toilet was
broken. oh my god. and Glen
threw up, i feel so bad for him.
he didn't even ask how the con
went with the costume he
made for me.
      but the biggest thing that

makes that other stuff seem
so stupid is that there's this
superhero vigilante girl called
Unknown on campus. it is crazy!!
me and zia (who is the best!)
were walking back from work
and there's that part of campus
leading into the city where it's
just swampy, wooded kind of
road without anything nearby
really, and this mugger ~~guy~~
guy jumped out from behind
a tree with a KNIFE and
I nearly had a heart attack
and almost barfed all over
the place and he goes GIVE ME
YOUR MONEY or something! then
before he could even do anything,
this Unknown girl drops out of
a TREE and knocks the guy out!!!!
it was amazing!! for a second i
thought i was totally in love at
first sight, but now that i'm
writing it down and thinking
more about it, i think it would
be a bad idea. PWS there's
Myrtle AND Mara and... fuck,
what is even going on in my
life??! Unknown?! am i crazy??
besides that i do feel a ~~lot~~ lot
better about walking at night,

though, knowing that Unicorn
is out there keeping people safe!!
i know she can't be everywhere
at once (could she have a
partner or sidekick??) but just
knowing she's out there makes
me feel better about muggers
and rapists. somebody told me
there were a couple girls who
got raped in the Forest of Doom
near the campus park. i wonder
if that was before Unicorn
showed up. i wonder how long
she's been out there. i can't
imagine it could be that long
without me hearing about it,
without rumors going bonkers
all over school!! sometimes i
hear people talking about how
Wet Moon sucks, how it's such a
stupid, lame, boring city with
nothing to do and how they're
moving out the first chance
they get, and i used to be like
that, i think, but as i got older
the more i see how great it
is in a lot of ways. except for
the weather being so hot all the
time and i wish it would snow
just once. can you believe i've
never seen REAL snow besides

in a movie!?

also, i told Trilby about me and mara, and she totally knew already, ugh! she tried to act like she didn't care about myrtle, but i know she cares about this thing with mara. tiny changes in her tone of voice and i know next time i see her she'll have equally tiny changes in her body language. she can't fool me. i wish she was okay with all this, but i know she's kind of... i don't know, i don't want to say homophobic, but she's definitely weirded out by all the girl/girl stuff even though there's Audrey and now me... sigh. and mara being our friend, not a stranger like myrtle was, i know Trilby is uneasy with it. maybe i am too.

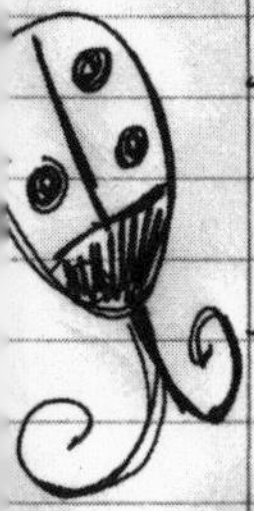

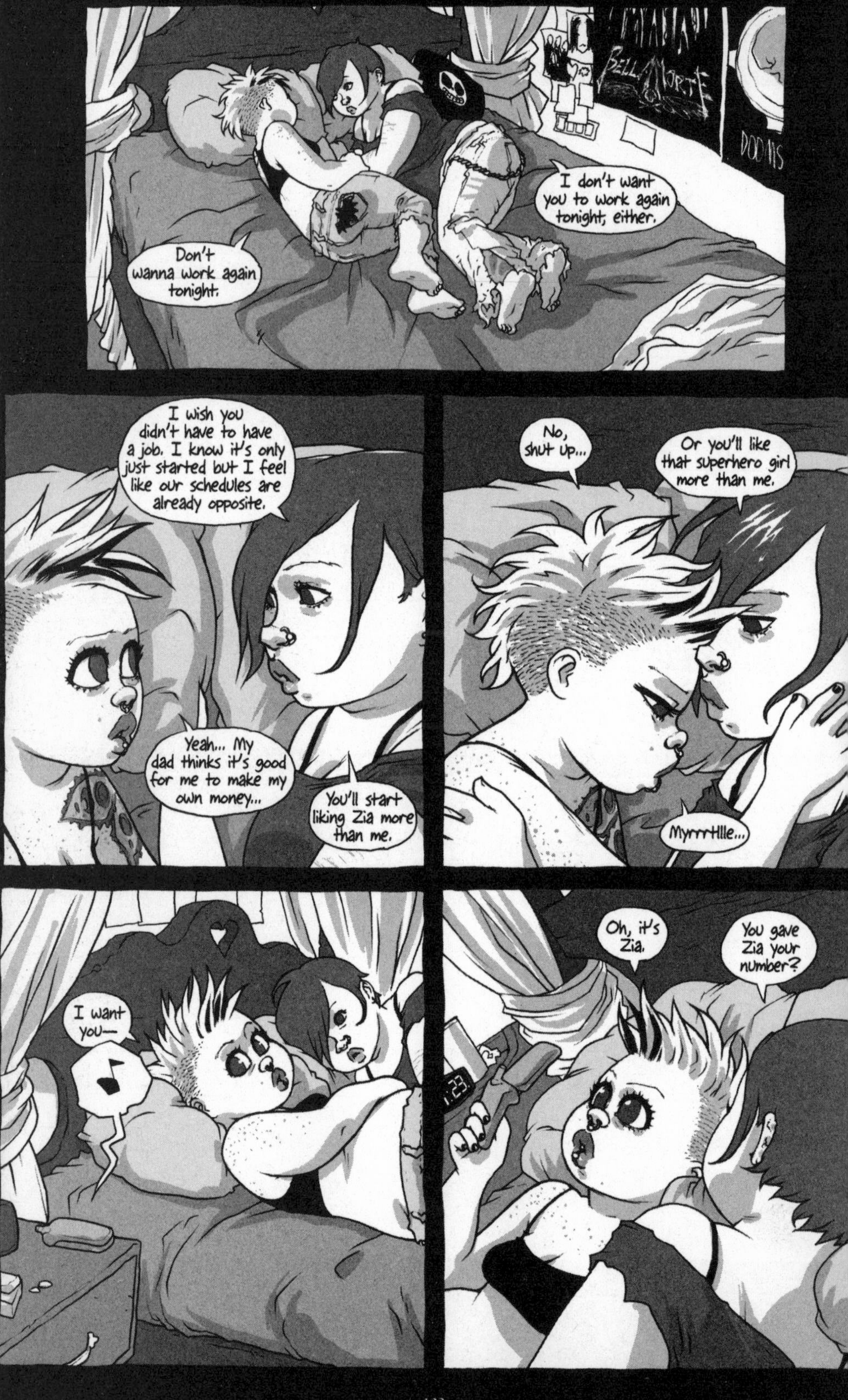
I don't want you to work again tonight, either.
Don't wanna work again tonight.
I wish you didn't have to have a job. I know it's only just started but I feel like our schedules are already opposite.
Yeah... My dad thinks it's good for me to make my own money...
You'll start liking Zia more than me.
No, shut up...
Or you'll like that superhero girl more than me.
Myrrrtllle...
I want you—
Oh, it's Zia.
You gave Zia your number?

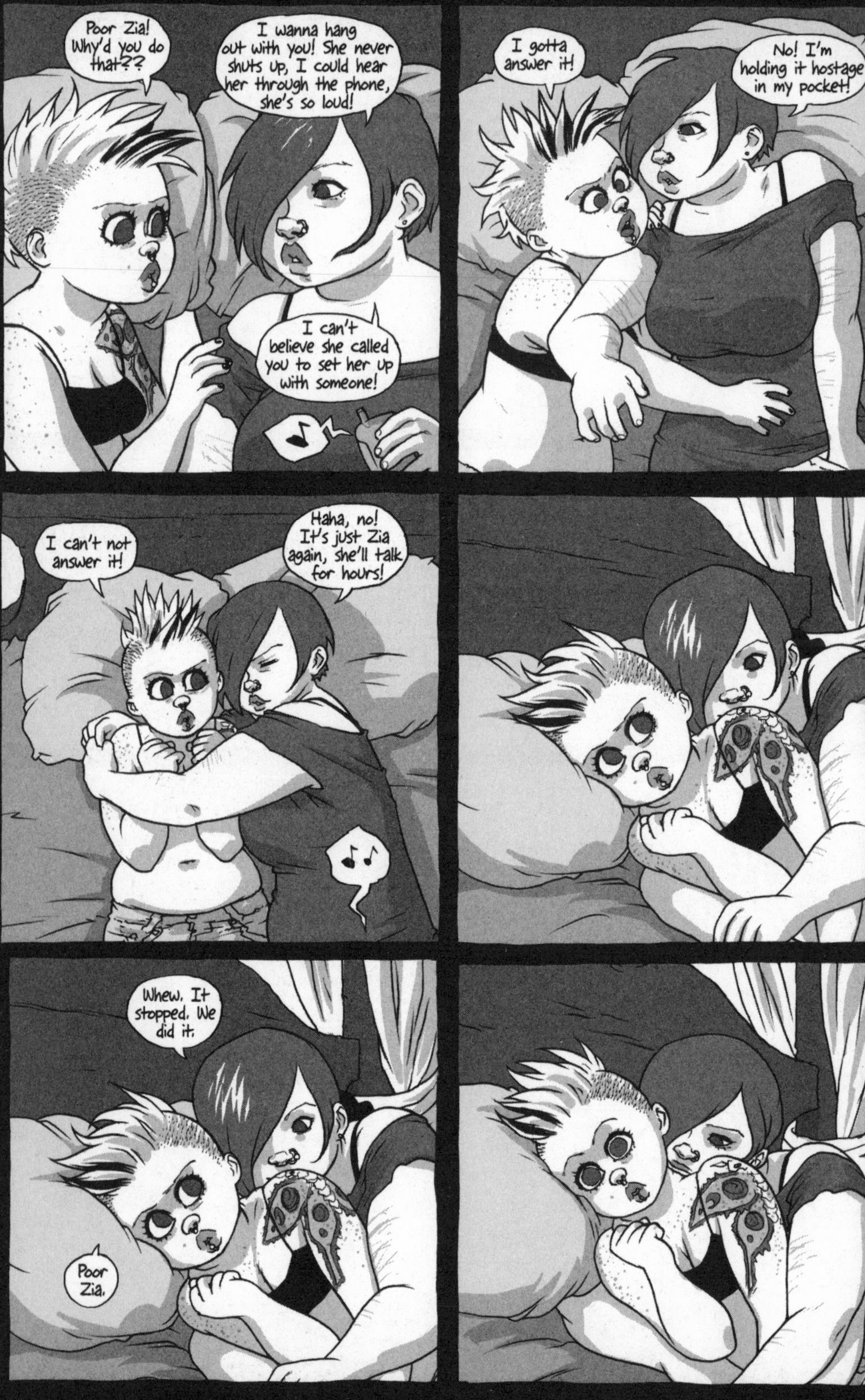
Poor Zia! Why'd you do that??
I wanna hang out with you! She never shuts up, I could hear her through the phone, she's so loud!
I can't believe she called you to set her up with someone!
I gotta answer it!
No! I'm holding it hostage in my pocket!
I can't not answer it!
Haha, no! It's just Zia again, she'll talk for hours!
Whew. It stopped. We did it.
Poor Zia.

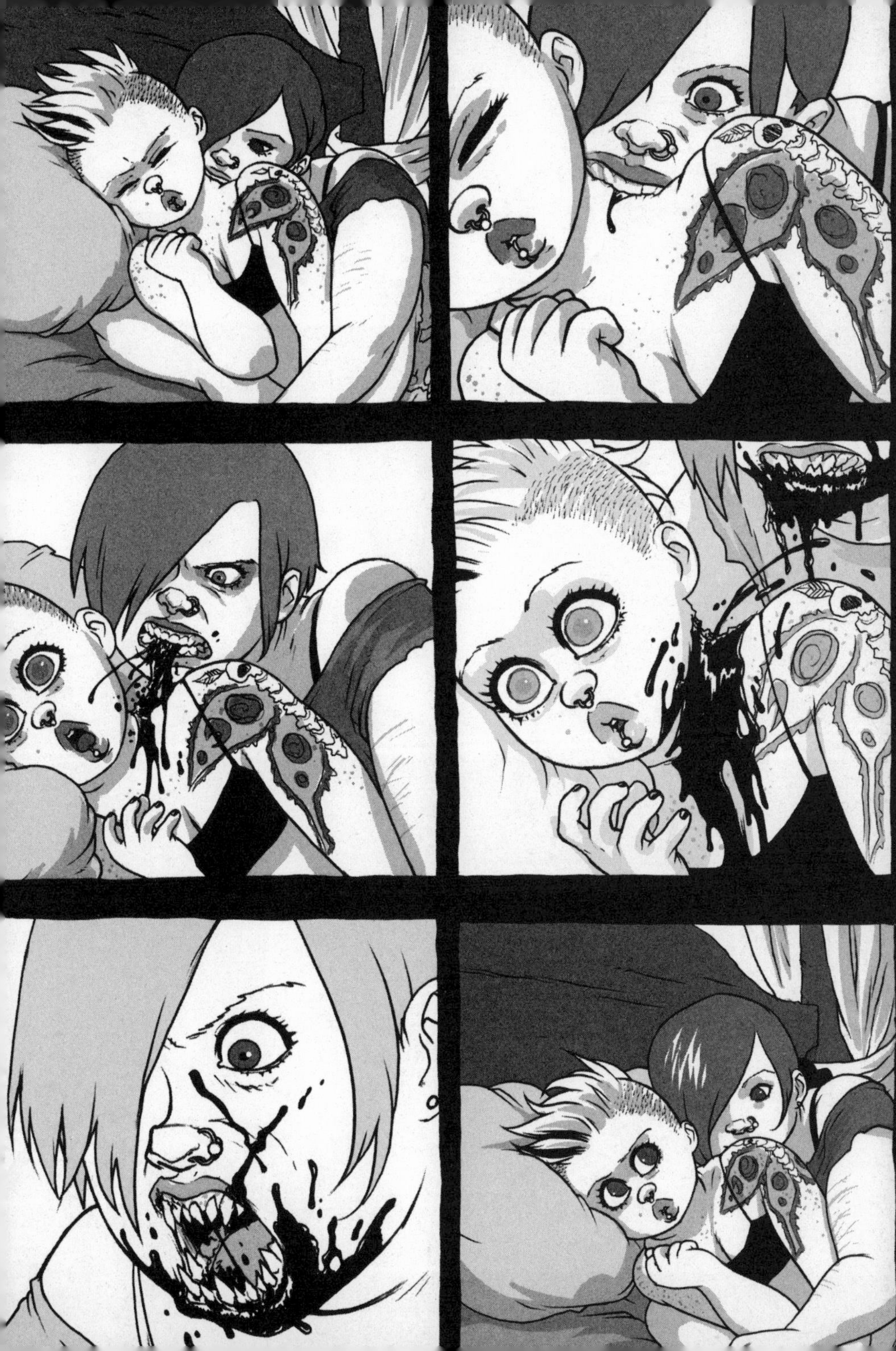

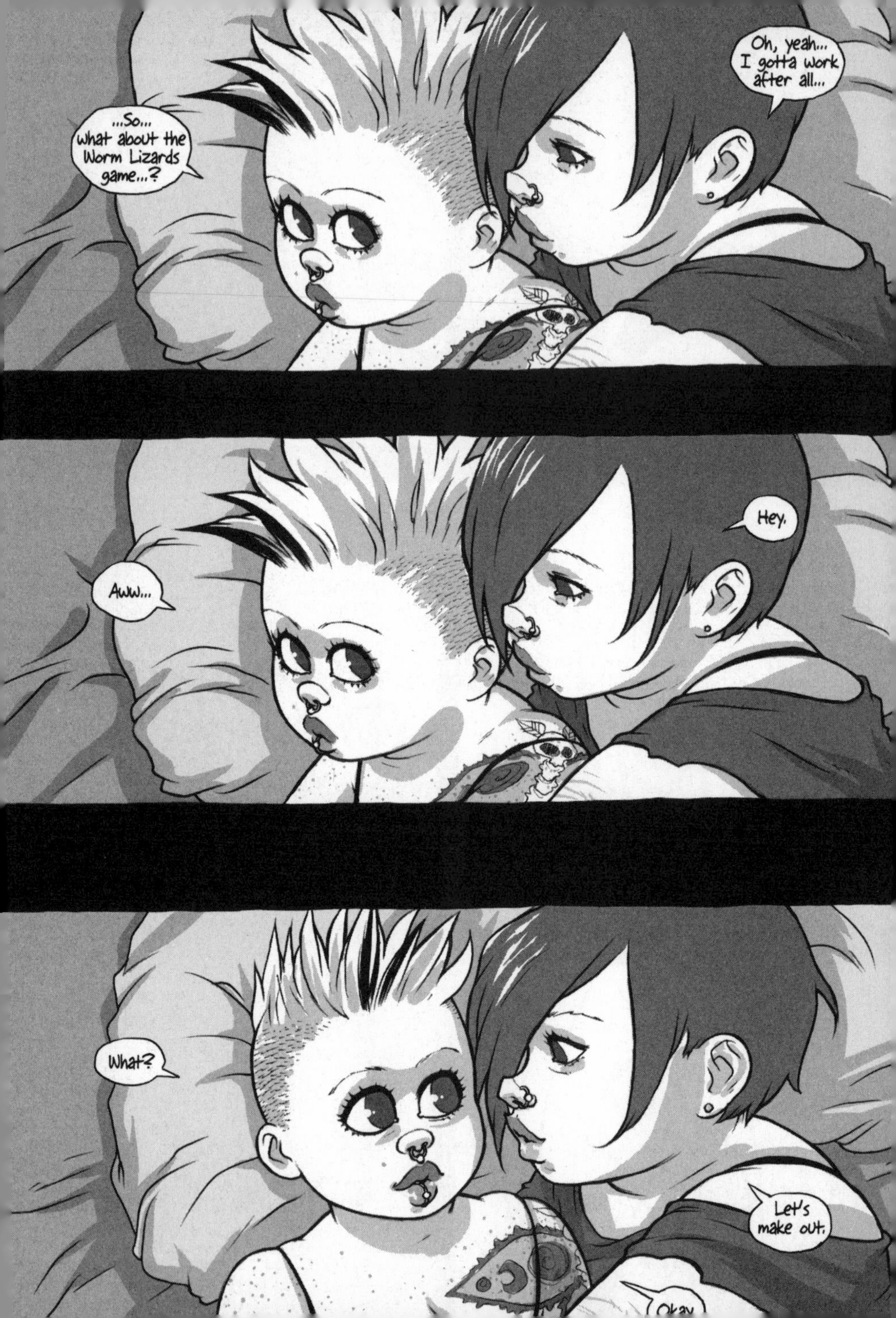
...So... what about the Worm Lizards game...?
Oh, yeah... I gotta work after all...
Aww...
Hey.
What?
Let's make out.
Okay

# Skeleton Season
audrey richter

Previous 20

ofile

ittyhawk1

## Who knows.
November 3rd, 7:26pm

What the heck. That babysitting gig... where do I start? It is definitely the worst one I've ever had, the kids were absolute terrors. The oldest one is 15, she turned out all right except... well, I don't want to write what happened with her. It's got nothing to do with me, it wasn't a malicious thing, but boy... yeah, I can't say it, it doesn't seem right. Everyone's always on me about spilling the beans when i shouldn't, so this is me going against that.

The other two kids were young, and they both insulted me, threw things (including an entire CAKE) at me, locked me out of the apartment, poured beer on me... yes, they actually managed to get beer and got drunk. I know, I'm the worst babysitter. I finally got them in bed, at least, but not before being covered in frosting and beer and being thoroughly humiliated. I won't get into the rest.

I like to think that I have a generally strong self-esteem, at least compared to most girls I know. I try not to obsess over my body and I don't beat myself up over not being "good enough" at something or worry too much about if somebody likes me or anything like that. At least not usually, but everyone does once in a while. One of the kids called me the ugliest girl he's ever seen (his actual words were a bit nastier), and on one hand it's like, okay, he's 8, he probably doesn't even LIKE girls in "that" way yet, and he's already a big jerk, who cares. But it really struck me in a bad way and I still feel down about it. I know, it's so dumb... a jerky 8-year-old boy, sigh. I guess part of it, I hate to drag this aspect into it, but often I feel like nobody, as in the masses or "society" or whatever, will ever think I'm pretty. Because I'm a Woman of Color, and everything is steered away from presenting us as attractive... Sometimes I look in the mirror and I think I'm "too much," my face, my hair, my butt, everything... I've been really fighting it, though. I used to straighten my hair and I only stopped recently, and I'm much happier with it now. But I feel bombarded by everyone trying to get me to buy straightening stuff and "tame" my hair or whatever, and all these magazine ads where they lighten Black women... It's really sad. I know I've written a little about this before in Social Abattoir, but I want to tackle more about it, it's such a big, sprawling issue that's really important to me. I actually sort of don't like writing about it because I'm so upset by it, thinking about all those little girls who never see positive images of girls who look like them (well, there are SOME but not nearly enough). I don't want to write about it but I have to, I think it's important to get stuff like that out there. So stay tuned on that.

I'm also putting together some stuff on crime in Wet Moon since there's so much; not really street-level stuff, but forensics and crime investigation. I've always been really interested in the topic but I've thought more about inserting it into the zine because of this FBI guy that's around town recently, and an actual masked vigilante my friend told me about! I was sort of skeptical at first but I believe it, I'm going to try to set up an interview with her somehow, wouldn't that be amazing? Anyway, I want to talk to some forensic science people and maybe have some articles about historic crime in Wet Moon, too.

**Mood:** gloomy

### Latest Month
November

| M | T | W | T | F | S |
|---|---|---|---|---|---|
| 2 | 3 | 4 | 5 | 6 | 7 |
| 9 | 10 | 11 | 12 | 13 | 14 |
| 16 | 17 | 18 | 19 | 20 | 21 |
| 23 | 24 | 25 | 26 | 27 | 28 |
| 30 | 31 | | | | |

View All Archives

nks

byhatescomics

ndtoroaches

p-dead

ckyard Birds

gans of Color

ntheshadows.com

nosha's tomb

0,000 Years Hence

ters of Battle

retcrystal

il Galaxy

tflame

llow oasis

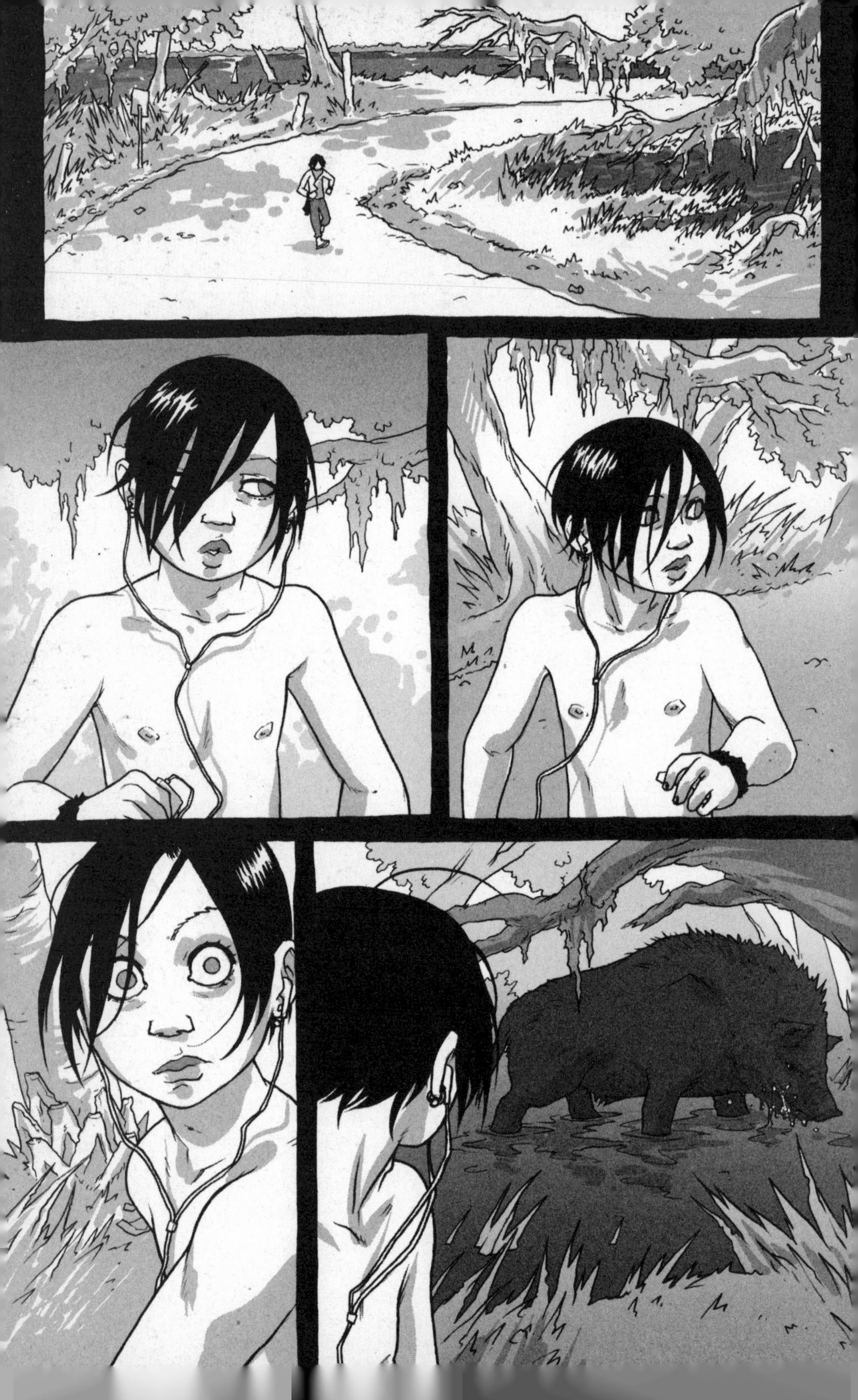

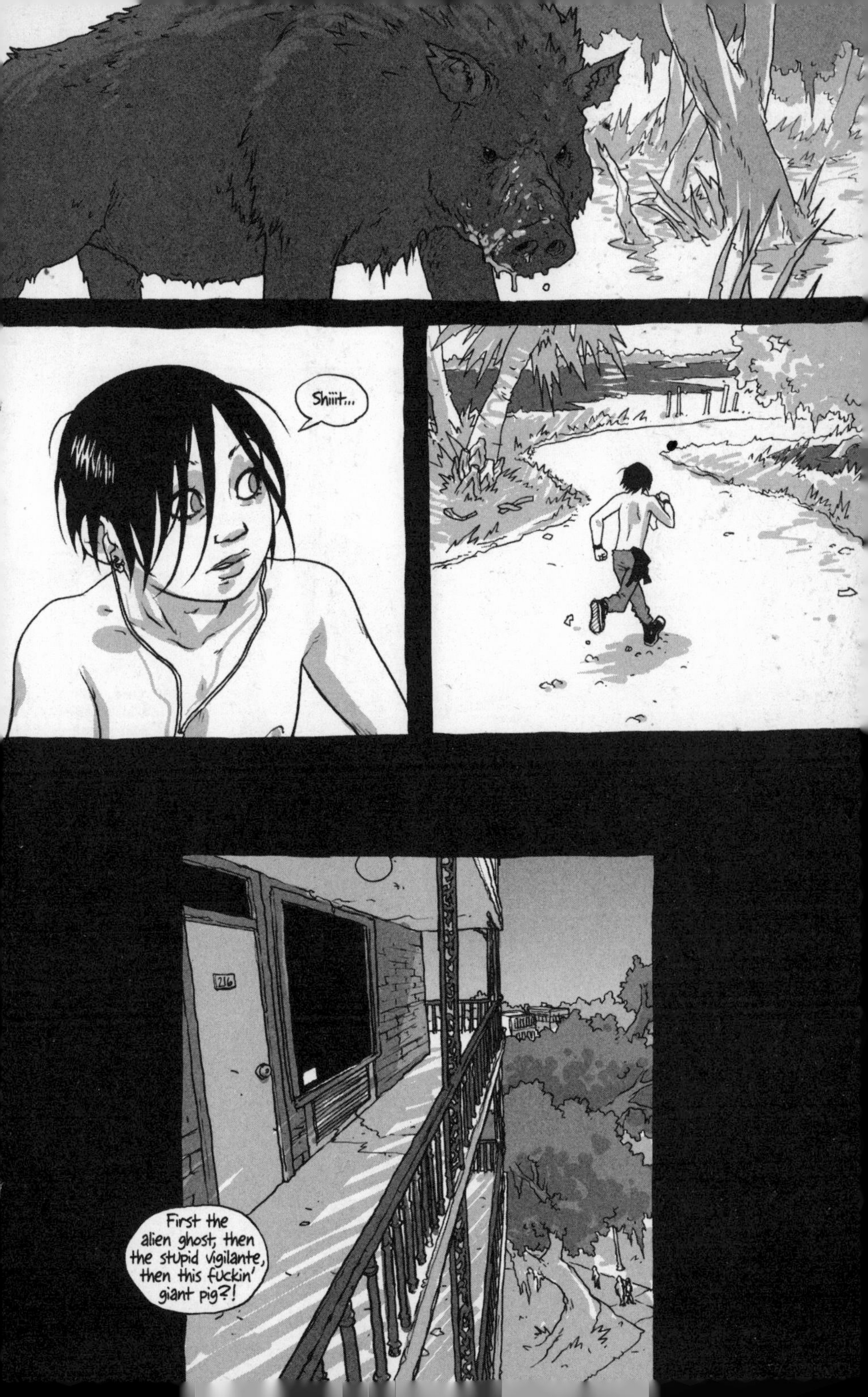
Shiiit...
First the alien ghost, then the stupid vigilante, then this fuckin' giant pig?!

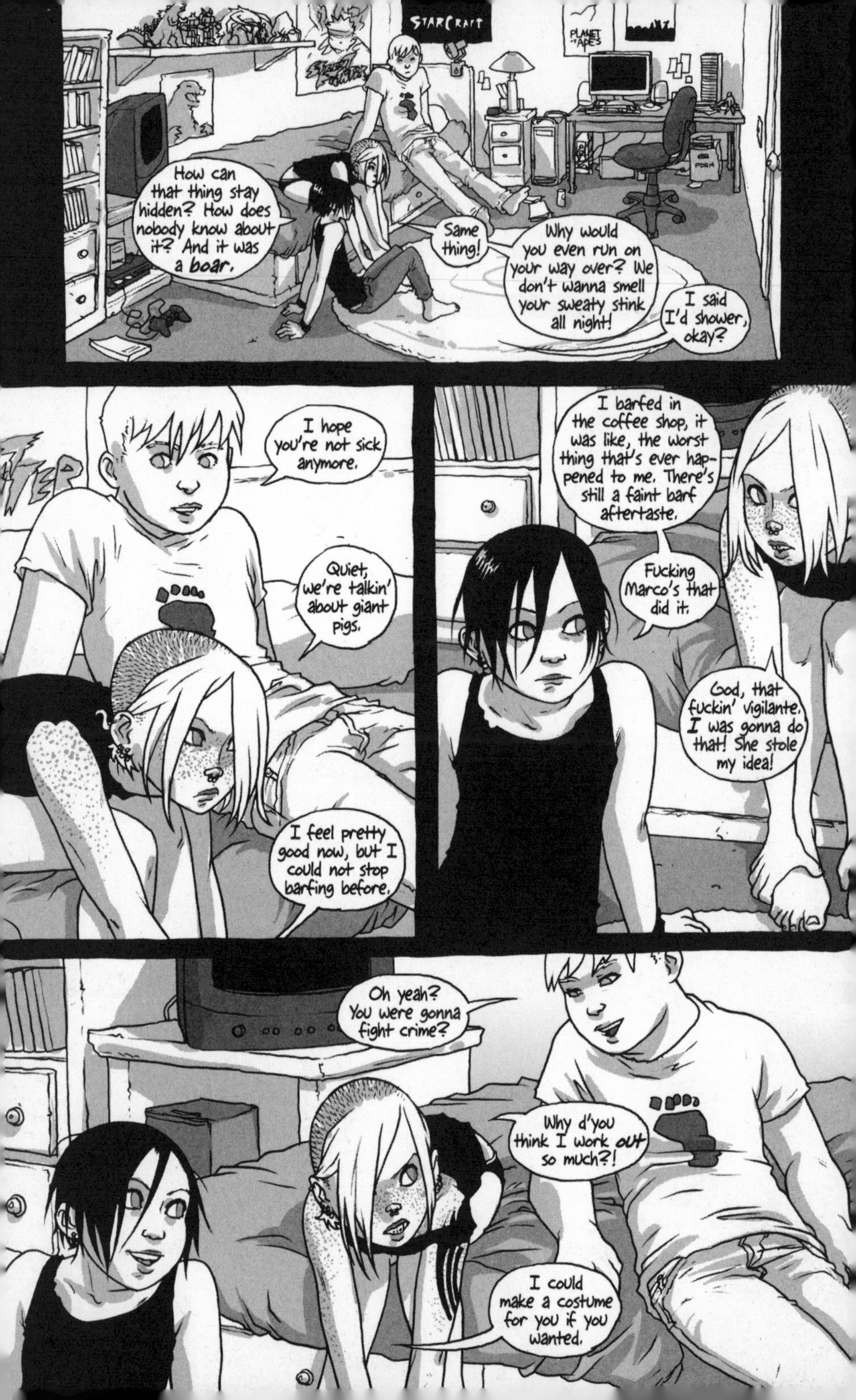
STARCRAFT
PLANET APES
How can that thing stay hidden? How does nobody know about it? And it was a **boar.**
Same thing!
Why would you even run on your way over? We don't wanna smell your sweaty stink all night!
I said I'd shower, okay?
I hope you're not sick anymore.
Quiet, we're talkin' about giant pigs.
I feel pretty good now, but I could not stop barfing before.
I barfed in the coffee shop, it was like, the worst thing that's ever happened to me. There's still a faint barf aftertaste.
Fucking Marco's that did it.
God, that fuckin' vigilante. *I* was gonna do that! She stole my idea!
Oh yeah? You were gonna fight crime?
Why d'you think I work *out* so much?!
I could make a costume for you if you wanted.

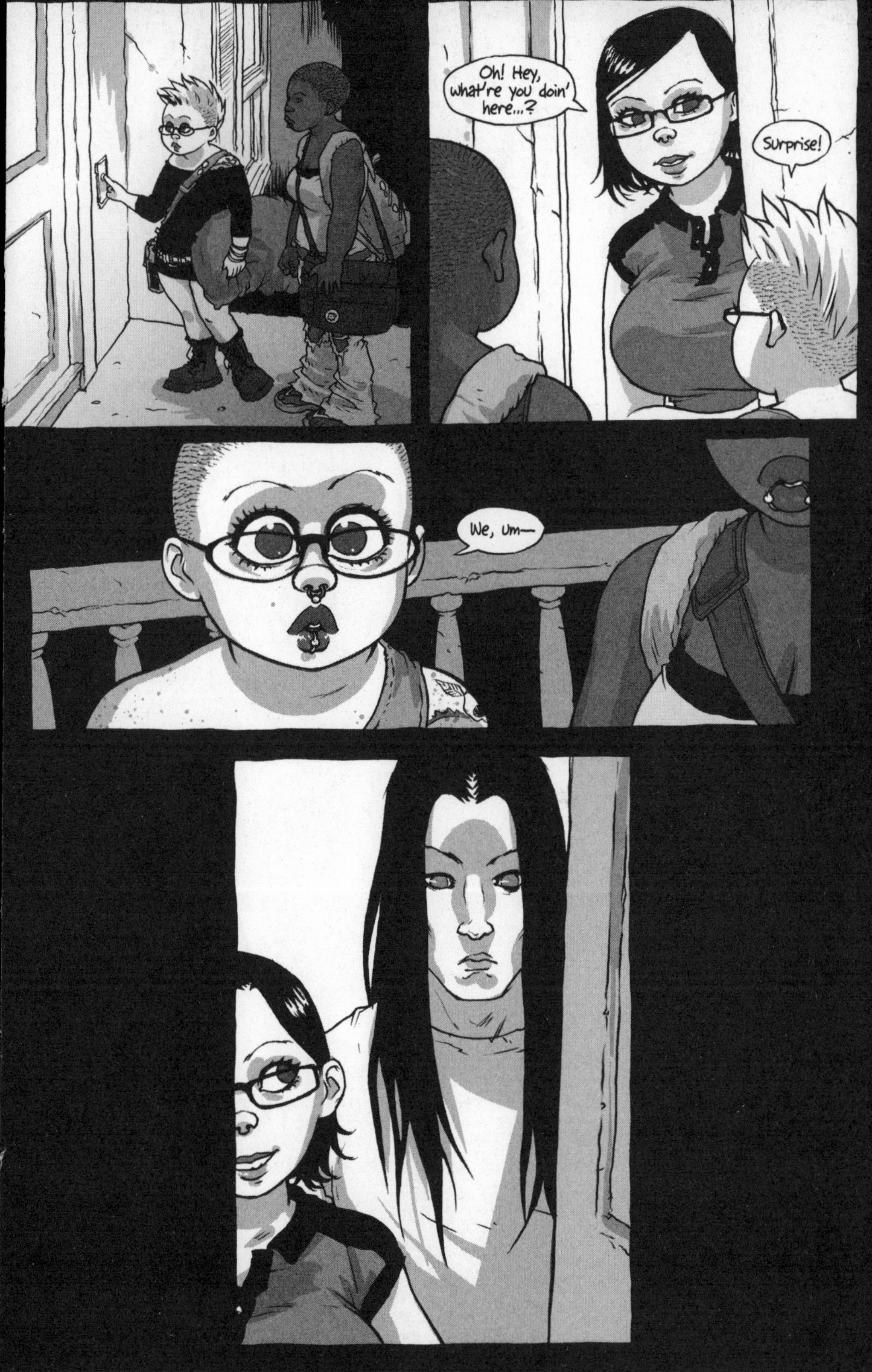
Oh! Hey, what're you doin' here...?
Surprise!
We, um—

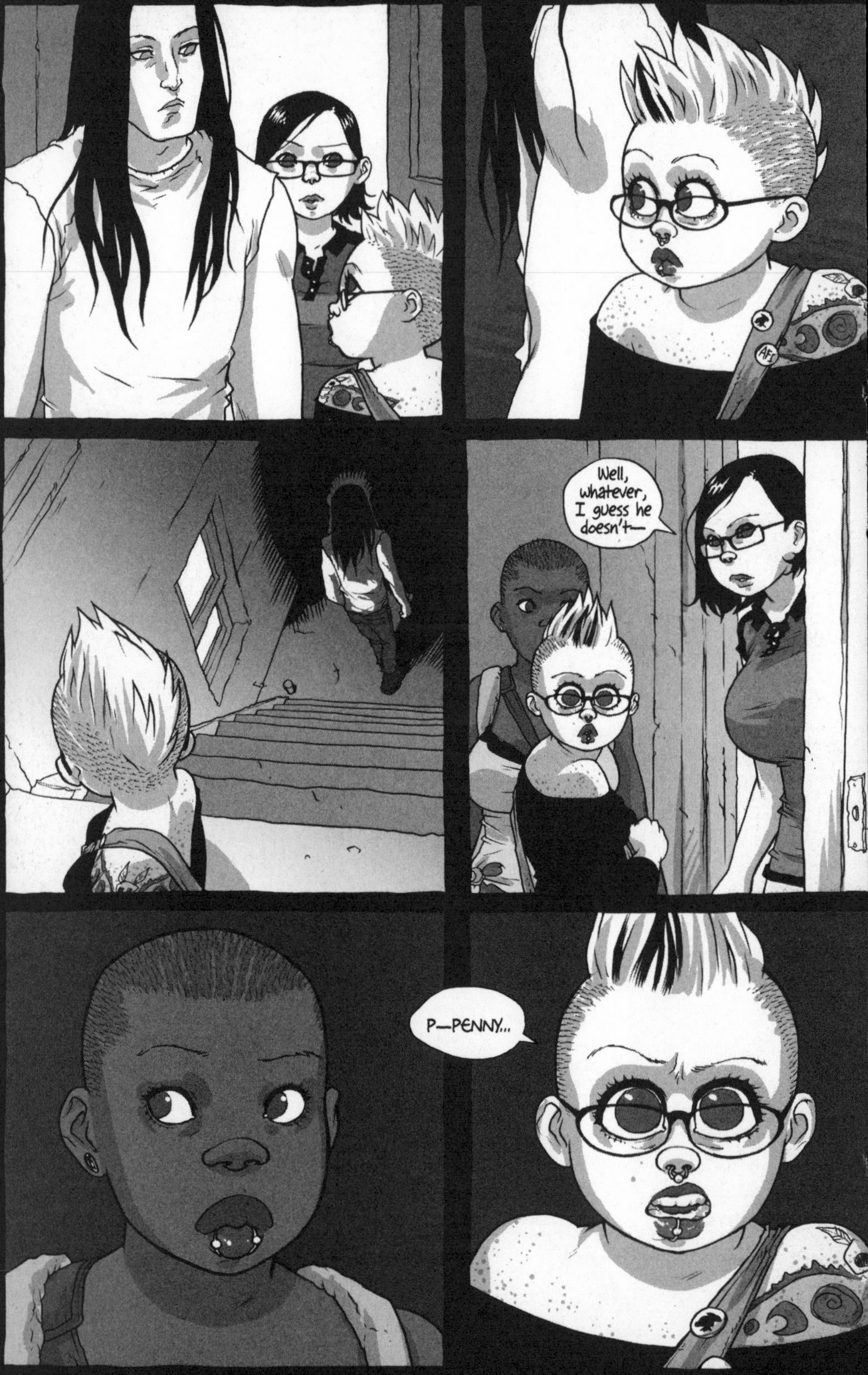
Well, whatever, I guess he doesn't—
P—PENNY...

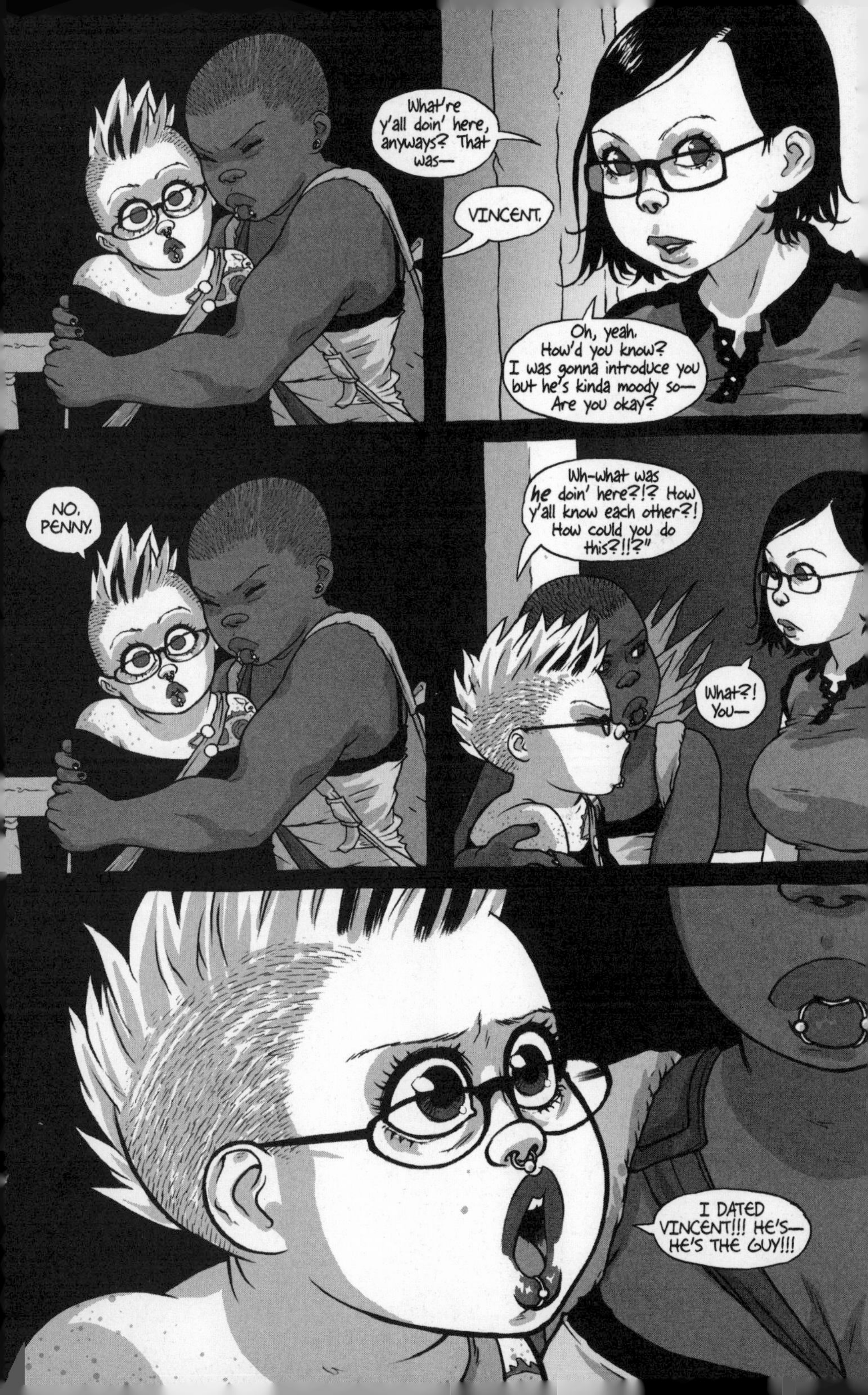
What're y'all doin' here, anyways? That was—
VINCENT.
Oh, yeah. How'd you know? I was gonna introduce you but he's kinda moody so— Are you okay?
NO, PENNY.
Wh-what was he doin' here?!? How y'all know each other?! How could you do this?!!?"
What?! You—
I DATED VINCENT!!! HE'S— HE'S THE GUY!!!

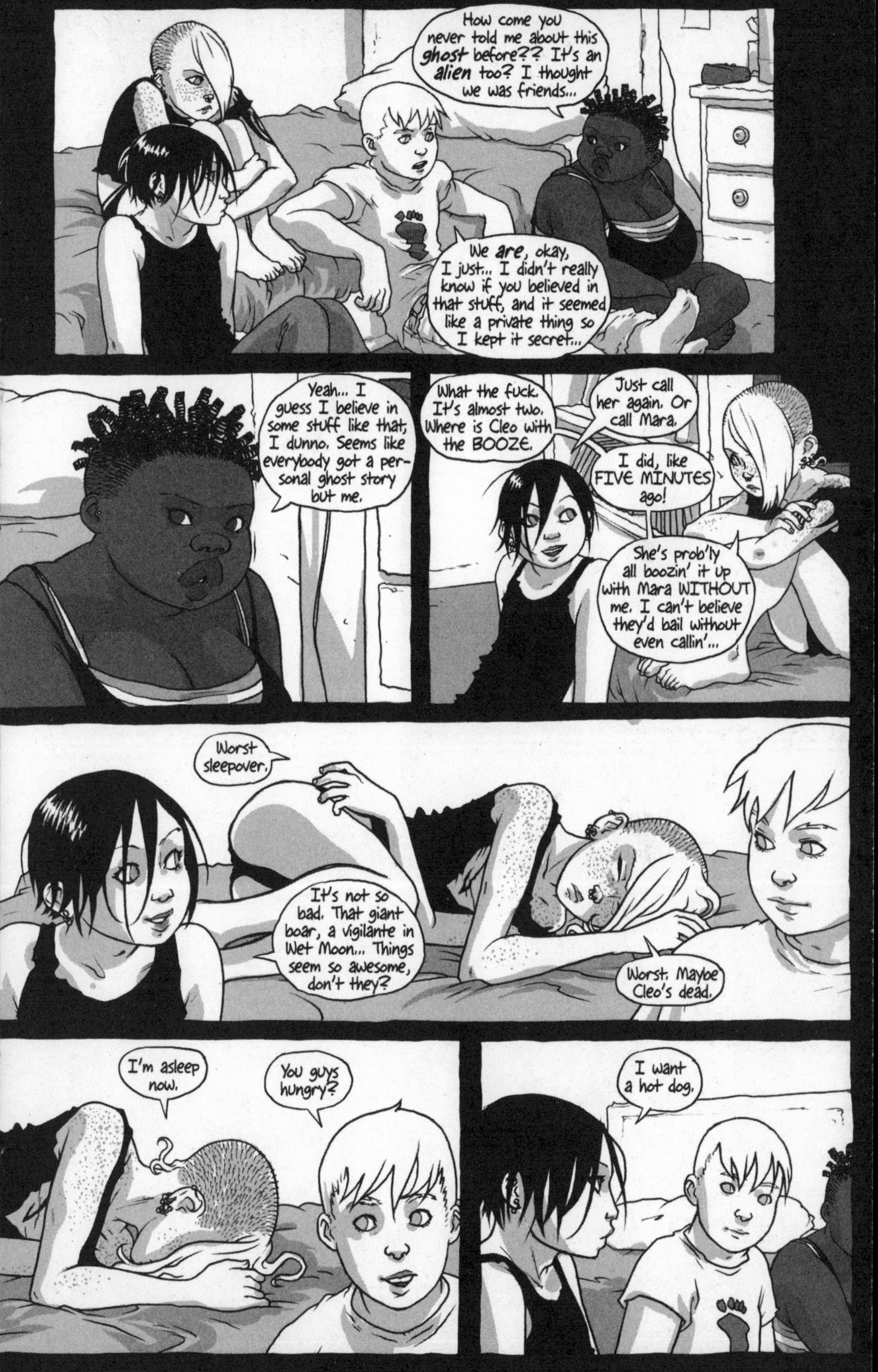
How come you never told me about this ghost before?? It's an alien too? I thought we was friends...
We are, okay, I just... I didn't really know if you believed in that stuff, and it seemed like a private thing so I kept it secret...
Yeah... I guess I believe in some stuff like that, I dunno. Seems like everybody got a personal ghost story but me.
What the fuck. It's almost two. Where is Cleo with the BOOZE.
Just call her again. Or call Mara.
I did, like FIVE MINUTES ago!
She's prob'ly all boozin' it up with Mara WITHOUT me. I can't believe they'd bail without even callin'...
Worst sleepover.
It's not so bad. That giant boar, a vigilante in Wet Moon... Things seem so awesome, don't they?
Worst. Maybe Cleo's dead.
I'm asleep now.
You guys hungry?
I want a hot dog.

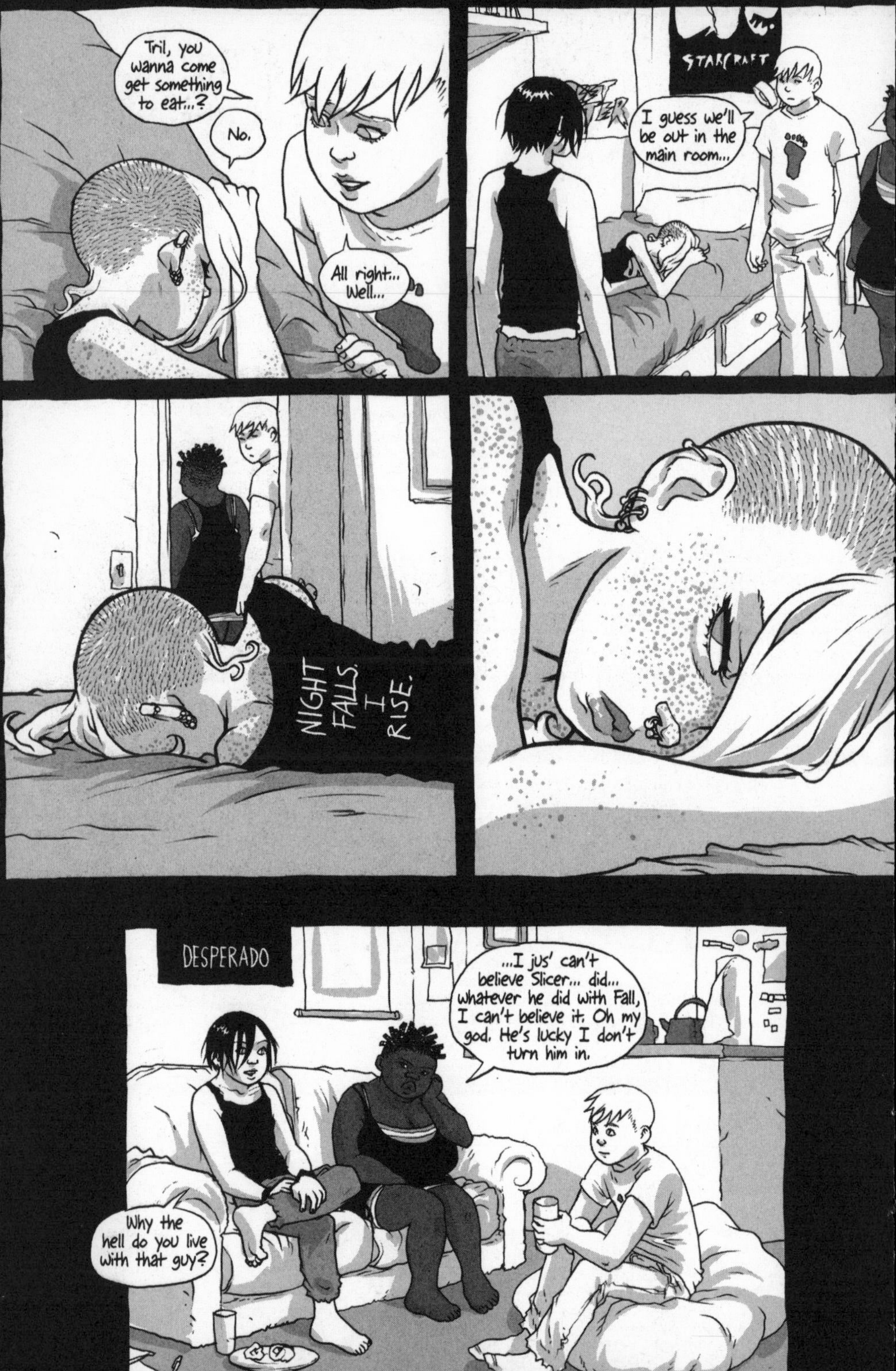
Tril, you wanna come get something to eat...?
No.
All right... Well...
STARCRAFT
I guess we'll be out in the main room...
NIGHT FALLS. I RISE.
DESPERADO
...I jus' can't believe Slicer... did... whatever he did with Fall, I can't believe it. Oh my god. He's lucky I don't turn him in.
Why the hell do you live with that guy?

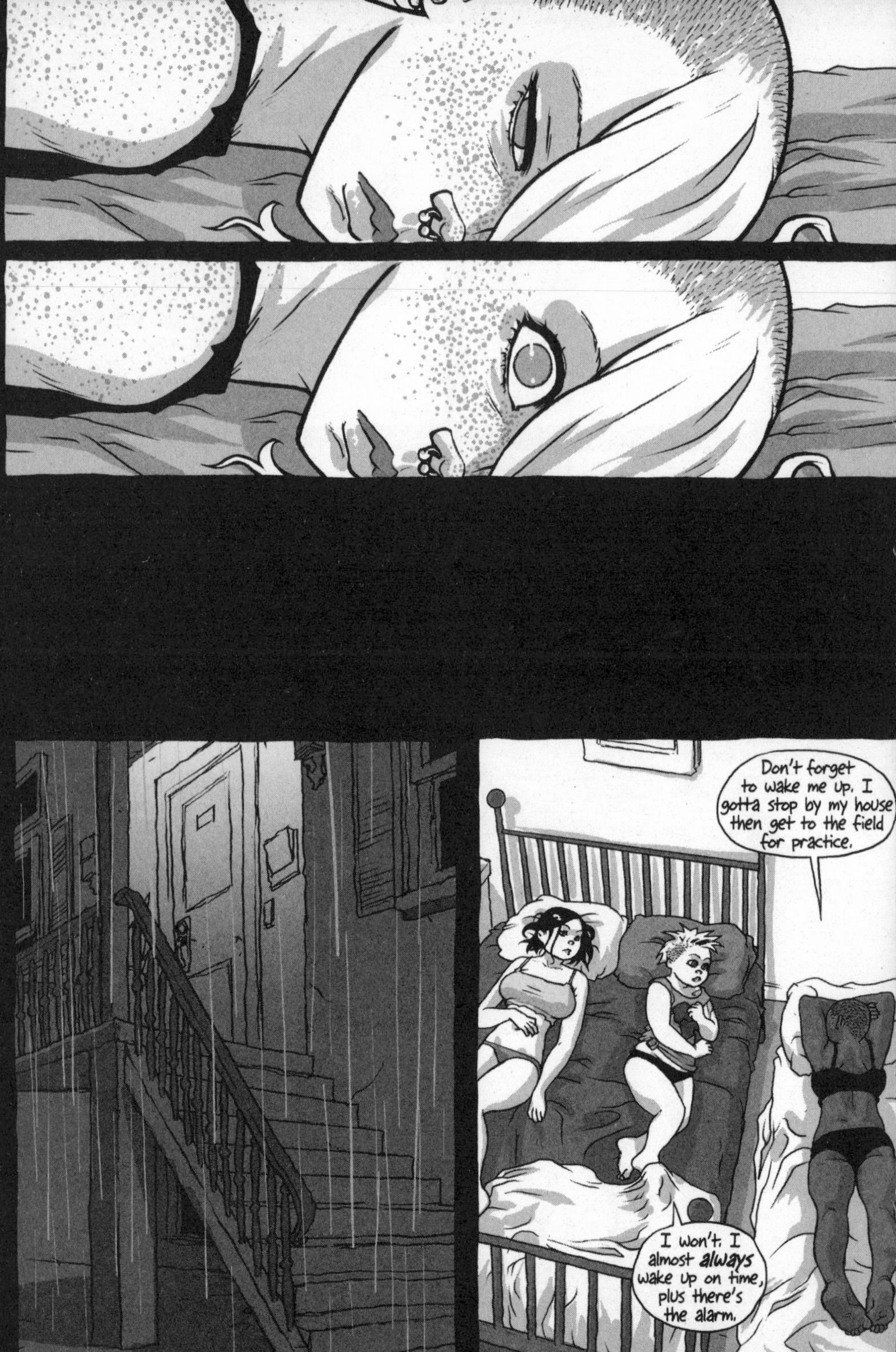
Don't forget to wake me up. I gotta stop by my house then get to the field for practice.
I won't. I almost always wake up on time, plus there's the alarm.

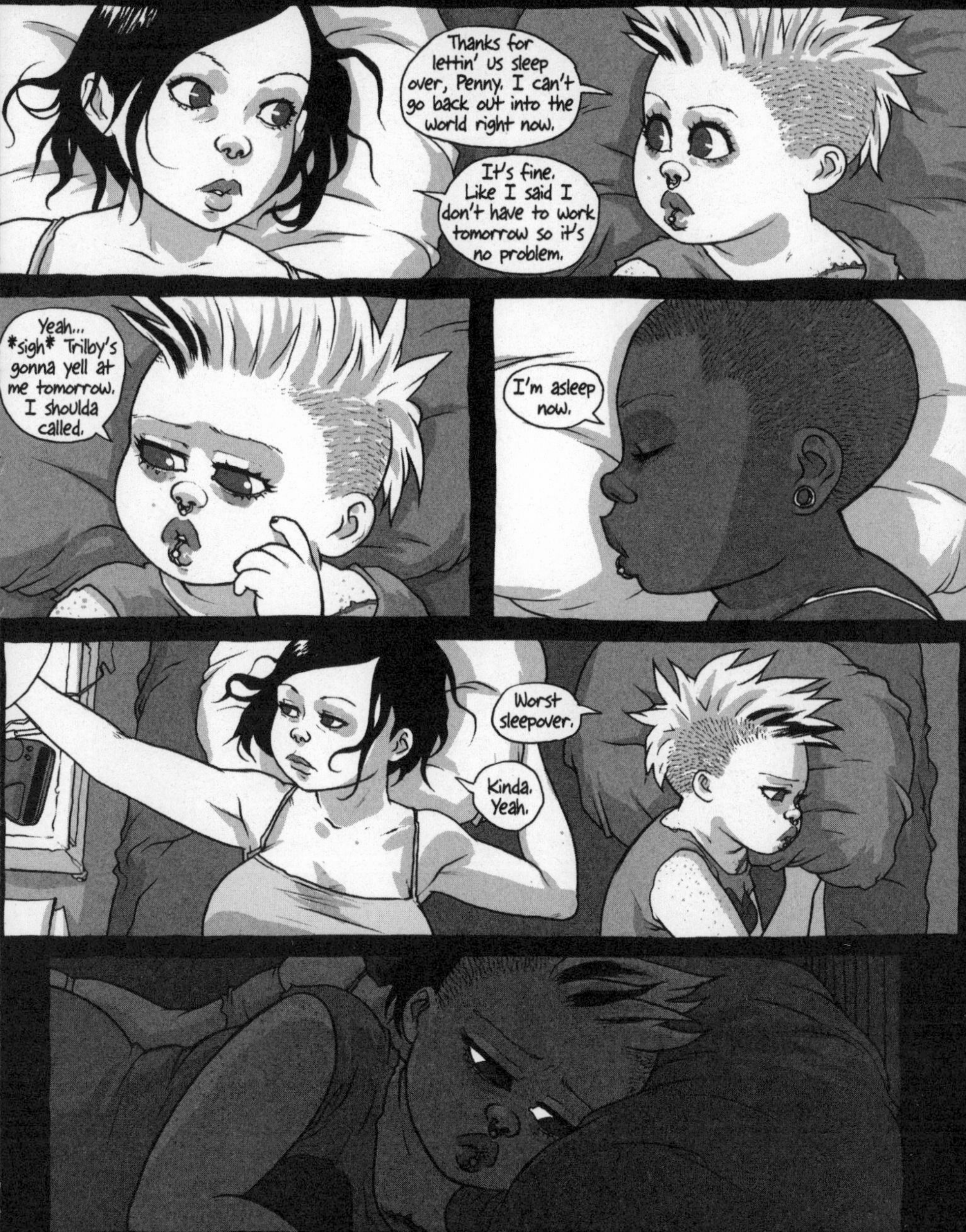
Thanks for lettin' us sleep over, Penny. I can't go back out into the world right now.
It's fine. Like I said I don't have to work tomorrow so it's no problem.
Yeah... *sigh* Trilby's gonna yell at me tomorrow. I shoulda called.
I'm asleep now.
Worst sleepover.
Kinda. Yeah.

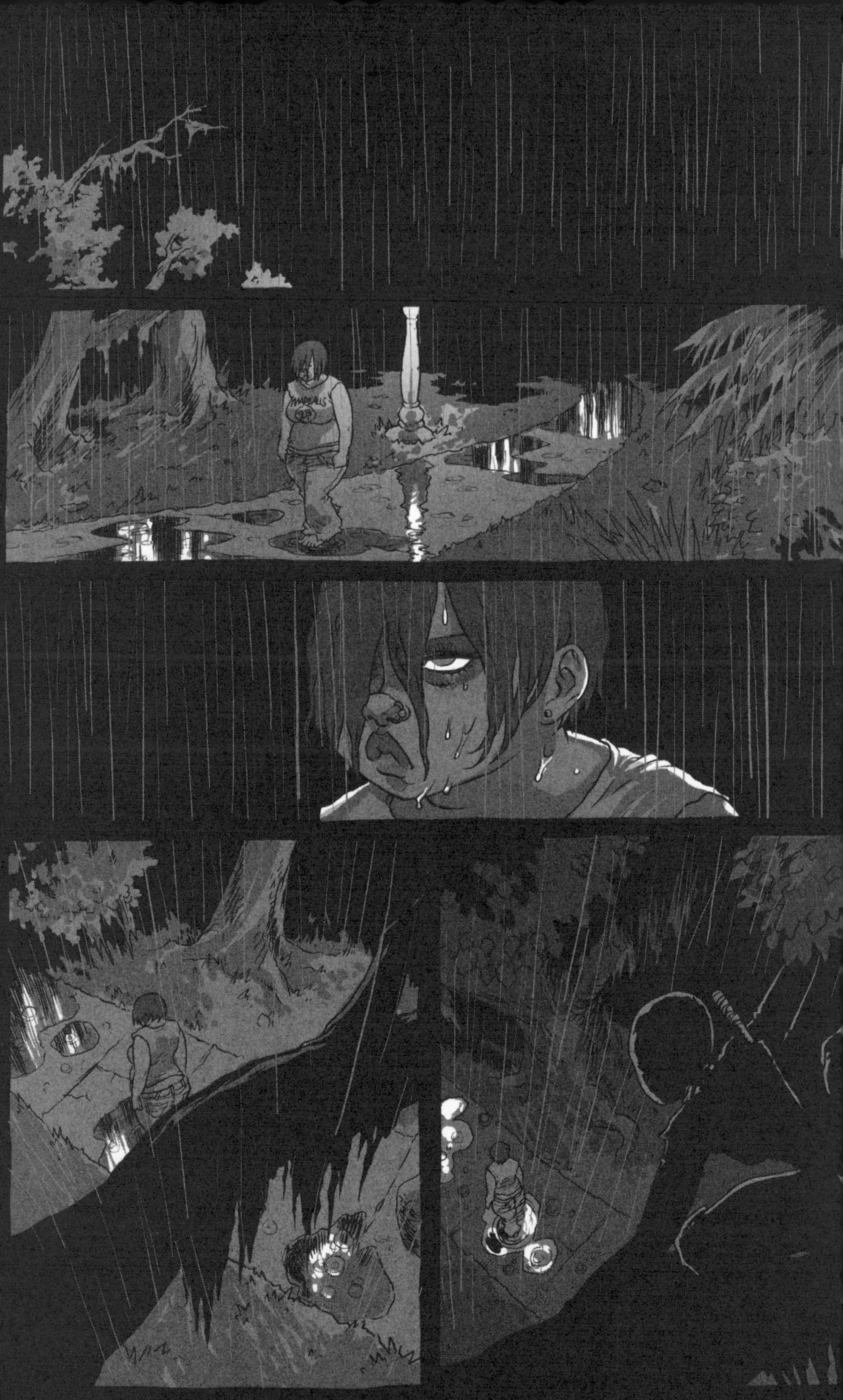

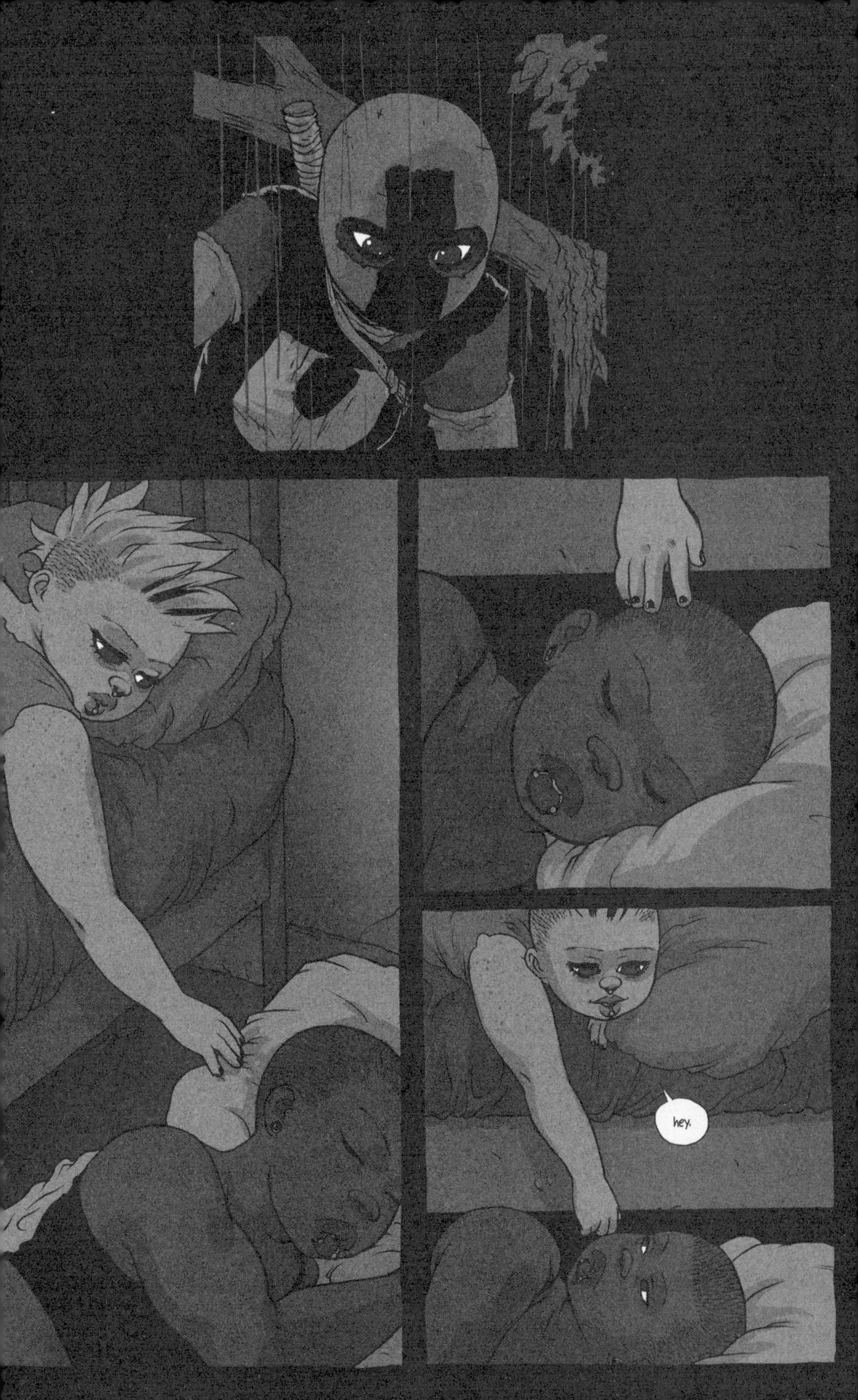
hey.

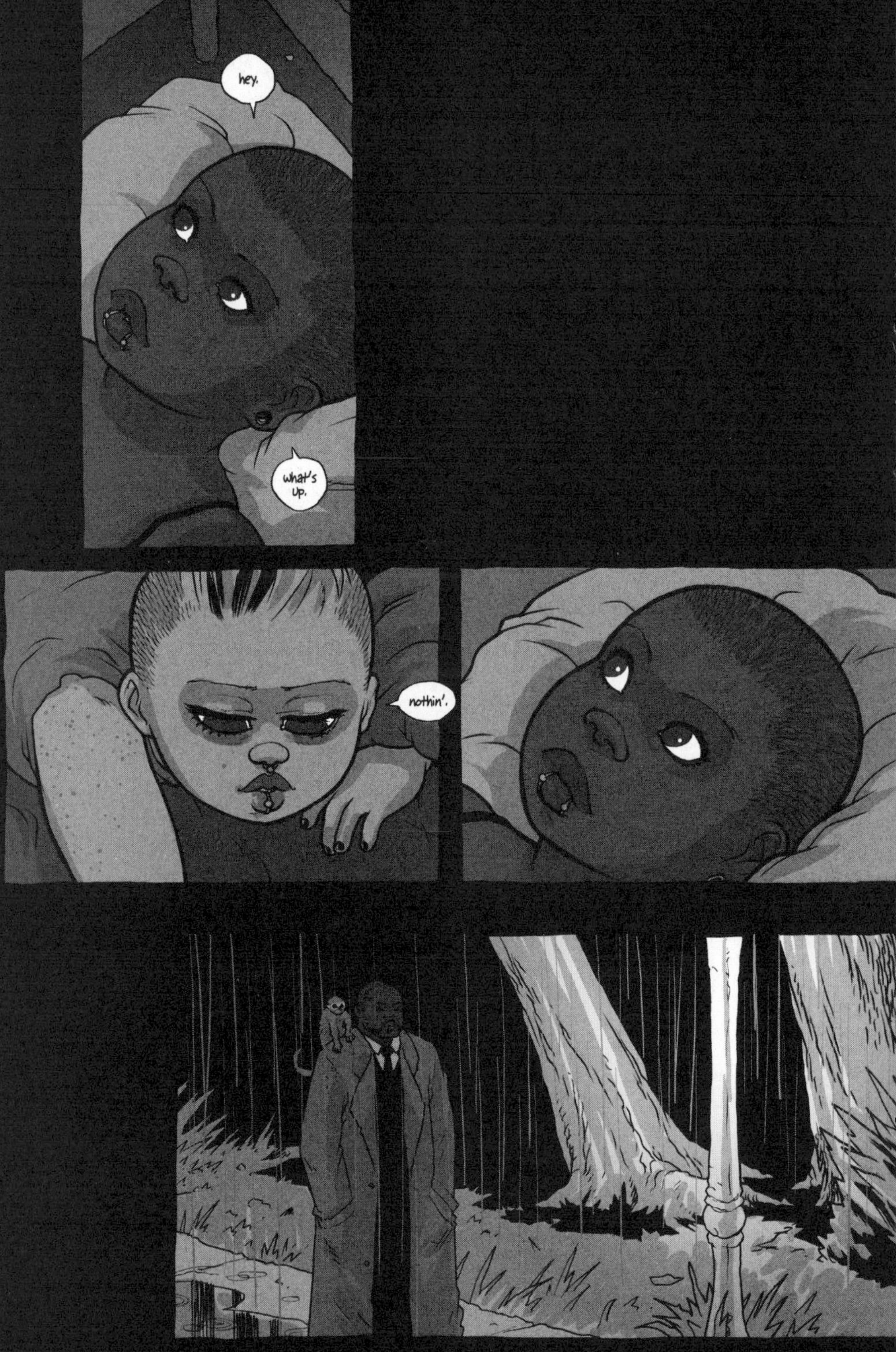
hey.
what's up.
nothin'.

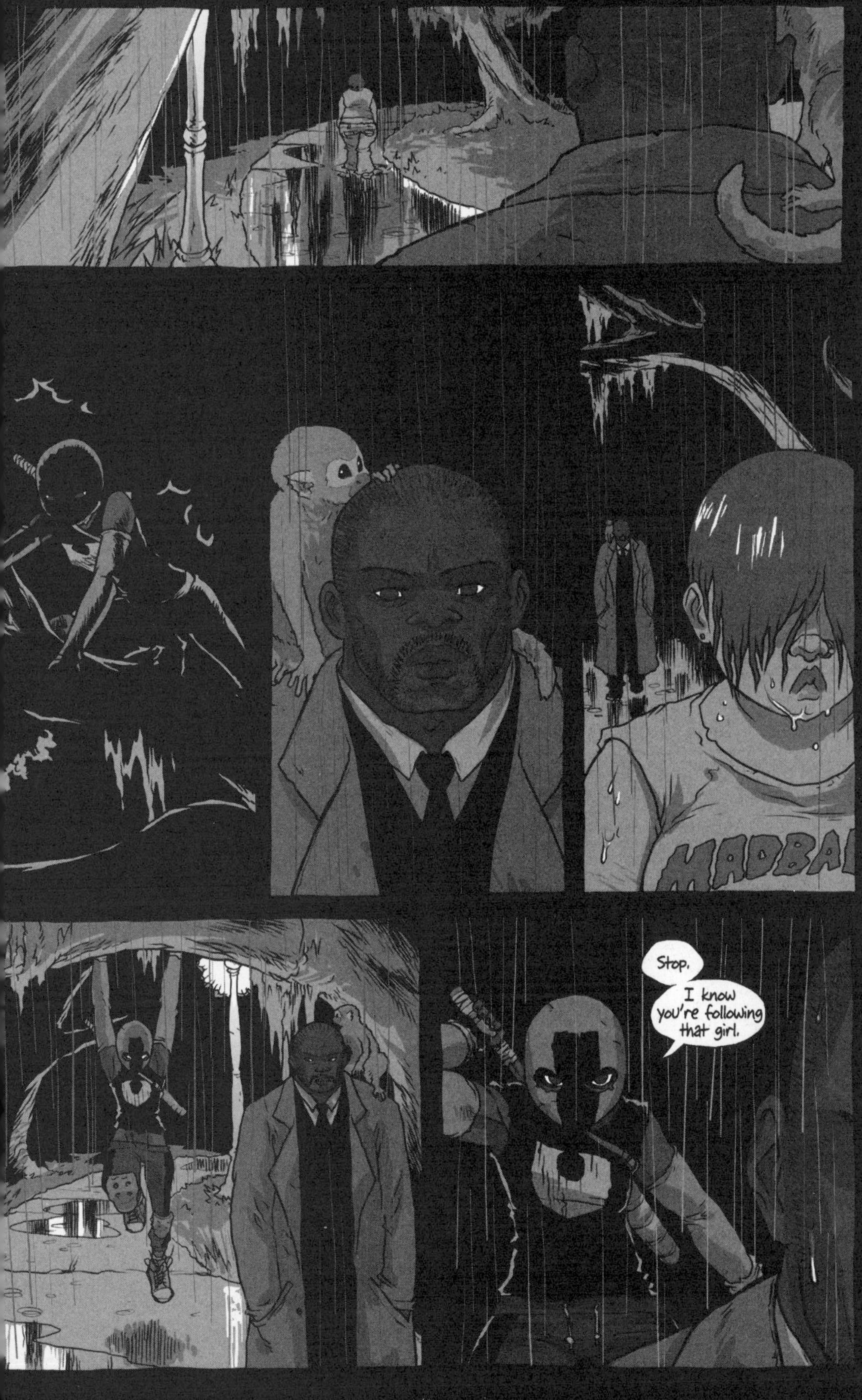
MADBA
Stop.
I know you're following that girl.

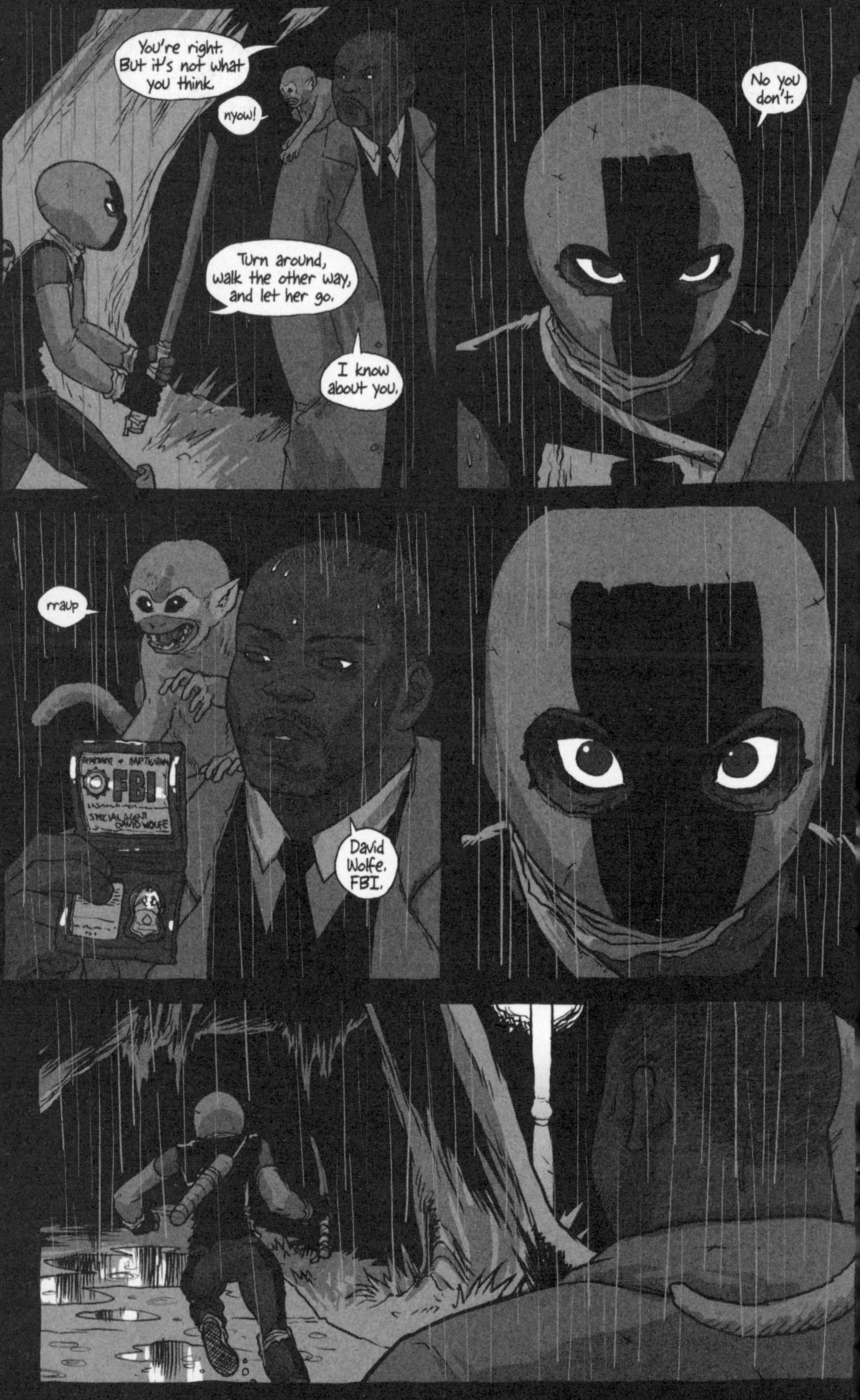
You're right. But it's not what you think.
nyow!
Turn around, walk the other way, and let her go.
I know about you.
No you don't.
rraup
FBI
SPECIAL AGENT DAVID WOLFE
David Wolfe. FBI.

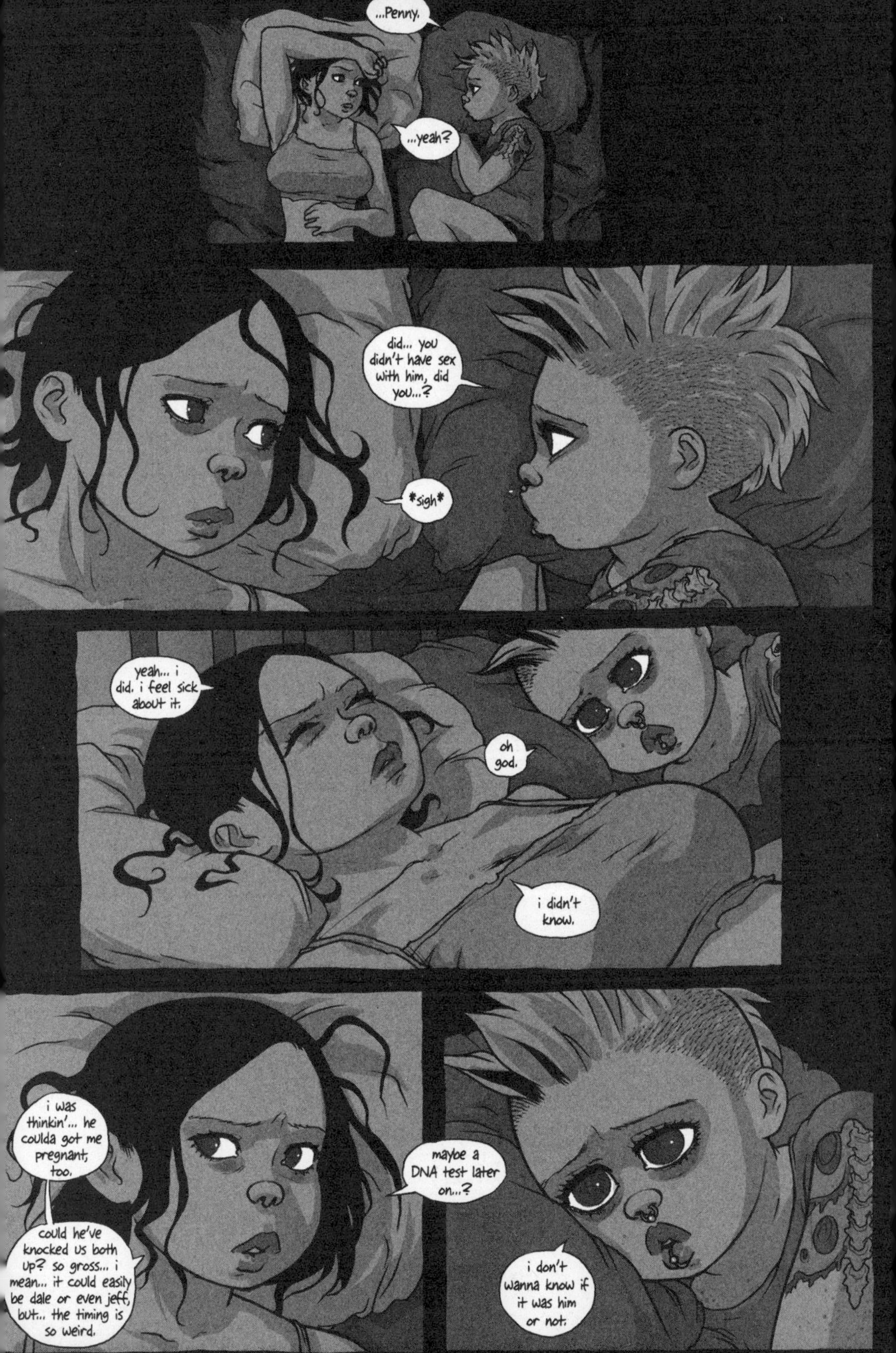
...Penny.
...yeah?
did... you didn't have sex with him, did you...?
*sigh*
yeah... i did. i feel sick about it.
oh god.
i didn't know.
i was thinkin'... he coulda got me pregnant, too.
could he've knocked us both up? so gross... i mean... it could easily be dale or even jeff, but... the timing is so weird.
maybe a DNA test later on...?
i don't wanna know if it was him or not.

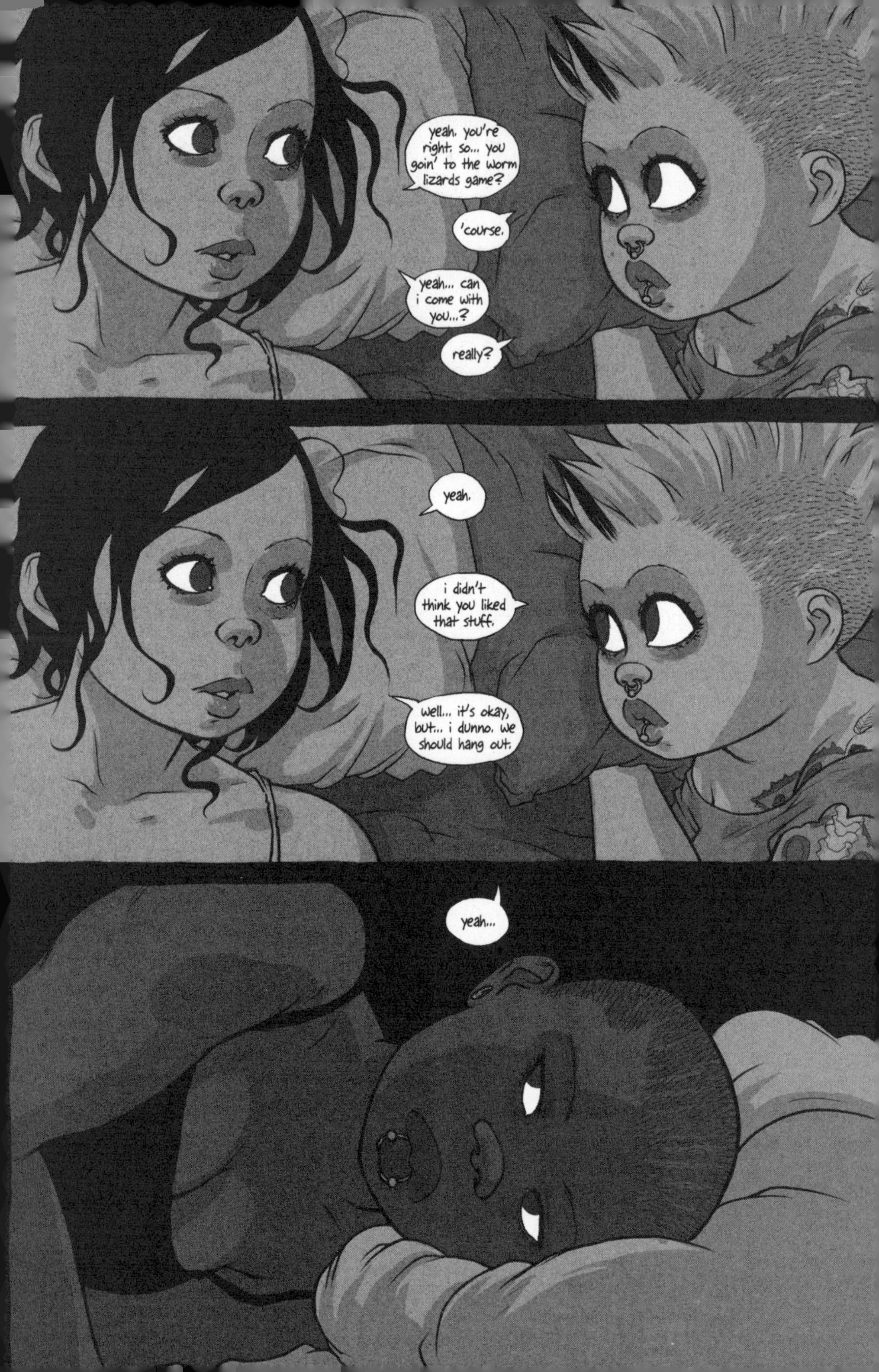
yeah. you're right. so... you goin' to the worm lizards game?
'course.
yeah... can i come with you...?
really?
yeah.
i didn't think you liked that stuff.
well... it's okay, but... i dunno. we should hang out.
yeah...

November 3
i'm writing at Penny's in secret
while she and Mara are asleep.
the worst thing. so many great
(but confusing) things and now a
terrible and also confusing thing
has happened. i found out that

Penny was seeing Vincent. he
was one of her guys. he was at
her apartment and i totally
froze like i was a zombie or
encased in ice, i completely didn't
know what to do or how to
do anything. i'm not mad at
Penny. she never met Vincent
when i was with him, she had
no way of knowing who he was.
but it is still agony. i feel like
even though we're not together
that i don't want anyone to have
him or know him except me. i
say to myself that i would never
go back to him, that i don't
even want him at all, that i
even want to hurt him like
how he hurt me, but i'm afraid
because i think if he ~~did~~ did
want me back i'd be powerless
to say no. my heart feels like
it's on fire, burning inside my
chest with sticky bonfire, and
it hurts more than anything.
writing this now is almost
unbearable. ~~my~~ my heart can't
take it. literally. tonight when
i saw Vincent . . . usually what
happens is that i either paint or
throw up; I throw up when i'm

on my medicine and faint the
other times if i forget to take
it... but tonight neither of
them happened. i was immobile.
i don't know what that means.
   everything reminds me of him.
even though i had a bunch of
flings with guys over the years,
i always believed in indomitable
love, but after Vincent i don't
anymore. it's simply not how
things are. but i'm still consumed
by all this emotion swirling
around the idea, like i can't escape
it. like Vincent is a walking
manifestation of an ideal that
i don't want to believe in but
from which i can never escape,
like it's part of my beliefs whether
i want it to be or not and i
flip-flop between the idealist
that i used to be and who i
am now while also being both
simultaneously.
   i'm writing about something
else.
   i'm not surprised Vincent went
for Penny. they're both gorgeous.
i don't know why he ever got
with me in the first place, he's
perfect and i'm... me. how much

did Penny and Vincent do? how
far did they go... i don't know...
i don't know. was penny better
than me? did he enjoy her
more? probably. how could
he not. i don't blame him.
    i think after vincent i'm a
little afraid of sex even though
i really want to have it all
the time, and i'm especially
afraid of getting to the sex
level with myrna. it seems
nice thinking about it, but i know
actually doing it will be a
totally different thing. i'm not
sure i could go through with it,
i wonder if i could even feel
satisfied sexually with a girl,
but i know things will have to
arrive at that point sooner
or later. i remember having
sex for the first time, still
vivid. i was 13 and he was 18.
it was disappointing like pretty
much everything in my life
after that. and now possibly
having sex with a girl is
like doing it all over again
for the first time. the first
time with a guy i was eager
and curious, but this second

first time, seems frightening and insurmantable. the first time with that boy, it wasn't anything like i imagined, i guess nothing is or ever will be, like i never imagined that what happened tonight could've happened, or anything in the past we could have happened but it did.

Penny told me she is definitely pregnant for sure. i didn't want to write about it at first but i have to at least a little. i don't know. i don't know how to feel about that. i know it was Vincent. he did the same thing to Penny as he did to me, and i feel like even though this is happening to Penny, its happening to me all over again at the same time. except i don't think Penny ever really cared about him like how i did. he's just another guy to her. no, that's mean. i know she cares ~~about~~ about the guys she gets with, but... i still know it was different for me. i guess in some ways he was also just another guy for me too.

i really really hope Penny keeps
the baby. i know how possessive
that sounds and i know its totally
up to her and it would really
change her life and she's
still so young, i guess, but....?
wouldn't it also be great....?
i'm even sadder thinking about
her baby possibly being snuffed
out. but i know that sometimes
that's how it has to be.
   i'm crying as i write this. i
feel like my life is over. i feel
like when i put down this pen
and go to sleep, that i'll never
wake up because my life is
plainly over and simply doesn't
have the momentum required
to continue. I will slip into
a coma because that will become
my natural state. i don't think
i would mind that. except i
would feel sad for my dad,
Trilby, Aubrey, Penny, Meiko,
Myrtle, Zia, Glen... and
Meira! she might be the
saddest. sad everything.

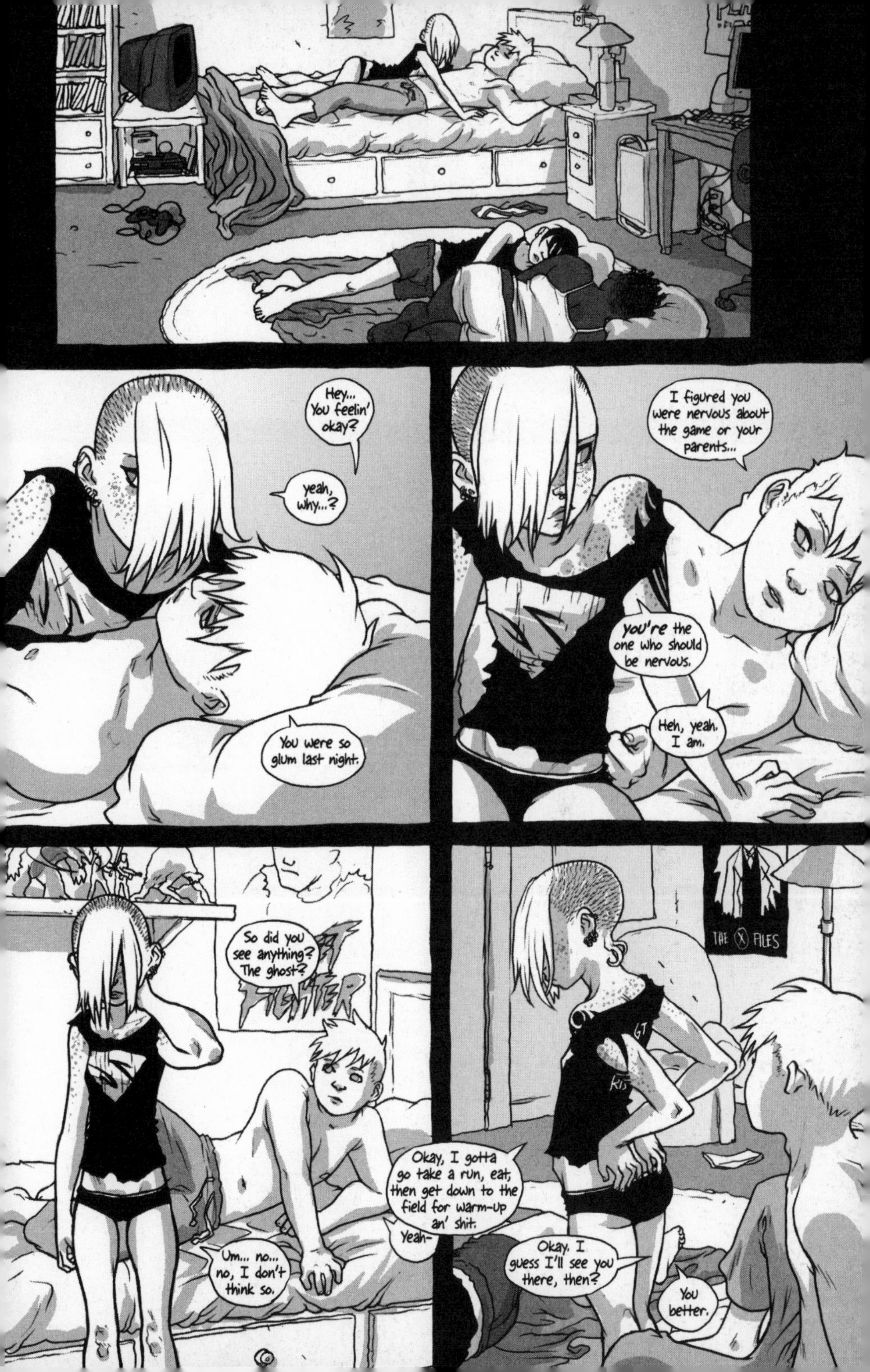
Hey... You feelin' okay?
yeah, why...?
You were so glum last night.
I figured you were nervous about the game or your parents...
you're the one who should be nervous.
Heh, yeah. I am.
So did you see anything? The ghost?
THE X FILES
Um... no... no, I don't think so.
Okay, I gotta go take a run, eat, then get down to the field for warm-up an' shit.
Yeah-
Okay. I guess I'll see you there, then?
You better.

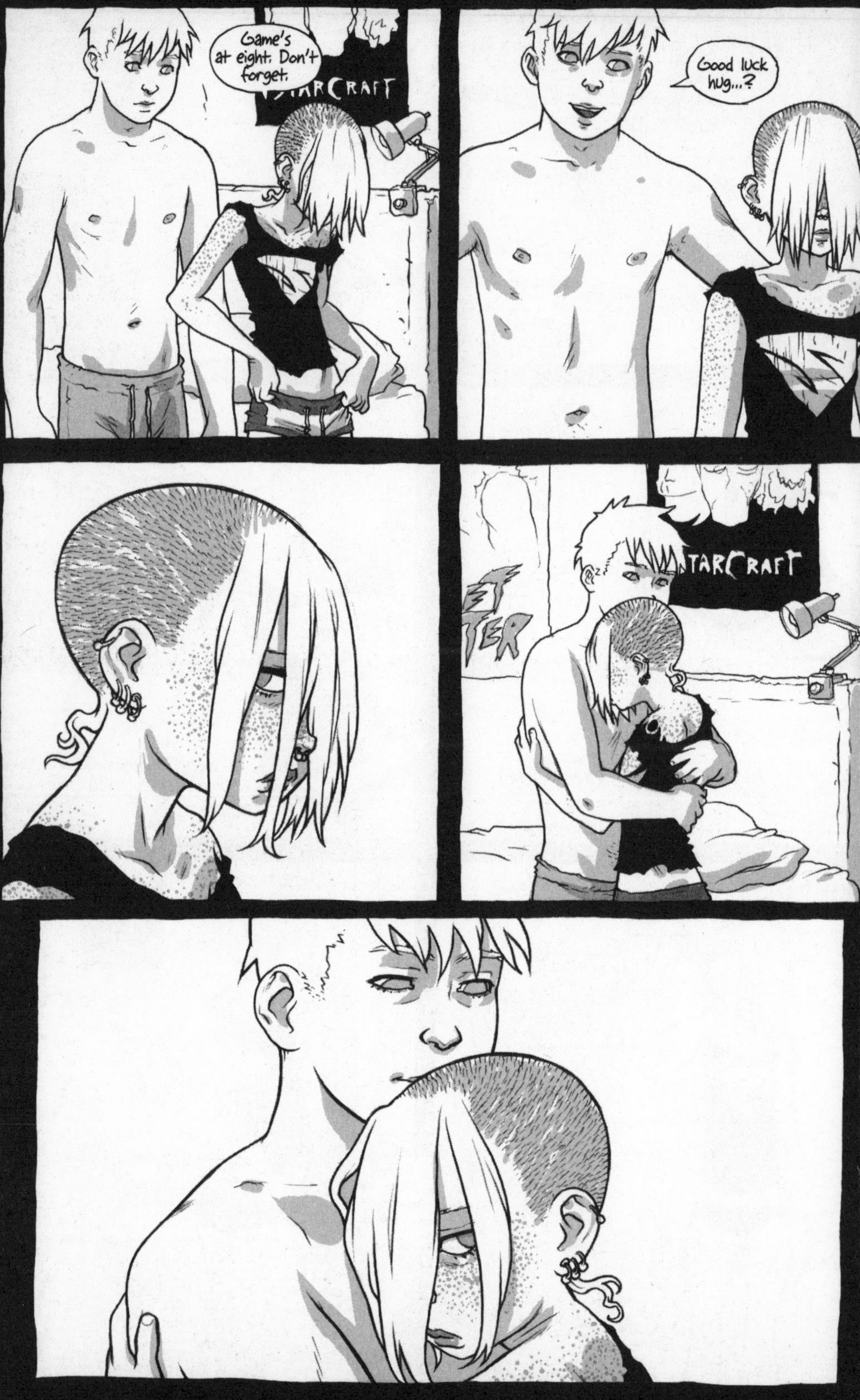
Game's at eight. Don't forget.
STARCRAFT
Good luck hug...?
STARCRAFT

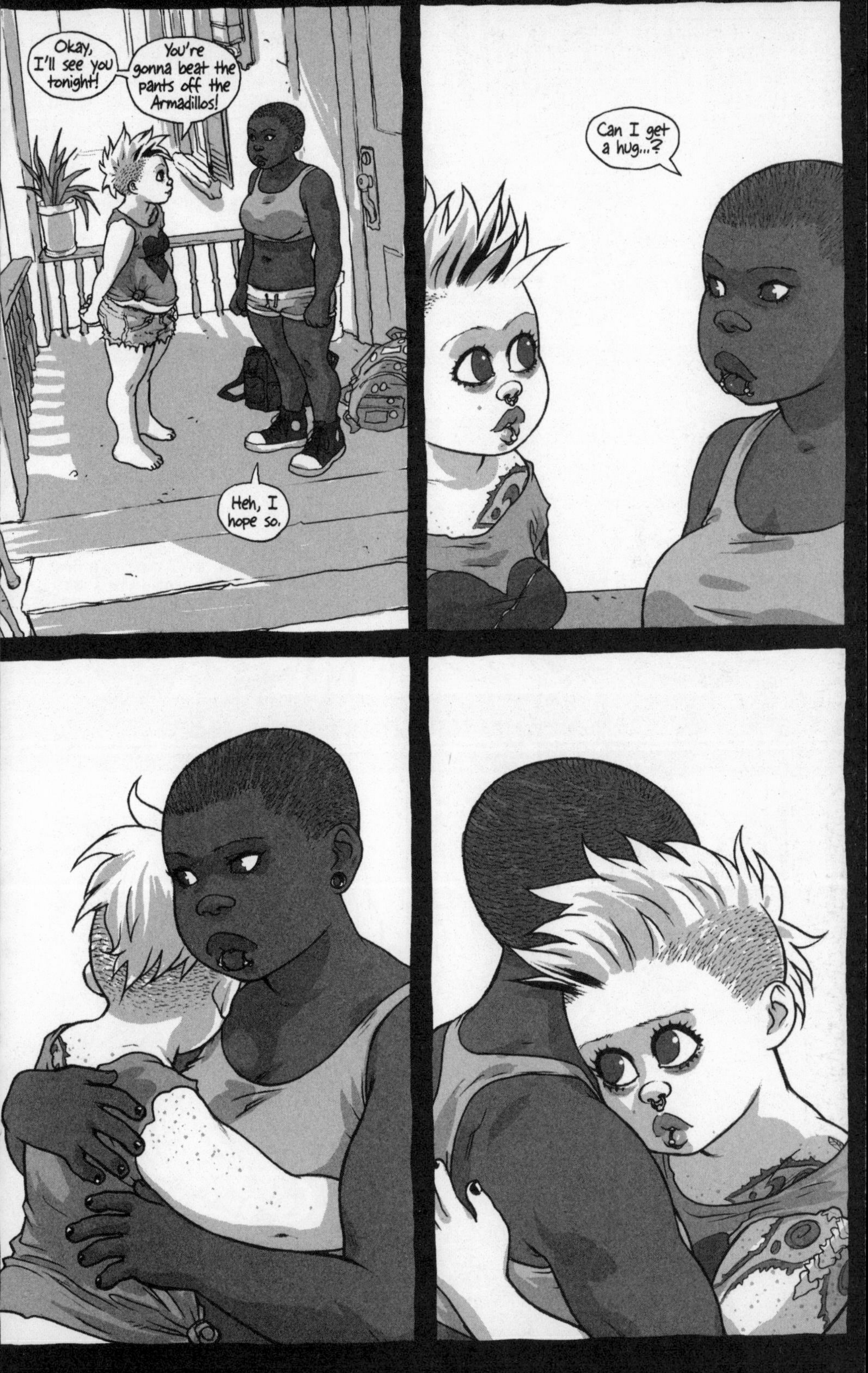
Okay, I'll see you tonight!
You're gonna beat the pants off the Armadillos!
Heh, I hope so.
Can I get a hug...?

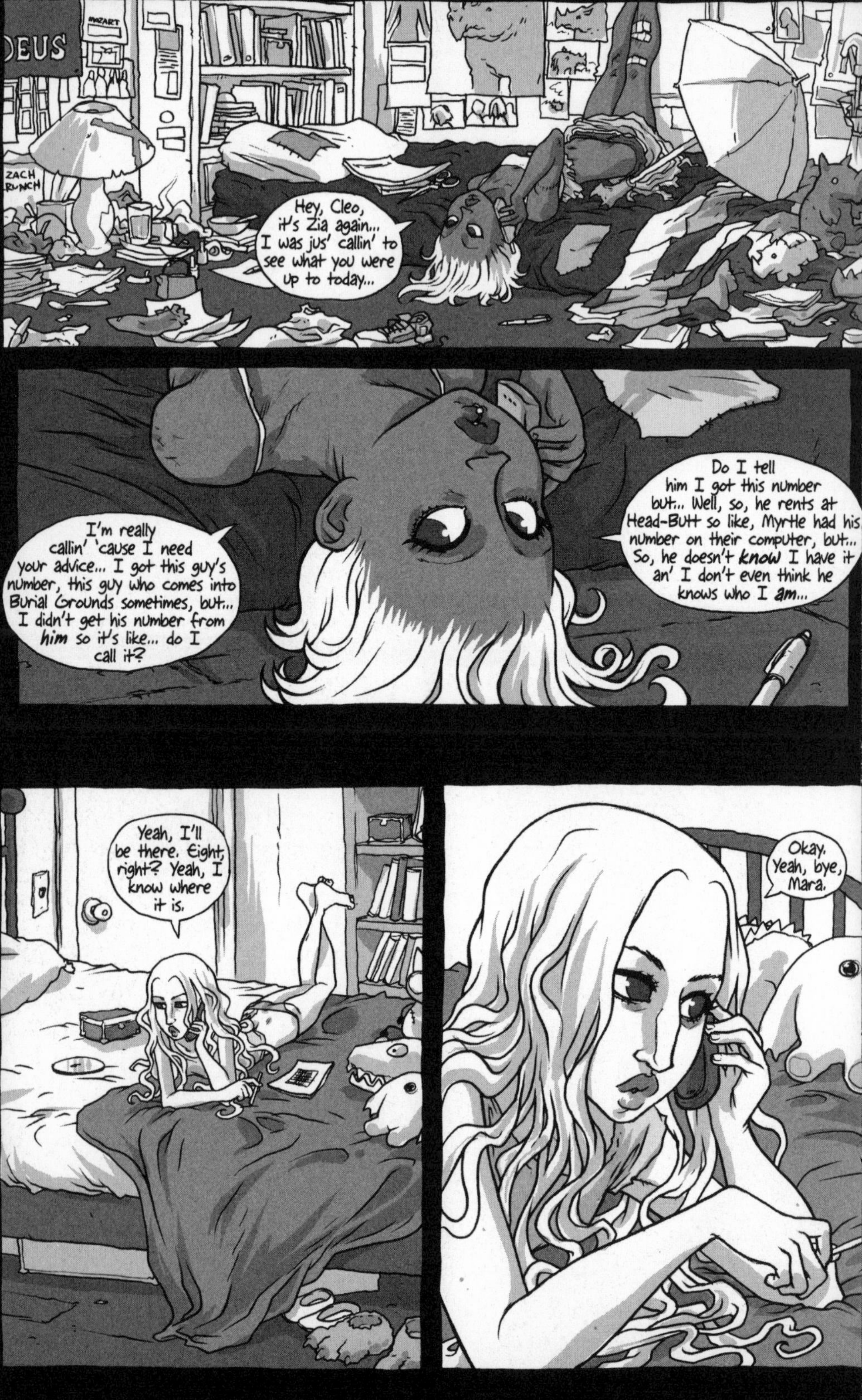
DEUS
ZACH
RUNCH
Hey, Cleo, it's Zia again... I was jus' callin' to see what you were up to today...
I'm really callin' 'cause I need your advice... I got this guy's number, this guy who comes into Burial Grounds sometimes, but... I didn't get his number from *him* so it's like... do I call it?
Do I tell him I got this number but... Well, so, he rents at Head-Butt so like, Myrtle had his number on their computer, but... So, he doesn't *know* I have it an' I don't even think he knows who I *am*...
Yeah, I'll be there. Eight, right? Yeah, I know where it is.
Okay. Yeah, bye, Mara.

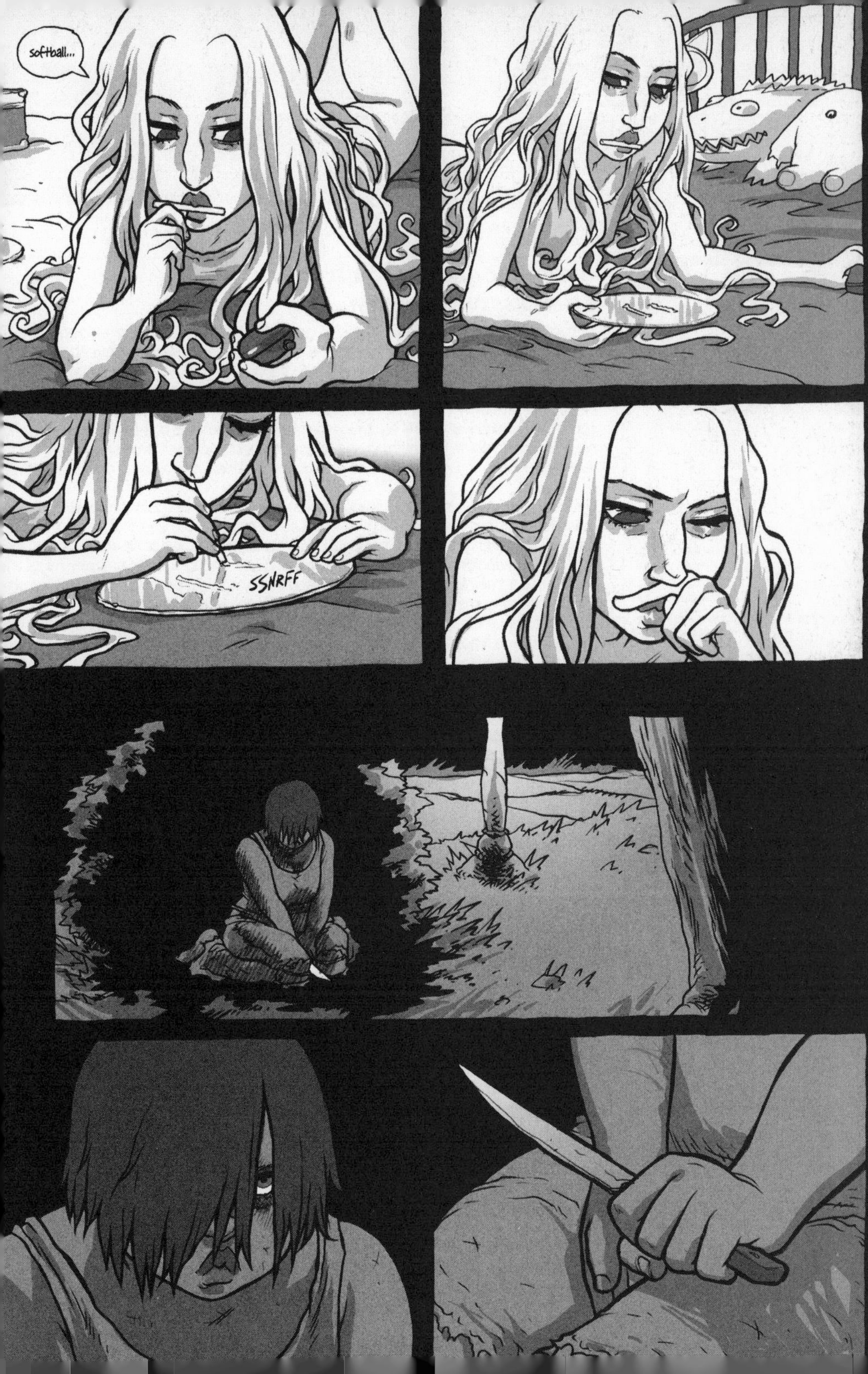
softball...
SSNRFF

# The Wonders At Your Feet

[ friendtoroaches@gmail.com ]

Recent Entries Archive Friends User Info

## mara's journal

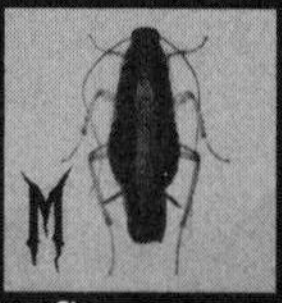

profile

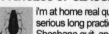

## *November 4th, 11:35am*

### *PRINCESS OF SLAUGHTER.*

i'm at home real quick before i go to the field for practice. we're doing one last serious long practice before the game at 8. i think i wrote before about how Shoshana quit, and now we have this new girl Galaxy (crazy name) who is o but i feel really uncertain about her. whether she can perform out there. Nisha pretty flakey recently, i don't know what the hell is up with her. Paquita is good, we can count on her. and Fall, she is an awesome player but she's the biggest flake of all, you ca never count on her to do anything and i always expect she won't even show up. she's really into boxing, i guess, i think she spends more of her time focusing on that. whateve

yestrday i dumped a ton of my old clothes off at goodwill. all the goth shit i was into for those three or four years or whatever. i kept some of it, i still like some of the cool pants i had that aren't so gothy. i thought about giving some of it to Cleo since she's still kind of i that shit, but i decided to get rid of it without telling her. i thought about how she might sh up wearing some old outfit i used to wear and that would just be weird. our sizes are so different anyway. my tits are huge. it feels liberating to get rid of that stuff, i don't even wa to look at it anymore. good thing most of my old clothes still fit. i'm a little bigger now, mos muscle i guess (i hope), but at least my ass seems to be pretty much the same size.

i wrote a big chunk on my serial killer screenplay yesterday, too. i still haven't come up wi a title, that's seriously the hardest part for me. i can make up dumb story after story but th title always stumps me. i kind of hate how the real reason things have titles is to separate them from other things, or to describe the material to somebody who hasn't experienced like Gremlins, or Escape From New York, while others don't even have anything to do w the movie. and titles are also good so you can remember a movie or find it or talk about i okay i guess titles are pretty useful. but i wonder if movies could be numbered somehow instead of named, i don't know. something more technical. then my screenplay could jus be 17334876X or something. actually that's not a bad title.

i made this a custom post because now i'm going to talk about what happened at the co i decided i should. a while ago Cleo was talking about getting a livejournal, i'm sort of dreading it because then i'll have to have her on my f-list and then she'll get to read all my posts unless i make them totally private. but i also like your guys input. i don't know. okay so Cleo and me kissed at the con. it was totally weird and spontanoeous. that guy pushe her and she fell on her face and got a bloody lip, so we were in the bathroom and then i don't know what i was thinking but there was a weird pause between exchanges and i bent down and fucking kissed her. not a long sloppy kiss but a little more than a peck. it lasted for less than two seconds. right then i was afraid i ruined everything between us b things actually seem fine. we even kissed again after that, a little longer. i don't know if it means anything, i know some girls who've done shit like that with their friends all the time and it's not a romantic thing or awkward. i think i want this to be a romantic thing though. except Myrtle is in the way. i really don't give a shit about Trilby or whoever giving us shit about a possible relationship. i say fuck off. i don't even care what my parents would say. the other big thing is that i know Cleo, even though she's with Myrtle, is still seriously hun up on this guy Vincent she dated. turns out Penny was also dating him recently but she didn't know Cleo had dated him or something, it's all kinda fucked up. we ran into him at Penny's last night and Cleo flipped out, i thought she was going to melt or go into a coma or something. she actually didn't cry that much at all, she was more like... i guess shocke or like beyond tears or something. she really seems okay, though, i'm glad. oh someone at the door i think its Louisa to pick me up. wish me luck at the game tonight.

*mood: hungry*
*current music: his name is alive - your cheating heart*

[ 3 comments | leave a comment ]

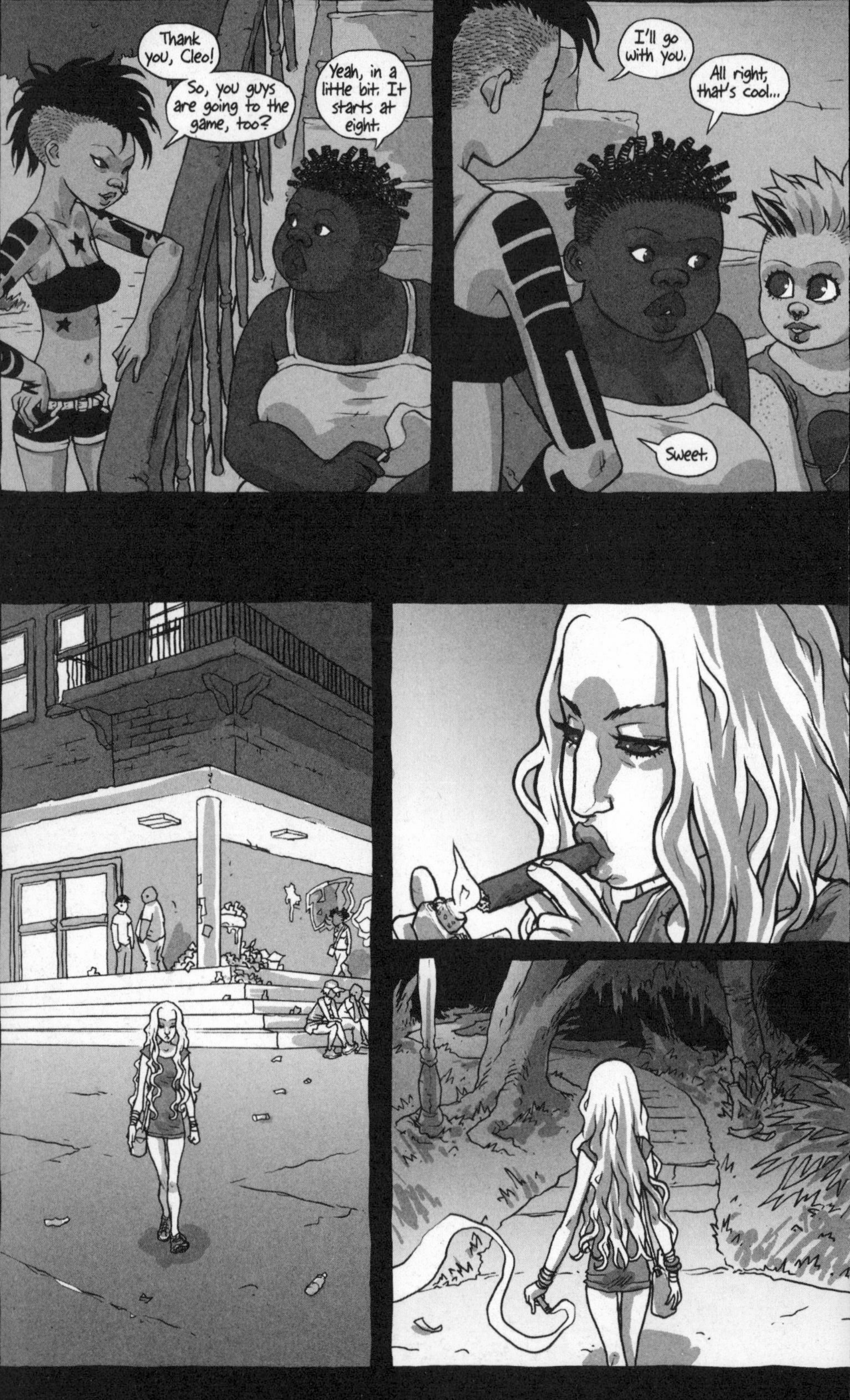
Thank you, Cleo!
So, you guys are going to the game, too?
Yeah, in a little bit. It starts at eight.
I'll go with you.
All right, that's cool...
Sweet.

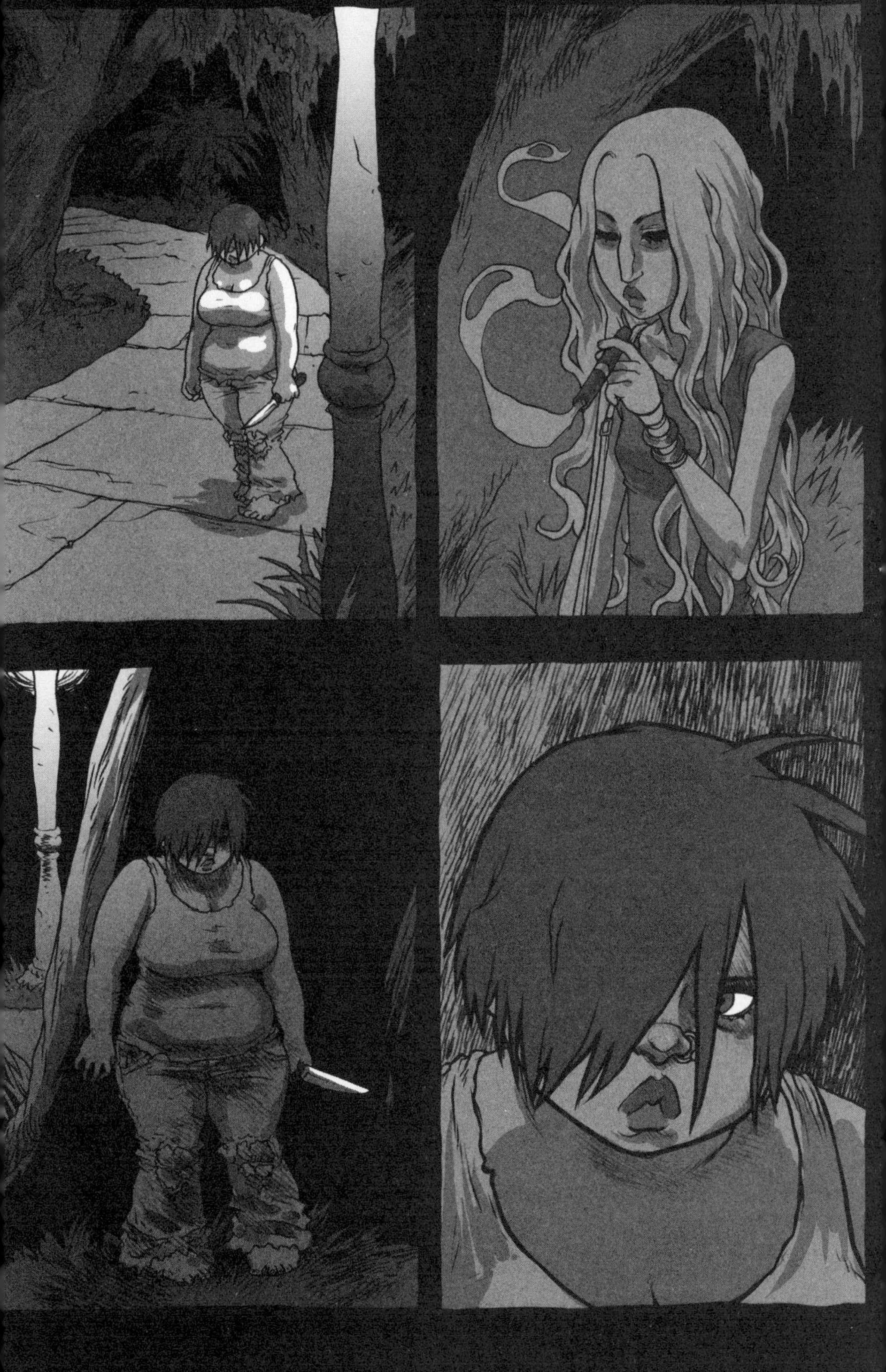

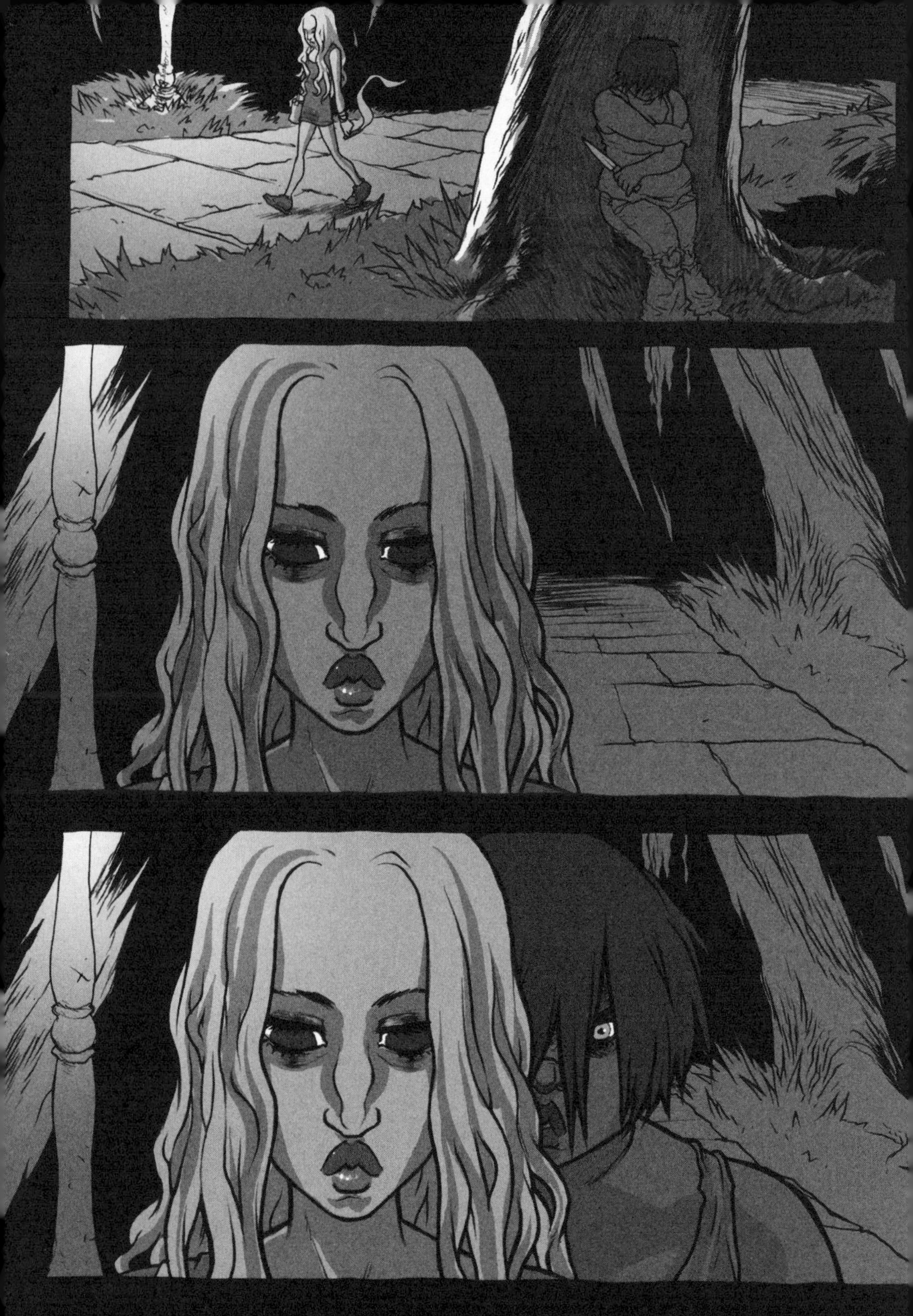

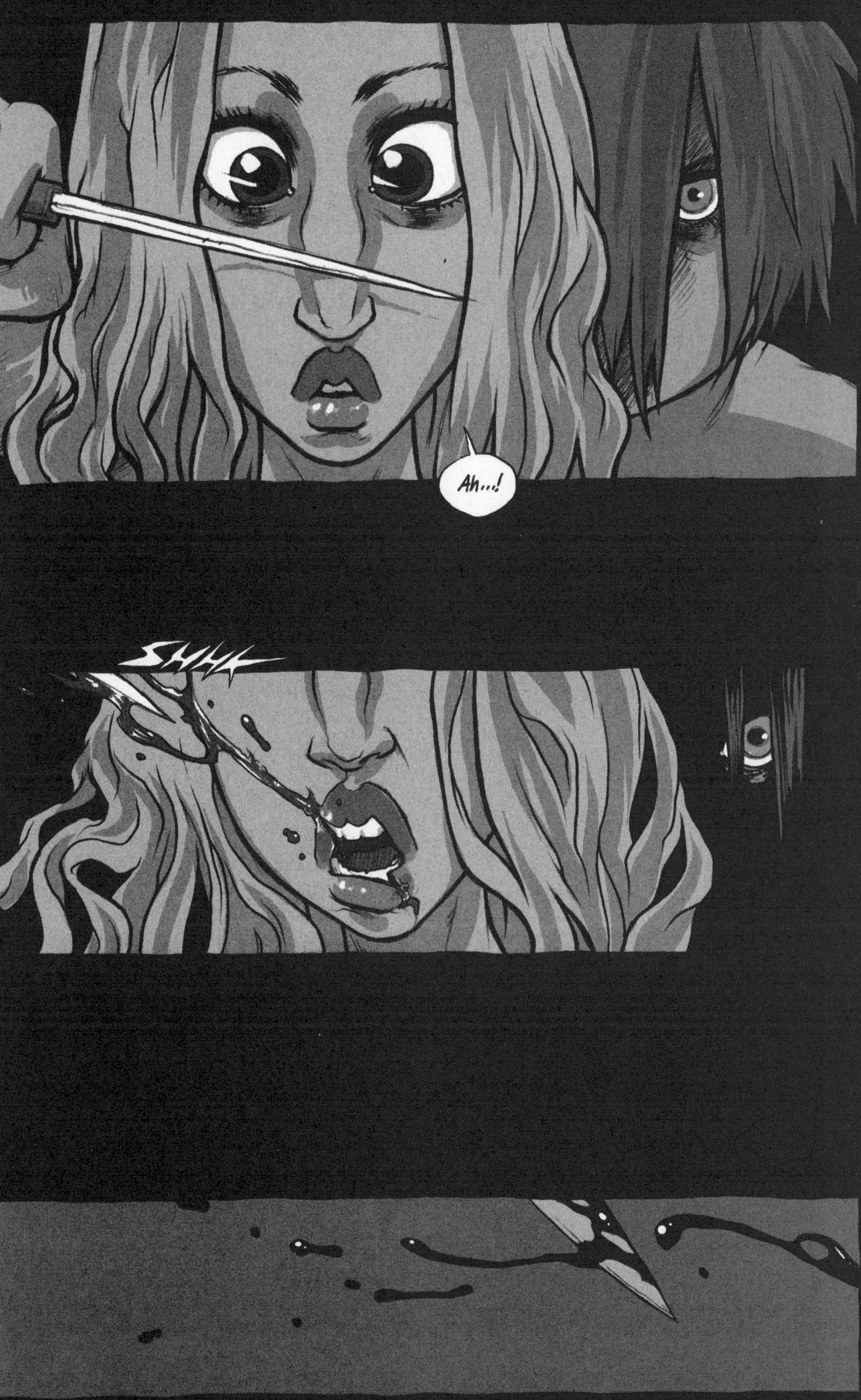
Ah...!
SHHK

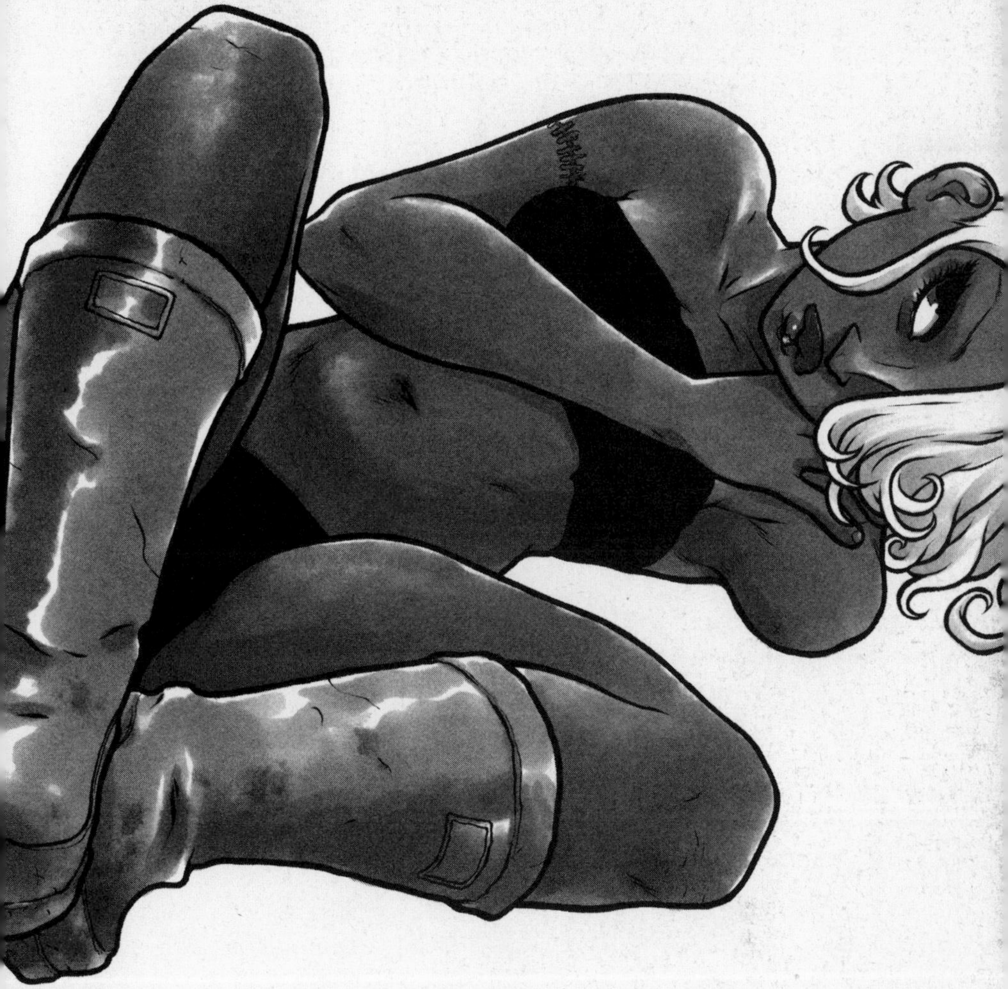

to be
continued

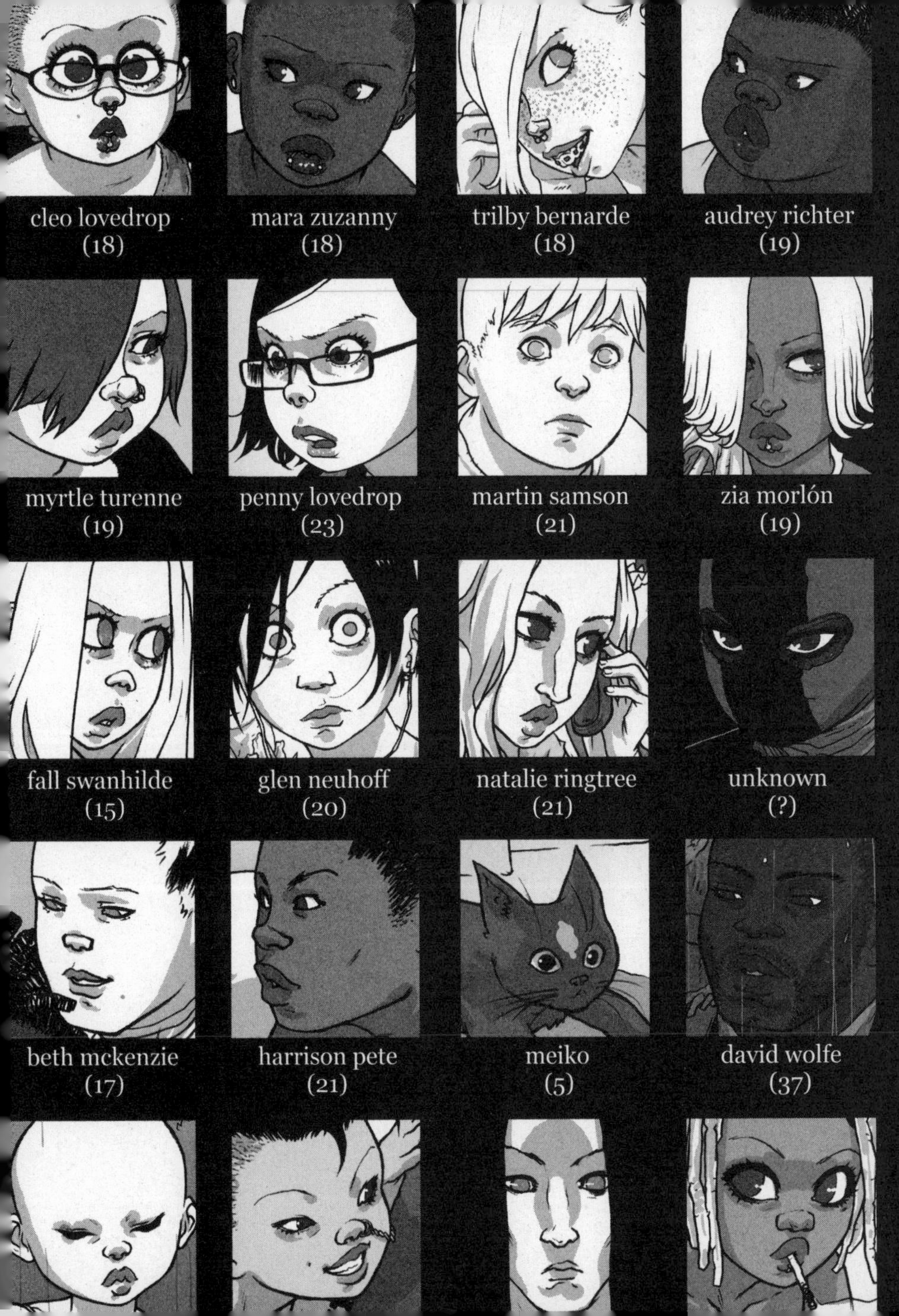
cleo lovedrop
(18)
mara zuzanny
(18)
trilby bernarde
(18)
audrey richter
(19)
myrtle turenne
(19)
penny lovedrop
(23)
martin samson
(21)
zia morlón
(19)
fall swanhilde
(15)
glen neuhoff
(20)
natalie ringtree
(21)
unknown
(?)
beth mckenzie
(17)
harrison pete
(21)
meiko
(5)
david wolfe
(37)

*Special thanks to:* mom, dad, joe, james, jess, zach, dan, rea, michelle, jessica, shelly, dave, julie, the Bella Morte guys, robert haines, becky, vasilis, kirk, everyone at deviantart, everyone who reads my books, and everyone who's bought artwork or mini-comics from me.

*No thanks to:* bill goodin, noise

*Plugs:* bellamorte.com, thismeansyou.com, theprotomen.com, cadaveria.com, synthetic-division.com, roaringshark.com

*About the author:* Ross Campbell is an art monk who currently lives in Rochester, New York. His personal website is www.greenoblivion.com, and his deviantArt gallery is at mooncalfe.deviantart.com. He likes monsters, zombies, Tifa Lockhart, Fefe Dobson, unsolved mysteries, great white sharks, alien artifacts, tea, outer space, and cats. He hates neighbors, ketchup, frogs, traveling, sunny weather, and pretty much everything else.

*Other books by Ross: Spooked* (written by Antony Johnston/ Oni Press), *Wet Moon* volumes 1-3 (Oni Press), *The Abandoned* (Tokyopop), *Mountain Girl* #1-3 (self-published), *Water Baby* (DC/Minx.)

# OTHER BOOKS FROM ROSS CAMPBELL & ONI PRESS...

wet moon
book 1: feeble wanderings

wet moon
2 : unseen feet
ross campbell

WET MOON, VOL. 1:
FEEBLE WANDERINGS
By Ross Campbell
168 pages, 6x9" trade paperback
black and white interiors
$14.95
ISBN 978-1-932664-07-2

---

WET MOON, VOL. 2:
UNSEEN FEET
By Ross Campbell
176 pages, 6x9" trade paperback
black and white interiors
$14.95
ISBN 978-1-932664-47-8

wet moon
3: further realms of fright

wet moon

WET MOON, VOL. 3:
FURTHER REALMS OF FRIGHT
By Ross Campbell
200 pages, 6x9" trade paperback
black and white interiors
$14.95 US
ISBN 978-1-932664-84-3

---

WET MOON, VOL. 5:
WHERE ALL STARS FAIL TO BURN
By Ross Campbell
168 pages, 6x9" trade paperback
black and white interiors
$14.95 US
ISBN 978-1-934964-25-5

wet moon
6
yesterday's gone
Ross Campbell

WET MOON, VOL. 6:
YESTERDAY'S GONE
By Ross Campbell
168 pages, 6x9" trade paperback
black and white interiors
$17.99 US
ISBN 978-1-934964-83-5

ONI PRESS
REVOLUTIONIZE COMICS
www.onipress.com

For more information on these and other fine Oni Press comic books and graphic novels, visit www.onipress.com. To find a comic specialty store in your area, call 1-888-COMICBOOK or visit www.comicshops.us.